NICOLAS WINDING REFN
AND THE
VIOLENCE OF ART

ALSO BY JUSTIN VICARI
AND FROM MCFARLAND

*The Gus Van Sant Touch: A Thematic Study—
Drugstore Cowboy,* Milk *and Beyond* (2012)

Mad Muses and the Early Surrealists (2012)

*Male Bisexuality in Current Cinema:
Images of Growth, Rebellion and Survival* (2011)

Nicolas Winding Refn and the Violence of Art
A Critical Study of the Films

Justin Vicari

McFarland & Company, Inc., Publishers
Jefferson, North Carolina

LIBRARY OF CONGRESS CATALOGUING-IN-PUBLICATION DATA

Vicari, Justin, 1968–
  Nicolas Winding Refn and the violence of art : a critical study of the films / Justin Vicari.
     p. cm.
  Includes bibliographical references and index.

  ISBN 978-0-7864-7182-9 (softcover : acid free paper) ∞
  ISBN 978-1-4766-1498-4 (ebook)

  1. Refn, Nicolas Winding, 1970– —Criticism and interpretation. I. Title.
  PN1998.3.R426V53 2014
  741.4302'33092—dc23
  [B]   2014009353

BRITISH LIBRARY CATALOGUING DATA ARE AVAILABLE

© 2014 Justin Vicari. All rights reserved

No part of this book may be reproduced or transmitted in any form or by any means, electronic or mechanical, including photocopying or recording, or by any information storage and retrieval system, without permission in writing from the publisher.

On the cover: Ryan Gosling, left, and Vithaya Pansringarm in Nicolas Refn's challenging *Only God Forgives*, 2013 (RADiUS-TWC/Photofest)

Manufactured in the United States of America

McFarland & Company, Inc., Publishers
  Box 611, Jefferson, North Carolina 28640
  www.mcfarlandpub.com

In memory of
HARRIS SAVIDES
(1957–2012)
and
ROBIN WOOD
(1931–2009)

"from his eye subversive beauty"

Table of Contents

Preface	1
1. Seven Disorganizing Principles	11
2. The *Pusher* Trilogy	51
3. *Bleeder*	68
4. *Fear X*	89
5. *Nemesis*	120
6. *Bronson*	128
7. *Valhalla Rising*	151
8. *Drive*	178
9. *Only God Forgives*	192
Conclusion	208
Chapter Notes	215
Bibliography	227
Index	231

Preface

> In the postmodern moment, mass media increasingly operates through strategies it shares with experimental art. Dana Polan argues that it tends to work with "montage that produces collisions of messages that continually destabilize and negate each other." Confronted with this kind of practice, we can only posit a spectator who goes to cinema precisely for a loss of reality, to continually reactivate that loss in simulation effects.—Sharon Willis[1]

> I loved the idea that Walt Disney had this dream of a place and then made it a reality. It's the same way I felt when I saw *Blue Velvet*. It's so clearly one person's singular dream. The fact that someone believed in their idea so much to make it a reality ... I want to be that kind of person.—Ryan Gosling[2]

Does mass culture delude us and remove us from reality, or does it help us to actualize realities that have formerly existed only as dreams? It is likely that mass culture does neither of these things on an exclusive basis and therefore cannot be subjected to blanket judgment. Yet it cannot seem to stop inducing blanket judgments. In the above quotes, what scholar Sharon Willis denigrates and artist Ryan Gosling celebrates as "simulation effects" amounts to the main fork in the road of aesthetic sensibility in our time. The project of denigration depends upon an archetype of capitalist mediation that has not been updated since the digital revolution of the new millennium. It is not my aim to formally and comprehensively update it here in this book about the films of Nicolas Winding Refn,* but rather I would suggest, by way of intro-

---

*Pronounced Vin (rhymes with shin) ding Revfun.

ducing Refn, that the ways in which that mediation functions now—as Willis herself attests[3]—are far more spontaneous and "responsive" than they are centralized, although this change to the order of things often goes unremarked or uncredited. Instead, there remains the limiting and self-defeating perception that our natural responses cannot be trusted, that our consciousness (even at its most subversive) has been thoroughly colonized for corporate interests, that violence in narrative art is synonymous with anti-humanism, and that finally no pleasure, no fantasy, can be concocted or savored outside of the production-consumption nexus.

This line of thinking derives from the post–Marxist "negative dialectics" of Adorno and the Frankfurt School, and must be understood as a direct reaction against Nazi Germany. It requires the politicization of desire itself as an antidote against potential fascism. But this has become in its own way a totalization and therefore a dead end. Plus, in the U.S. it has never been the case that Hal Hartley and talk radio, say, are in direct competition with each other; the proliferation of the latter is not, either accidentally or intentionally, blocking the former from mass popularity. Rather, these need to be thought of as entirely separate cultural phyla rather than merely separate root-ends of the same rhizome. The multi-channel, multi-tracked, multi-tasking culture that we have is not a cause but a symptom of a certain worldview whereby we can derive a range of different (not necessarily superior) pleasures and satisfactions from reading great literature versus graphic novels, for example. But the basic need for some kind of aesthetic pleasure and satisfaction is more or less always the same.

This is what has proven much more difficult to admit: our instincts are to defend high culture against the encroachment of "trash" in whatever form, when it is actually the case that to deny the significance of graphic novels (talk radio is harder to validate, I admit) is to simultaneously deny the intoxication of great literature, or rather to fail to fully grasp the neural-cognitive aspects of what leads us to art in the first place. Appreciation is not categorical or "rote," just as the most important culture now does not attempt to have the last word in its field (a territorialization that we recognize from obsolete canonical thinking) but, quite the opposite, to blast open difficult conversations and break messy new ground.

In a literary context, the Chilean writer Roberto Bolaño spoke of "the great, imperfect, torrential works ... that blaze paths into the unknown." He compared the, shall we say, anal-retentive love of what is pure but minor, sacrosanct but irrelevant, to a boxer sparring rather than actually fighting (a metaphor that recognizes some violence even in the act of reading books) "against that something that terrifies us all ... that cows us and spurs us on, amid blood and mortal wounds and stench."[4]

Birth processes are unique forms of violence. It is becoming less and less relevant, and even a species of reactionary thought in itself, to demonize the seductions of a culture that is increasingly diverse and driven now more than ever by individuals at the grass roots level. Today, authors of all kinds, far from dead, are just as likely to emerge autodidactically from the audience for culture as from specialized zones of training and discipline. Everything in culture now, both the new media and the old, takes place somewhere beyond our previous formal expectations.

• • •

In general, the academic world, somewhat anhedonically, has reflexively chastised the play of fantasy (in mass culture especially) as denying or dysfunctional; nothing good, it is thought, can come from indulging the unconscious, which is where atavistic prejudices and antisocial tendencies to violence ostensibly lie. On the contrary, everything good comes from the organized triumph of higher reason over human instinct. In pursuit of this, academia has moved away from that very humanity which once gave a crucial empirical basis to the hypotheses of theory.

Even though most of its practitioners probably identify as freethinking and even non-religious, academic theory is, ultimately, the last bastion of that form of abstract Western thinking which moved from religious to psychoanalytic dogma over the course of the 19th century, held together by the central premise that man is essentially made bad or ill by wishing for inappropriate things, and that redemption lies in bringing an abstract idea (whether logic or faith) to bear upon desire and unconscious processes.

These latter processes are viewed as particularly egregious in the case of mass media because it is assumed that those who wander into its range immediately fall under a Circean spell and revert to the barnyard; that they are manipulated even when they think they are not being manipulated (i.e., even where their higher reason deludes them into thinking that they know better). As anyone can see, though, this formulation is condescending and infantilizing, especially considering that we have been hearing nearly nothing but this for close to a century now. The all-points bulletin has failed to snare any legitimate quarry, yet it keeps going out to all and sundry, its guilt and terror now self-perpetuating and ubiquitous.

Thus, it stands to reason that mass art, considered a savage devolver even at its best, is particularly alarming when it takes savagery as its main subject and modus operandi. It is thought that such works carry contagions of violence. Recently, academic study has begun to catch up to exploitation cinema, but always still with the distinction that it is not "art" but instead something ironic in which we can revel in clever wordplay and the personal response; whereas I believe that anything worth watching on any level is automatically a kind of art, and that pleasure is a determining factor in judging works of art, albeit an amoral one. But the fight for a moral cinema clings to film theory by its bitten-to-the-quick fingernails, even though we find it philistine to speak of "moral painting," "moral sculpture," "moral theater," "moral music." At some point we will have to fully account for the reasons why films continue to be burdened not only with moral judgments but with narrow political ones as well; as if film has become more real than reality and therefore more crucial to police and contain. Intriguingly, we accept a lot more "inappropriateness" or antisocialness in literature, because reading is seen (wrongly) as ineluctably reflective and individualistic in ways that watching or listening are not. As Stephen Greenblatt notes, in postmodern literary theory we have long been accustomed to the idea that aesthetic pleasure is not only intrinsic to our understanding of a text but that this pleasure can and does go hand in hand with something like "disturbance."[5] In film theory, however, there is still a tendency to separate the two responses as being antagonistic: pleasure in itself is already reductive or escapist; when it is linked directly to disturbance, then all chaos is on the verge of breaking loose.

But stability, like the moral self-righteousness which impels us to turn disturbance away from pleasure and toward flagellation (of the self and others), is a canard. Greenblatt writes: "Virtually every form of aesthetic pleasure ... is located in an intermediate zone of social transaction, a betwixt and between. It is this mobility, a mobility that includes the power of ready mutation, rather than disinterestedness or stability, that enables the pleasures provoked by certain works of art."[6] Again, all manner of "simulation effects" draw us in. We advance unconsciously, and later we stop to realize how far we have come and what it has meant. Uncertainty is a signpost of progress—or, as Nicolas Winding Refn says, "I really like when I don't really know where things are going" during the making of a film[7]—just as praxis often trumps theoretical models.

It is time to revise some of our less than productive assumptions about individuals and society: for example, although the capitalist hegemony that it was designed to support and propagandize is still, unfortunately, very much with us, the "culture industry" as a regime (the way it was envisioned and diagnosed by Adorno and others) no longer exists. Today production and consumption mirror each other's distrust of large investments. Filmmakers, for example, generate work on their laptops or with digital video cameras, and become overnight sensations[8]; so do musicians.[9] It would be naïve, to be sure, to assume that these cases amount to a fully accomplished revolution in culture, or even an end-run around capitalist production; and it remains to be seen whether the internet, which has sponsored these endeavors and made them possible, will become a true haven for creativity or only an unprecedented high-tech citadel of direct marketing. Meanwhile, the fields of culture continue to expand. TV programming competes with video blogs and uploads on YouTube; even professionally-produced porn is given a run for its money by the proliferation of amateur sites and real-time live streams. Spontaneity will become more and more part of "official" culture, even as our former spontaneous pleasure centers get clogged with pop-up ads and blocked by payment-info screens. At the same time, the big-budget blockbuster or solid indie film (these days, usually with upwards of fifteen different production backers) is no longer any guarantee of reward, whether commercial in the former's case or artistic in the latter's.

This is not necessarily bad, however. The unstable conditions produce distinct anxiety in those who have worked hard to create the storied "level playing field" of social-political enterprise. The field of culture is once again bumpy beyond any leveling, no longer entirely due to various forms of discrimination (although these problems have not gone away), but instead due to more chaotic and intangible processes of buzz, momentum, timing, access and exposure. Indeed, with so many "niche markets," it is now more difficult to account for cultural success and failure by the former models of patriarchal or racist conditioning. Theoretically, anyway, in this world of remote-and-mouse-controlled living-room culture, there are more avenues to public attention (even as that attention naturally becomes more deficit-disordered with the plethora of choices), and the topsy-turvy-ness which now prevails can lead, perhaps unexpectedly, to climates ideal for a certain kind of controlled anarchy beyond old regimes of left and right.

There have been other attempts to consider culture as a dynamic of give-and-take rather than strictly as a function of conditioning and totalitarian control. In 1983 (when I would assert that an Adorno-esque model of the culture industry was still more or less operational in the U.S.), T. J. Jackson Lears wrote: "The changes in the dominant culture are not always deliberately engineered; at times they stem from attempts to resolve private dilemmas that seem to have little to do with the realm of class domination."[10] There are private zones of pleasure, desire, problem-solving, that are a priori human; moreover, these pleasures are likely to be the same at all points along the continuum of the class spectrum, regardless of whether the upper class takes advantage of consumption more and benefits from it more (which is clearly indisputable). Although affirming that it is "the ruling groups [who] continually refashion the prevailing structure of feeling," Lears nonetheless states that this process occurs without them "conspiring to do so, sometimes with wholly other ends in view ... [and instead] to express—more or less—... changing social experience."[11]

Let me not be misunderstood here. Our vigilance against totalitarian systems must remain strong. In an era when corporations are able to rival, undermine and overrule the will of nations and peoples, the power of the consumer dollar (stretched to the limit as never before) is little more than a cold comfort at times. But our perceptions of these problems are, among other things, historically determined. And solutions often come inevitably from within the very zones of hegemonic-capitalist infection. In 1951 Adorno wrote, "The subjective precondition of opposition, uncoordinated judgment, is dying out, while its gesticulations continue to be performed as a group ritual."[12] I would argue that today we have an optimal ground for the resurgence of the uncoordinated judgment, the defiance of received orthodoxy in the name of free thought (e.g., Ryan Gosling's visionary linking of Walt Disney and David Lynch). Indeed, in terms of art today, success might be best measured not by critical certification or box office (in the case of movies), but by how our art, which can literally be anything now, understands its new mission precisely to acknowledge the uncertain conditions under which it operates, and to play them up, instead of courting, as Greenblatt writes, "the risk of absorbing the … rupture of human relatedness into an abstract, prepackaged schema."[13]

Thus, the "lack of positioning" which Sharon Willis cites as concomitant with the rise of simulation effects[14] might be the unique vertigo arising from terrain opening up beyond our frequently impacted ways of thinking, seeing, reading, listening, creating. Where it truly exists, "total access" to ideas and entertainment, as it turns out, can potentially privilege those quixotic ventures that were formerly compartmentalized (and often lost) within now-defunct categories of ideology and aesthetics: communist and capitalist; "difficult" and "entertaining"; abstract and realist-representational; high-canonical and trashy. The multiple-leveled culture allows for our responses to art to be separate and equal, if you will, like speaking different languages or enjoying the company of unlikely friends.

• • •

Time to come a bit clean. If this opening gambit has sounded at all defensive, it is because I do feel somewhat defensive about something which I nonetheless feel compelled to admit. I have always had a penchant for extremely violent films—sadistic, twisted, graphic—the kind of films that carry warnings to watch only with caution. I am like Mrs. Bubis, that creation of Bolaño's, who chuckles delightedly at the obscene George Grosz caricatures which disturb and depress her more mature-minded peers.[15] I do not pretend that this penchant is post-structural or semiotic or quasi–Marxist or politically correct or wholly ironic or anything other than what it is: I enjoy watching visceral displays of physical power, even though I want neither to be on the giving nor receiving end of such displays in real life. I have even secretly rooted for non-violent movies to suddenly turn violent, while never knowing exactly how this squares with the rest of my core beliefs. Basically, I'm for nonviolence; but my taste in entertainment tells a different story.

At some point I made personal peace with these seeming contradictions by deciding that it is the place of fantasy to experience *vicariously* (and perhaps it is not merely coincidental that my very name is contained within this word that I have struggled with so much throughout my life) things that I would be horrified to live out in reality.

Nicolas Winding Refn has made violence central to his films. But there is much more to his movies than their quotient of expressive, propulsive, heady, imaginative violence. Or, perhaps more accurately, there's more to the violence than "simple violence" (as if there were such a thing). One might come to his work initially for its thrills and end up feeling as if a new way of seeing cinema is being revealed. For Refn is a kind of whip-smart visualizer and mixmaster such as we have not encountered lately on such a grand international scale. While always remaining distinctly his own man, he combines elements of ascetic art and Euro-decadence, cinéma-vérité and Abstract Expressionism, Mafioso spectacle and old-fashioned surrealism, ancient epic saga and po-mo melodrama. The result is uncanny. His films, sometimes set to trancelike techno music, seem to go into fugue states right before your eyes.

Imagine a virtual-reality application in which you could project yourself into any scene from any film. The ending of *Casablanca*, for instance—you are there on the airport runway, everything in motion and three-dimensional. You could watch from the sidelines, or choose a protagonist to inhabit. Rick or Ilsa. Or both. You could even be Laszlo if that is your fancy, or good old Inspector Renault. And, of course, you would not be limited to merely replaying the scene as is; you could throw the game. Rick could convince Ilsa to give up the Resistance and come away with him to Argentina. Sam could get to do the love scenes—why not? Laszlo could masochistically give Ilsa up and fly off alone, picturing her and Rick making love all night, everywhere, forever.

And then again, for a really jaded thrill, you could make Conrad Veidt and the other Germans-speaking-broken-English arrive in time to polish everyone off. Is there any harm in that? It's only *virtual* reality, after all. Is it only honest respect for the dead that makes this idea sound appalling, or rather an attenuated and reflexive political and historical superstition whose weird burden the dead themselves would most likely cast off if they could be miraculously brought back to their (in many cases) apolitical lives? Might they even urge us to live more, to live again, to live unrestrainedly for their sake?

If we allow ourselves to view "the Nazis" as something quaint for a moment, will we be enabling their return somehow, or will we come to see that the next Nazis or even the current Nazis are not going to be wearing those same uniforms or speaking those same sentences? What is this unique piety that polices representations? Can we call it a true survival mechanism or just a holding pattern? Have our old myths failed us while still claiming too much space inside our heads? And how do we generate new, more useful myths to enhance humanity today, to summarize our public emotions of pride, hope and fear?

Finally, why is Hitler more ubiquitous today, more on our minds and more the stuff of legend than, say, Elie Wiesel? A new film has recently been made about Hannah Arendt[16]; but what is this dilatory response compared to the hundreds of films that have been made about Nazis and the Third Reich? When do we begin to replace our "negative myths" about Nazis with "positive myths" about those who opposed them? By myths I do not mean untruths in need of debunking, but *stories* that cement the actual history within mass consciousness. Why can't we overcome our obsession with the bad guys in order to move beyond them once and for all? Are we forever stuck with trauma, fatalism and *mauvaise foi*, fearfully repressing every trace of what neurotically consumes and excites us?

Leaving open these admittedly somewhat crazy-sounding questions for the time being, let's add another twist to this hypothetical app. Not only can you walk around inside any film and change its action at will, now you can bring two different films together in an interlacing of disparate artistic effects and intentions. You could splice-in the ending of *Casablanca* with *Cannibal Holocaust*, for example. It is a wide, infinitely varied world (also a globally interlinked one), and when we set out to save the world, just as when we set out to exploit it, we should always know how the parts work together—romance, glamour, solemnity, nudity, screams, blood, all taking place in the same mental battleground, all finding a common denominator of human emotional truth. After all, what ultimately makes us hate the Nazis so much when we watch *Casablanca* is nothing overtly political or even historical, but instead precisely the fact that they have the power to deform the natural ending, to make the true-hearted lovers, Rick and Ilsa, violate the logic that would otherwise reign supreme: that it's the crazy, mixed-up world that's the hill of beans, and it's love on which all of life depends—love which cannot be faked or controlled, at the extremes of romanticism, a reason to die that removes the fear of death.

Meanwhile, "cinema," that elusive poltergeist, plays in the shambles of its own contradictions without needing to apologize, because we accept that its chaos makes us feel less lonely, less haunted. We drive toward the projector's flickering light that we think we see on the horizon, uncertain whether it is a new dawn or the last violent spasm of the setting sun.... So let's play *Casablanca-Holocaust*. On the airport runway where Laszlo still waits for Ilsa, the figures of jungle cannibals emerge, watching, waiting. They begin to come closer. They are naked except for necklaces of dangling bones; but one of them is wearing Bogart's trench coat.

– 1 –

Seven Disorganizing Principles

1. *"I don't consider myself a director"*[1]

Refn has directed ten films: *Pusher* (1996), *Bleeder* (1999), *Fear X* (2003), *With Blood on My Hands: Pusher II* (2004), *I'm the Angel of Death: Pusher III* (2005), *Miss Marple: Nemesis* (2007, for BBC Television), *Bronson* (2008), *Valhalla Rising* (2009), *Drive* (2011), and *Only God Forgives* (2013). Many of these films have come to note as commercial and critical successes, possessing a distinct and visionary sense of style. Although barely into his 40s, the Danish-born Refn has been hailed as an Emerging Master at the 2006 Seattle Film Festival, and he also won the Best Director award at Cannes in 2011 (for *Drive*). Yet I would like to begin considering his work in light of the above comment. Why would he say that he does not consider himself a director?

    Perhaps part of the answer can be explained etymologically. The Danish word for "director" is "Instruktør"; "direction" is "Instruktion." Although these words literally do mean "director" and "direction" in the same cinematic sense that we understand, they have secondary meanings identical to the English words they closely resemble, "instructor" and "instruction," as in to teach, to explain, to demonstrate, or, more generally perhaps, to *set an example*.

    There is something unique in this Danish derivation. By contrast, the French "directeur" and the English "director" unmistakably denote one who oversees, one who leads or commands; while the Italian "regista" and (the French and) German "Regisseur" seem even more imperial and kingly, likely etymological links between the Latin *regius* (regal) and the modern Spanish *rey* (king) and English *regent*. Only Danish seems to conceive the film director's role as something other than a kind of overlord. Without wanting to place too much weight on a single word, this nonetheless might be symptomatic of what currently seems unique about the Danish sensibility in general, especially as it is being revealed in an ever-expanding and ever more attention-grabbing cinema.

It is clear that some of the best and most exciting films (and filmmakers) are coming now from Denmark. Expert Mette Hjort writes: "The transformation of a previously moribund national cinema into a form of cultural production commanding considerable interest within a national communicative space and on a festival circuit with global reach is, I suggest, the result of initiatives on the part of what I call a hebephilic state. What I have in mind, more specifically, is a state [Denmark] that values creativity and innovation, with the qualities in question being attributed to young people who thus in principle become deserving of unique forms of state support."[2] "Hebephilic," an interesting word which I interpret as the love of youth and youthful ideas, suggests a background in pedagogy as much as "Instruktør" does. Put otherwise: Danish cinema is an open classroom, a shared learning experience in which even the state is happy to play a supportive part.

There is an element of benign anarchy in Hjort's semi-utopian conception of the hebephilic state. After all, if we follow the linguistic logic we have been pursuing, one who instructs is an exemplar, a mediator between ideals and realities. An instructor is not necessarily humbler than one who directs; but we might think of instruction as a vertical movement, aiming upward, whereas direction is a lateral movement (albeit structured hierarchically, with top-to-bottom power differentials) aimed at the covering of ground. One can impersonally "direct" masses of tourists or traffic flows. In fact, we have signs and automatic lights designed to do just this. However, one can only instruct *as a human*, and then only in relation to another human (animal training is already anthropomorphic). Moreover, the patina of didacticism has an objective, borderless, calming neutrality which transcends or encompasses disparate ideological grounds: it might appeal equally to Bertolt Brecht and John Stuart Mill.

Such borderlessness, in particular, has a special meaning in the world of film, whose best practitioners have often been freely moving citizens of the world (rather than provincial types). Denmark, specifically its language, has given us a place to begin this investigation of contradictoriness and even benign anarchy in the work of Nicolas Winding Refn, but no more than a place to begin. Refn innately grasps the idea of transcending the limitations of borders; there are numerous reasons why we should not label him as a "Danish filmmaker." Although born in Copenhagen (in 1970), he grew up in New York City from age eight to seventeen,[3] and is now more or less an internationalist:

he has made less than half of his films in Denmark, the rest have been made in the UK, the U.S., Asia and elsewhere. Moreover, Refn's freedom is intellectual as well as geographic, for it is clear that Refn does not think monolithically, or from an exclusively centralized position, crediting his "alienated," deracinated upbringing as sparking a creative sense of belonging everywhere and nowhere.[4]

In keeping with this, he believes in encouraging a certain amount of artistic freedom in those with whom he collaborates, "because you're dealing with human beings. You only make good stuff if your collaborators are a part of your process and a part of your ideas, and there's no point in fighting them or them fighting you."[5] Here is where the idea of the capital-D Director begins to yield to the new idea of the instructor. Or, as Refn himself explains what he does as opposed to "directing" in the classic sense: director is merely "a title. It's more like I make films and I just want to control it."[6] Authority is static; whereas Refn's sense of "control" (I am not fond of this word, but it's Refn's) would seem to be dynamic, active, a way of effecting continuous change. Control, perhaps best understood as a constant balance between growth and containment, is where the instructor's skill comes into play, and where one *earns* the authority only promised by the ephemeral title.

Refn himself wears different cinematic hats. Originally he wanted to be an actor, and he also worked with special effects, but he had difficulty submitting to authority.[7] Could Refn be as much an anarchist as I have described Mette Hjort as being? In fact, one constant theme of the films which Refn has written and directed is the distrust of authority and the movement away from artificial hierarchies. The one who officially commands, in Refn's films, is nearly always a hollow figure, unworthy of the title he holds; while the real hero is thwarted, kept from power, placed in a position of having to revolt, and sometimes martyred in the end. One of the most important things about Refn is that he is definitely committed to bringing back to movies a credible and mature vision of heroism—in which the hero generally has no place in the world for which he fights and dies.

In Refn's films, then, we will find that the hero is not a social construct, an aggregate of fixed social values, but an entity outside of and perhaps above society, or, rather, his own epoch. This idea is not new, but Refn's interest in it runs somewhat against the grain of what we have come to expect from recent action cinema, for example. These are not the typical flawed, shabby heroes who adapt to difficult times; Refn's heroes have an exacting and almost mythic superiority, forcing them to stand alone in life. This kind of hero appears in *Fear X*, *Bronson*, *Valhalla Rising*, *Drive* and *Only God Forgives*. What makes them heroic is that they demand for chaos to take on a moral shape and order.

Indeed, behind the idea of heroism are issues of moral right and wrong which Refn claims have become taboo in current Western society. He has said that his films are "about consequences, how every day, everything is consequences. You come out of your front door, you either walk this way or that way, and your decision has consequences. And I think the biggest fear in the West is confronting that idea."[8]

Confronting an idea is, of course, never the same as endorsing it, but let's say that Refn is correct, that morality has lost that sanctified public aspect which made it cohere and have influence. After all, if our random decisions had only random consequences (sometimes they do, though), then the consequences would hardly matter more than the decisions themselves if we wish to rise above a relativism that is as much related to physics (time and motion) as to ethics. It is reminiscent of that memorable Grace Jones lyric, "Everybody Hold Still," in which she is caught up in a bank robbery and traces her steps backwards to reveal the everyday science of congruency: if she had watched another TV show, if she had run back to answer the phone that rang as she was leaving, etc., she would not have ended up in the wrong place at the wrong time. But what appears as a paranoiac form of Murphy's Law from the standpoint of a hapless "victim" amounts to more of an existential gamble for the bad actor,

Born in Demark, raised in New York City, and comfortable making films in such diverse places as Thailand and the UK, Nicolas Winding Refn offers hope for a new vitality in international cinema. His role is that of mythmaker, creating compelling characters who exemplify great themes such as loss of innocence, heroism, and the universal oneness of existence.

the criminal who chooses to do wrong. Refn: "I like crime movies that deal with moral issues within the genre, where, at some point, the protagonist is forced to choose and realizes that there are consequences to his choice."[9]

However, Refn stresses that his sense of heroism within the crime genre doesn't break down neatly into "villains and good guys."[10] We see through Refn's often impassive and inscrutable male characters only to the extent that they allow us to, only to the extent that they see through themselves. There is little irony in *Bronson* when "Charlie Bronson" says, "A hero is made for better things. I had a calling. I just didn't know what it was."

Above all, the hero is an affront. He is not accounted for by the system that inadvertently produces him, nor is he wanted. He is concerned with breaking free from an entrenched order, as in *Valhalla Rising* and *Drive*, or at least defying it as best he can from his own enchained position within that order, as in *Fear X* and *Bronson*. Dismantling artificial hierarchies enables organic hierarchies to arise, based on strength, or determination, or virtue, or truth. These, too, are anarchic, stemming from the spontaneous flow of world and life. As Georges Bataille wrote, "Nothing seems more miserable and more dead than the stabilized thing."[11] A constant play of chaos is really order, or the only order that can support a healthy, not moribund, existence. Authority grows fallow when it rests on wilted laurels. So in order to grasp control at any given moment, one cannot stay standing still; one must keep on the move, dodging and weaving, subjecting oneself to new tests of skill or new environments— as so many of Refn's hell-bent, compromised heroes discover, or as Refn himself has done in his questing, peripatetic career.

Indeed, it is not difficult to see this vision of the hero—as one who alters reality as it stands to produce something more harmonic, more just, and also one who establishes a free-floating space of individual freedoms—as a metaphor for the work of a film director. What the "instructor" imparts is not so much the teaching of all the separate processes which come together in the making of a film, the specialized skills of the crew, but instead the collective means by which so many different individuals are able to set themselves aside in the service of a greater enterprise. The diverse film crew mirrors the delicate responsibilities of citizens in social citizenship. It is difficult to get people to set themselves aside, and all education aims at it fundamentally, regardless of the area of knowledge: ideally, the ego is subsumed to the general category of knowledge itself through the quest for it. One begins by loving process for its own sake, specifically the process in which an abstracted idea crystallizes into facts and actions, setting the example of having visions and then getting out of the way of those visions as much as one can.

Finally, we should consider the possibility that Refn does not consider himself a director because, as cultural figures, film directors have lost a great deal of the clout which the generally passé auteur theory built up for them during the '50s, '60s and '70s—the Age of Power Directors. Today's directors, even at their best, are more like mixtures of technical managers and public relations brands. Clearly emerging as one of our most fascinating and gifted cineastes, Refn is a true throwback to the Age of Power Directors in one defining sense: he gives enthralling, maddening interviews. (This first chapter is sectioned around some of his more provocative aphorisms, what I am calling "disorganizing principles.") One feels charged with energy to hear him speak or read his words. Recall what Somerset (Morgan Freeman) says to Mills (Brad Pitt) in *Se7en* (1997): "It's impressive to see a man feeding off his emotions." Refn feeds like that—he needles, he lobs questions back at his interviewer, he radiates productive anxiety and the coveting of adrenalin, he says things he probably "shouldn't say," he expounds on philosophy and even goes so far as to discuss what his films are "really about." He understands the longing for creative friction; for the exalted or the grubby; the truly sacred or the totally profane; the insane gamble, the throw of the dice; the Blakean marriage of heaven and hell—in proto-cinematic-mythic terms, the bad and the beautiful, the holy whore, the two weeks in another town, the cinema paradisio, the road to nowhere.

2. *"I'm happy I didn't go to film school because I don't think I would have survived it"*[12]

Theodor W. Adorno begins *Minima Moralia* by making the point that academe is not a refuge from capitalist hegemony but a reification of it, in noble, altruistic drag. He does not assert this, as we might assume today, by taking up the cause of educators as underpaid drones, taken for granted and exploited, but instead by hypothesizing an independently wealthy genius who chooses to go into higher education as a way of "defecting" from his own elite ruling class and thereby questioning the tyranny of leisure. The passage is worth quoting at length:

> The departmentalization of mind is a means of abolishing mind where it is not exercised *ex officio*, under contract. It performs this task all the more reliably since anyone who repudiates the division of labour—if only by taking pleasure in his work—makes himself vulnerable by its standards in ways inseparable from elements of his superiority. Thus is order ensured: some have to play the game because they cannot otherwise live, and those who could live otherwise are kept out because they do not want to play the game.[13]

1. Seven Disorganizing Principles

The game which must be played involves the reasons why students seek higher education at exorbitant cost, because the license of "professionalism" is available only to those willing to wend through the socially prescribed labyrinth, i.e., willing to accede to the formulaic structure of society. It is precisely "independents" who threaten the perceived stability of the process by which one submits to training and discipline in the first place. In the largest sense, what is really being taught in academic systems is the following of rules, what Adorno calls "departmentalization of mind," which turns mental work into drudgery and further cuts off the potential for truly new ideas. Everything is filtered through "domineering competence,"[14] which demonstrates that it is worthy of joining the intellectual tradition by mastering the endless parroting of previously absorbed and assimilated thought, thereby agreeing to validate rather than question the assumptions by which that tradition maintains itself. "Ambition aims solely at expertise in the accepted stock-in-trade, hitting on the correct slogan."[15]

Needless to say, there is no room for anarchy. Ultimately, this is true of personal as well as professional dealings within universities. We know that education as a formal system is really nothing but a process of normative socialization. Just as art is made from a combination of talent and experience (none of which can be properly "taught"), the essence of scholarship finally lies in reading and research skills, which can be honed autodidactically. The purpose of superintending a student's practice of these skills is not an objective and unbiased process, but a careful herding of nonconformist tendencies. Like any piece of status in a status-driven society, advanced degrees are not only awarded for merit but for being a dependable part of the social combine.[16] (It does not matter that many, if not most, academics are leftists in an age when the right-wing is engaged in challenging every centrist societal assumption; they are so often leftists who have been submitted to a training of circular thinking and outmoded concepts, giving rise to an essentially unempirical, non-social, non-reality-based leftism.)

Likewise, the constant exposure to one's peers over the years of education is a kind of de facto method of indoctrinating students with socially acceptable norms. Adorno: "Society is integral even before it undergoes totalitarian rule."[17] One learns to get up on time every day, to groom oneself, to cooperate, to compromise, to work side by side with others, to complain only in whispered confidence, to gradually betray one's individual mentality for something molded more and more to fit the ethos of the group. Above all, one learns to refrain from asking those questions which as yet have no official, certified answer; and from re-posing insistent questions that have official but unsatisfactory answers. The scientific method (in philosophy and the humanities) has been suppressed, but even though this method remains essential to the illusion of academic integrity, scholars denounce it in their colleagues by resorting to negative social paradigms: "awkward," "unfriendly," "fascist" are words that get bandied about behind the backs and occasionally to the faces of those who ask uncomfortable questions.[18]

No one gets through university without learning this socialization process, for humiliations both inside and outside the classroom attend upon those who are clearly and visibly failing to learn it. It isn't that one cannot be a hipster, a radical; indeed, one can be those things all too easily in university, but only to the extent that these roles demonstrate the proper deference and humility within the structural hierarchy, and do not attempt to transcend what has gone before. One must always ask permission to do the thing that seems new, and thus the gesture is never truly a break with tradition except on very superficial levels. This superficiality is what I call the "familiar new," and what Bataille calls the "educated vulgarity" of modern existence.[19]

The structure of knowledge and its dissemination is part and parcel with societal structuring. Meticulous referencing is the first indoctrination of the idea of "indebtedness," the full implications of which must be assimilated by everyone preparing for a future of cubicle jobs and credit-card peonage. Education is preparation for a world in which "standards" are not there to be transgressed upon in the form of innovation and ideas, but are instead a means of wielding control from above. Specialization and expertise become, as Adorno suggested, ways of containing, rather than liberating, the energies of mind, of art. Better to be a journeyman, a jack of all trades, than to subject oneself to that containment. Never before has specialization been the absolute sign of a contempt for true learning, true knowledge. Refn: "I always believe that a director should not be an expert at anything. But he has to know a little bit about everything."[20]

Unlike what film school might have provided, Refn's (film) education was entirely self-directed and sui generis. Living in New York City with his father, distinguished film editor Anders Refn, he discovered the grindhouse theaters that proliferated in Times Square in that era (the late '70s and the '80s), and spent endless hours in the dark imbibing double features of unabashed raunch and gore.[21] What nurtured young Refn's growing imagination was a culture of film untouched by highbrow notions. Grindhouse, or exploitation, films were cheap and shoddy; they were never self-important, yet indisputably they mattered. This is the most important thing: these films were cranked out to an audience that could not consume them quickly enough; they existed as a sort of constant ambient background to the life of the metropolis. And beyond Manhattan they lit up the enormous screens of rural drive-ins when those outdoor temples were still crucial, quintessentially American gathering places. It's not hard to understand the intoxicating, disinhibiting effects of these films. They were entertaining, escapist, but at the same time edgy and even uncomfortable; a kind of shared and even pagan experience, so shoddy and free in their assemblage that they depended on, and tutored, new ways of seeing and hearing, new ways of absorbing narrative.

There is a long tradition of this merging of sensationalism and didacticism in avant-garde 20th century art, so that when Refn did come to high culture (he learned to read only in high school[22]) he could experience its esoteric jeremiads through the influencing lens of exploitation films, not, as many other defenders of low culture have done, the other way around. What I mean is this: rather than reading exploitation cinema as a part of the long decay of the note that first sounded with Cézanne and *Le Sacre du Printemps*, Refn probably saw it as the blossoming fulfillment of something that had only been inchoate and partially realized in even the most radical productions of high culture. According to this line of thinking, Doris Wishman, say, is not a failed Godard because she threw the cinematic image and narrative realism into question *only* around issues of bodies rather than issues of language and politics (put simply). Rather, Godard is a "failed" Wishman, because the seventy-three-inch breasts of Chesty Morgan (Wishman's star in two '70s films) subsume all need for rhetorical argument or language-poetry. The spectacle of grotesque, real flesh—meant generally as sexual titillation, sexual purgation, or gory fake violence—contained a truth that escaped art's endless striving after (disembodied) meaning, and were also the sign of a nihilism so potent and complete that it acted implicitly as an indictment of anything and everything. Godard himself, in *Histoire(s) du Cinéma* (1988–1998), returns again and again to distorted scenes from antique porn as a way of underscoring the pragmatic survival of the moving image throughout ages of political and historical infamy. In a sense, Chesty, a stripper whose freakish mammaries constituted her entire acting and raison d'être, is more of a logical response to the concentration camps and the atomic bomb than all the circuitous, self-righteous nattering of art cinema. The critic R. H. W. Dillard even sees the nihilism of horror and exploitation cinema as a way of potentially breaking through to a new moral high ground if we so choose: such cinema gives us "a choice of energy, of free moral action and of light,"[23] while "revealing the good in its absence, wholeness in fragmentation, direction in apparently random motion."[24]

Could Doris Wishman really be "better" than Godard? Now, let me say I only partially believe this theoretical argument I am pursuing. I came to exploitation films after being immersed in Hollywood and art cinema, so for me exploitation was like a refreshing blast of slang or profanity in the midst of an elocution lesson. It was mainly great high fun, though I could see how the stories had a stronger quality of existential nihilism than the average Hollywood fare, thus often placing them closer to the most serious European and Asian cinema, and also how the slapdash camerawork, editing, sets and acting fed into an inchoately surrealist way of apprehending reality: a gaggle of nude manikins in a room where someone is freaking out on acid, as in *The Weird World of LSD* (1967), could be laughable, but in fact it is also genuinely creepy and somehow more effective than anything more subtle could be. The catharsis of these films, close to what we always assume ancient tragedy must have been like, is that they give a feeling of a short, fast ride to a horrible end, and one which can be read in social-universal terms; at their most potent and representative they bring a palpable uncleanness which hearkens back, again, to our sense of tragedy's exorcising body-counts, its anguished cleansing of communal wounds.

Here it would be helpful to refer to Antonin Artaud, whose prescriptions for theater were closely allied with depictions of brutality and violence such as we come to find in exploitation cinema. Artaud wrote, "A violent and concentrated action is a kind of lyricism: it summons up supernatural images, a bloodstream of images."[25] Theater would teach us two things primarily: "We are not free. And the sky can still fall on our heads."[26] Artaud believed that it was the role of theater to demonstrate that "we are no longer good for anything but disorder, famine, blood, war, and epidemics," but he viewed the revelation of this as paving the way for a purging of *actual* violence. The problem was one of being able to clearly see and own the (human, societal) tendency to violence in the first place. Exploitation cinema strips away a similar hypocrisy of denial in the individual spectator.

All serious art aims at this goal of being produced *urgently*, in a way that overrides the calculated gentility of the marketplace. Musician David Byrne bears witness to a similar phenomenon of finding an unlikely purity in a deliberate cultivation of cultural bastardization instead of a hypocritically exalted high art. "When I came to New York," Byrne says, "I guess I was very naïve, I expected the art world to be very pure and noble. I was repulsed by what I saw people putting themselves through, the hustling to try to get anywhere. My natural reaction was to move into a world that had no pretense of nobility."[27] It has only been in very recent history that art has become an experience prepackaged precisely as art; in all other times, those cultural products that ended up becoming the representative art of their time all began as dubious questions, and often as things that were not initially even considered to be art at all. Thus, because art has become so routinized and professionalized in our time, the true artist warily moves away from being defined, leaving it to history to sort out what will matter. Like the shocks that forge a growing consciousness, all of this must take place outside of any socializing academic structure. Indeed, in Refn's cinema of violence, "art" becomes the reiteration of lost innocence within more or less free liberal societies that must confront their own failings and their own violence.

3. "I do think that art is an act of violence"[28]

Violent action has always figured heavily into the narrative arts, both on the level of content (violence moves plots forward; it also resolves plots sometimes) and of form (we speak of brush strokes and paint spatters, contrapuntal harmonies, polyrhythms, acting styles, editing, and dialogue as all being violent, when they are). In his book *Deadly Musings*, Michael Kowalewski suggests "we begin by thinking of violence ... not as serving dramatic purposes but as both prompting and enriching stylistic prerogatives."[29] It is that violence of form which is most intriguing, from an interpreting perspective, and Kowalewski likens the expression of violence in various art forms as being generally connected with the imaginative faculties of artists, "an energy in motion."[30]

The overflow of aggression when we conceive and describe violent acts creates an opportunity for artistic imagination to overflow, to break the bounds, even push through to new forms and new mediums. This also promotes the haphazard but sincerely-intentioned founding of what Kowalewski hopes will become "an epistemology of violence."[31] But is form (or epistemology for that matter) ever completely neutral when it comes to violence? Kowalewski's epistemology of violence implies an a posteriori moral imperative to derive meaning or value from the description of violent acts; but energy in its pure state is as little subject to edifying interpretations as it is to any other automatic or contrived controls. Put otherwise: we might only be able to learn from violent representations in art insofar as we can identify our own necessarily complex response.

This is the crucial role of the hero, who mediates between unreconstructed violence and its ramifications. Kowalewski cites Robert Warshow, who states that movie violence is concerned with

> a certain image of man, a style, which expresses itself most clearly in violence. Watch a child with his toy guns and you will see: what most interests him is not (as we so much fear) the fantasy of harming others, but to work out how a man might look when he shoots or is shot. A hero is one who looks like a hero.[32]

Thus, there can be the distinct, shivering pleasure of a certain raw self-revelation in the representation of violence. For those of us who already tend to regard all art as raw self-revelation, art and violence are eminently capable of substituting for, or morphing into, each other.

At any rate, violence in art is usually larger than the art itself; it directs the art toward an immediacy that is more like raw experience (like Kowalewski's epistemology). In *The Aesthetics of Murder*, Joel Black has suggested that violence in a narrative always signals extratextual, metafictional intention (we can extend this to metacinematic intention), since violence, specifically murder, is itself an aesthetic category of experience, and "the act of murder will always appear more profound than the work of art that merely describes it."[33] The form of violence (or violent form) overtakes content, stops narrative flow, and "moves toward the experience of time suspended in an endless present" rather than on any linear or even nonlinear continuum.[34] "Confronted with a spectacle of destruction, the author can no longer create, and his narrator can no longer narrate; they can only bear witness to a mystery of unnatural violence ... beyond the customary limits of human experience."[35]

However, some of this might be overstated. The artist does find a way to assimilate "unnatural violence" into creation; this is the great link between myth and art. Some artists consciously take on the role of mythmaker to an exaggerated extent, requiring that the subjects who inspire them be partly or wholly buried in the mnemonic sands, ineffable sources of legend who would never have returned to life without the collaborative effort of the artist—the artist as Dr. Frankenstein, as resurrectionist, as mythmaker.

In film today, Refn plays this role of mythmaker. He has said that he is not particularly interested in crime per se, but his general interest in people (and in heroes) leads him toward subjects in which there is a tragic sense of fate, and where life and death are at stake.[36] This is the appeal of myth. It is concentrated—like an uncut narcotic—and reductive of everything, down to only the most elemental origins. But this is also what makes myth so vital in times of social change and upheaval, when it becomes, according to Pierre Mabille, "knowledge reflected in the collective soul for reference."[37]

Precisely because it insists on a Protean touching of common ground, insists on summoning the surviving tribe whose sheer determination made social evolution and refinements possible, myth helps societies retain their bearings through times of change. Societies who have entirely lost their trust in myth or their ability to generate new myths experience any changes as irreparable shocks to the system, like a body held so rigidly that its bones break on impact. It is in times of urgent, widespread social change that myths are most needed, although usually not the old endemic ones. New mythmaking tinkers with our perceptions until we can understand the need for change. This is literally the raison d'être of myth. Myth is finally what announces, "I want to live, I want to go on," or, "*We* want to go on," in spite of all uncertainties.

Therefore, rather than something fossilized from antiquity, myth is a power that needs to regenerate itself at periodic times throughout the life of a given civilization. Mass culture, in particular movies, might be the best conduit for the creation of myths that serve a function of transforming the world or of coming to terms with a world that is already (being) transformed. As scholar of violent cinema Laurent Bouzereau writes, "Through movies, we test our abilities to face certain fears."[38] It is from potent but controlled doses of the ahistorical (the pretense of myth is that it is always somewhere outside of history, no matter that it serves historically determined functions) that societies remain coherent enough to face up to their histories in meaningful ways, and to mark the achievement of confronting trauma and moving forward. In this sense it can be helpful precisely as a clearly delimited phase or stage of progressive acceptance that is passed through and finally overcome. Without this gently nursed dependency on some degree of amnesiac, ahistorical thinking, it is possible that no society would have been able to survive its worst losses, its worst atrocities.

Citing the Brothers Grimm and Western cowboy movies, Refn has spoken to the potential for myths, or "fairytales," to stir notions of social bonding around the figure of the hero "who comes in and protects the innocent from evil, sacrificing himself for purity."[39] Some of this wording—"evil," "purity"— might seem like red flags to a U.S. embroiled in misbegotten culture-warfare, but in Refn's films it is possible to see these as foundational reference points which we all possess (humans being the narratological species that we are). Refn says, "Fairytales are universal. Cultures all over the world have archetypes—the samurai, the Western cowboy."[40]

Myth has an exceptional (and exceptionalizing) quality; it has different peaks and trajectories from narrative in general, or art. Art emerges, like myth and everything else, from the same primeval violence, but it is also constantly striving to keep up with violence, since art, unlike reality and often unlike myth, has had the reflexive need to conceal its violence in symmetry, composition, rhetoric—in forms of conscious or seemingly conscious order. This ennobling pretense is breaking down, however, as reality itself becomes increasingly a refuge in symbolic orders. The artist is redundant, thwarted, bitter. Indeed, art has become the angel of death in Western culture, in whose movies art and artists are frequently associated with villainy and malice. Where art is not murderous it is openly suicidal. Like the experience of the sublime, which it attempts to imitate, art supposedly aims at death as the final resolution of its ongoing crisis of trying to make the invisible visible. Sooner or later the aware artist conspires in the visible world's revenge against him. There is a long history of this idea in modernism and postmodernism, where art itself is, again, a sort of naked Frankenstein monster, blatantly constructed from fragments ripped apart and pieced back together; or, as we see in the novels of Elias Canetti and Thomas Mann, the mind colonized by art comes to feel secondhand and eventually turns on itself in weary, enervated chaos.

Not only creation but something about the way art is received, or consumed, is affected by the specter of this angel of death, as when Black writes, "Both the terrorist-killer and the film-director know how to manipulate the media and how to play on the fantasies and the fears of their mass audience, and they are profoundly aware of the effect their actions will have on their enthralled spectators."[41] The artist seeks to reproduce his own shock, or to acknowledge and vent his own criminal impulses. "Every work of art is an uncommitted crime," Adorno wrote.[42] John Waters has said that his films are crimes that he wanted to commit.[43] According to Ruggero Deodato, his often banned and heavily censored *Cannibal Holocaust* (1980) was directly inspired by graphic TV news coverage of terrorist attacks in Italy at the time.[44] The attack itself, the replaying of it on the news, and then the horror film offer a kind of infinite regress of dread in which the same atrocity is committed again and again in "copycat" fashion. Deodato seems to have wanted to re-embody the actual violence as something more real than a media circus or a numbing loop, saying to his audience, "This is *your* Eros and Thanatos if you can stand to claim it," a teachable moment but one which requires artificial recreation as a story, again, as a myth.

Director George Miller has stated: "But violence is a part of us, and I don't think that we understand it very well. There is an ugly side to each of us, and I have tried to communicate it. I know sometimes people don't like to hear that."[45] The ability to give cultural expression to inchoate violence can also be seen as regenerative, like the periodic resort to myth, a way of recording what we have withstood and survived, and of orienting ourselves toward the future. It is all well and good for critic Michel Ciment to praise John Boorman's *Deliverance* (1972) for its supposed refusal to subscribe to "violence as an initiation" (even though this point is highly debatable): "The myth of regeneration through violence, a myth fundamental to American civilization, is portrayed as a pathetic delusion."[46] The truth is that there are things in art and culture which exist beyond the complacent piety that would condemn them. In fact, the profound truth of regeneration through violence (as act of survival, energy renewal, shamanistic transformation, sacrifice, rite, etc.) is at the heart of the Buddhist *Baghavad Gita*, for example, not to mention Baroque *Trauerspiel*— i.e., works and forms which we take seriously as philosophy and as history.

Rebellion, rioting and revolution have also been regenerative processes that point the spasmodic way forward toward equal rights and social inclusivity.

So the myths that we need are ones that come in the wake of revolutionary awakenings, to dramatize and make retellable the story of our progress. Some insight is provided here by Mark Fisher, in *Capitalist Realism: Is There No Alternative?* Fisher denounces the run of postmodern gangster films (Tarantino, Scorsese and others) as defenses of a moribund and cynical fetishizing of the real, of "capitalist realism," in "their common claims to have stripped the world of sentimental illusions and seen it for 'what it really is': a Hobbesian war of all against all, a system of perpetual and generalized criminality."[47] When "no way out, no hope of change" becomes folkloric, common wisdom, then we have a situation in movie genres which is comparable to the fact that everything is now connected back to corporate statehood. This is why Fisher calls such images of gangsterism "anti-mythical myth,"[48] a provocative term which suggests what is missing between the rote rehearsals of an assumed and incorrigible omnipotence in anti-mythical myth, and the potential for redemption in actual myth, also an alternative to capitalist realism perhaps, like that "unreal realism" which Refn has claimed to be working in. And Refn, too, views gangsterism as anti-mythical myth, when presented as it really is, as opposed to the abiding "fiction": real gangsters "don't have a lot of money. It's only in fiction that they have speedboats and yachts and thousands of bodyguards. This [criminal activity] is a nine to five job."[49] But in this, of course, there lies a new and more illustrative myth in the sense of story: the human side of something we had often considered as anti-human or unredeemable.

Even Milo (Zlatko Buric), the drug kingpin in Refn's *Pusher* trilogy, is seen as grinding out the day-to-day work of being a gangster. His rewards may seem greater than those of his underlings—he has, as Refn points out, "a nice house in the suburbs" which he is able to return to after dealing fake ecstasy and bumping off his rivals. But the house is antiseptic and lonely; in the last shot of *Pusher III: I'm the Angel of Death*, Refn shows Milo standing over the drained swimming pool in his backyard, an ice-blue pit that suggests a mass grave and whose emptiness reminds Milo that, as a gangster, he is always "in the hole," buying drug shipments that he might not be able to sell, partnering up with other criminals whom he might not be able to trust.

Refn has steered gangster cinema away from euphoria and glory, and toward "sadness." He has said that he tries to find and acknowledge the sadness in every aspect of his criminal protagonists' lives.[50] Likewise, on a formal level he has steered gangster cinema toward something almost like Italian neorealism: non-actors in lead roles, real locations, natural lighting, and tales of hard-luck urban losers.

Imaginative artistry and formal experimentation can be brought to bear on genre films, as well as unabashed moral stances in which love, for instance, can be un-cynically trumpeted as an end to the evil of that systemic, corporate-gangster criminality which Fisher says is usually allowed to flourish under "a kind of machismo of demythologization."[51] The demythologizers pose as "unflinching observers who refuse to prettify the world,"[52] while secretly identifying with corporate control and while offering only visions of hegemonic violence crushing the individual. Mythologizers, then, promote the idea that a heroic and concomitant violence against the system can liberate the individual, and they themselves as artists stand on the side of this anarchic overturning of the system.[53]

At the most basic level, of course, whether mythical or anti-mythical, narrative art has always been driven by irruptions of violence lurching toward resolution. This is for the most part so obvious that it is rarely considered. Yet, even the mere use of temporality—of time moving on, of the past recurring—proceeds by doing violence to an otherwise placid sense of stasis or resting in the present moment. Erich Auerbach comes close to saying as much in *Mimesis* when he places the recognition of Odysseus's scar as the first example of flashback in Western narrative art.[54] Homer's text itself bears this flashback like a (metonymic) scar on the page. Even when the manifold content of a story is not violent, narrative is pummeled and jostled along through a process in which described moments are externalized in a continuous presentness, leaving a series of (again) textual scars by which the reader's perceptions are altered and his or her identifications heightened.

Where narratives do concern themselves with violence and crime, they bear a more open relation to their own eras' concerns, fears and vicarious thrills. Historian Robert Muchembled states: "To varying degrees, the crime story, in all its many forms, questioned the morality of appearances and the order imposed by established society. It painted, and constantly updated, the picture of he who dared to resist, whether evil genius, youthful honorable bandit or disillusioned private eye with unorthodox methods."[55] According to Muchembled, the increasingly violent narrative over the centuries of early-modern Western culture set two disparate aims in tense, conflicted balance: on the one hand, exorcising violent instincts by giving them containable outlets in representational narrative art; and on the other hand, keeping those same instincts constantly simmering at low boil, as it were, in case we ever needed to tap into them again during times of war.[56]

Richard Bausch's novel *Violence* (1994) has been a fairly recent attempt to flesh out the links between violence and narrative. The book concerns an average man who survives getting caught up in a hostage crisis and subsequent deadly shoot-out in a convenience store one night; following this, he begins to see everything as a manifestation of the same basic Ur-violence of existence. "All of it was possible. It had happened. It was waiting to happen, everywhere."[57] Like Odysseus's scar, violence signals temporal shifts which allow for narrative to unfold, and also fold back upon itself, in traumatized fixations and repetition compulsions; for finally, in their jarring roughness, those shifts become indistinguishable from the neurotic symptoms they generate. Bausch's protagonist sickens from his new knowledge of time as a stasis waiting to be interrupted by violent action: "In the vast dark and sparkle of the city, people were going on with their lives in the aftermath of violence. And surely someone else's life was at this moment entering the heart of fright."[58] No matter what they might be describing, these blatant temporal cues— "going on," "in the aftermath," "at this moment," "entering"—suggest rupture, trauma, survival; they are also basic building blocks of telling a story. *Once upon a time*—but this time will soon be disturbed by the singular event promised by that "once." They lived happily *ever after*—but only by assimilating traumatic memories implied by that implacable "after."

Bausch goes further, stylistically. He begins to construct numerous sentences beginning with the most aggressive and altering of conjunctions, "but." "This was home.... But the violence was everywhere, and he should've known it."[59] "But the weeks and months ahead seemed blotted somehow. He could not imagine a time when his thoughts might belong to him."[60] "But he was convinced that something in him had been set loose by what happened in the convenience store, and it was floating around in his soul, dark, interested only in its own nourishment."[61] Bausch implies that narrative is not based on the use of a series of "and"s to signify adding the next thing to the previous thing, and so on, but instead a series of combative "but"s, which signify conflict, the other shoe falling. "And" is a laundry list; "but" is the beginning of a story. In this sense, Bausch's writing and narrative are functionally on the side of the violence, and it is only when he must pull back and resolve his hero's torment in a positive way that the novel suddenly loses its drive and conviction.

Indeed, aesthetic problems in general only seem to come into play when an artist is shown to be unaware or self-censoring of his own criminal tendencies, trying to have things both ways, as it were, by self-delusionally expecting social approbation and reward for making societal violence an explicit touchstone of his art. Kowalewski's epistemology of violence is nothing if not an entrée into self-knowledge. The megalomania of art today is not the belief that it can reproduce the world (as the encyclopedia-minded 18th century wanted to reduce all of nature to a beautiful garden, a naturalist's collection of specimens), but that it can undermine and destroy that same world with impunity. "We're gonna win an Oscar for this!" gloats the reckless documentarist Alan Yates (Gabriel Yorke) in *Cannibal Holocaust* as his crew film themselves gunning down unarmed natives.

Black argues that this megalomania relates to the perceived social meaninglessness of art:

> Often, however, the violence depicted in works of art ultimately seems directed against the idea of art itself, and should be seen as art's suicidal attempt to pass beyond its culturally conditioned self-image of falsity, and to achieve some transcendent or nihilistic—but, in any case, pre-aesthetic—"reality."[62]

Art again appears as dreaded angel of death. For Black, rather than coming together as an act of socio-psychological exorcism, art and murder share the salient quality of being at least partly bound up in issues of "style" overtaking and erasing the need for content. In this, he differs from Kowalewski: it is "not the motive" (a function of content, embedded in the text) that commands attention "but merely the external manner and circumstances."[63] Aesthetics become the refinement of a method in which the content is reduced to a summary of what the artist has literally done, what chain he or she has followed, to get to the accomplished work. (A disgusted reviewer once called Refn's cinema "the careful work of a serial killer."[64])

Here we have the fusion of the artist with his subject and with his materials. We see this in an intense, gruesome image from *Cannibal Holocaust* where the parts of a broken camera are bound up with the skulls and bones of the slaughtered film crew in an eerie jungle totem. In this image the filmmakers' medium is intimately connected with the literal life and death of their bodies. Although this fusion is presented by Deodato as a morbid extremity, it speaks to an ideal of art as an extraordinarily powerful experience, survivable or not survivable as the case may be. Thus, we see again what we have surmised all along: art, especially if it is *about* violence, must be made *with* a certain violence if it is not to become superficial and cynical. The morality of violent art is in the honesty with which the artist commits himself to his own rooting interest in violence as catharsis, if nothing else. Morality is identical to method and its labors; and these are probably not rigorous or cold-blooded labors. The artist's inner drive to identify himself through his art will compel a style that is non-neutral and therefore does not attempt to conceal the operation in which content (motive) is always made to define and express itself through style (means of execution). This might be pictured as the difference between a professional hit and a sudden crime of passion. Both are lethal, but the former, by its distanced, methodical nature, is a denial of the raw emotion behind it, while the latter is that emotion in the shape of a direct action.

4. "The Texas Chain Saw Massacre *was where I really saw film as an art form*"[65]

Violence in art, in fact, may be nothing but the bait, so to speak, for a new experience of art that reveals itself through the same nerve centers of stimulation which violence itself is meant to reach. Horror films are often unique in the way they become no longer mere movies but tests of stamina and will: can you stand to watch it? Can you even literally survive? Now and then a new and unprecedented horror film comes along that announces itself as an active rather than passive viewing experience: real consequences can supposedly result from the decision to watch. *Freaks* (1932) opened with a prologue advising people to leave the auditorium; *The Tingler* (1959) had theater seats wired for electric shocks; customers were warned that no one would be admitted to *Psycho* (1960) after the screening had begun, as if it wasn't a pre-recorded document but an unfolding, unstoppable happening; advertisements for *The Exorcist* (1972) carried disclaimers for people with heart conditions.

Specifically, for Refn, *The Texas Chain Saw Massacre* (1974), directed by Tobe Hooper and photographed by Daniel Pearl, "was about evoking emotions that you didn't normally get."[66] Gritty, surreal and satirical, *The Texas Chain Saw Massacre* taught Refn the power of the purely visual aspect of cinema, the way images can express emotions beyond words. In it, the cinematic image becomes "like painting."[67] For the image in *The Texas Chain Saw Massacre*, as it is in painting, is always supremely self-contained. It connects to other images (in montage) only obliquely; even when separate images work together, they do not "need" each other. Hooper's masterpiece is the greatest horror film ever made because it literally embodies in its style the terror of entropy and disintegration as skillfully and uncompromisingly as *Les Demoiselles d'Avignon* or Francis Bacon. "Seeing that," Refn says, "was like going into an abstract art form. Film was no longer about conventional storytelling, three acts.... Cinema could be just sound, or still images."[68]

Indeed, the larger claims of narrative and character (which belong to artificially ordering structures: the mind associates like with like) are subsumed within arresting moments that coalesce around startling chiaroscuro effects, sunspots, abstract patterns of roiling lava, disembodied close-ups of a bloodshot eyeball staring in deranged fright. Everything is on overload. Like the half-dead Pam (Teri McMinn) thrashing spasmodically out of a meat freezer, or the barely breathing mummy of the Grandfather (John Dugan), death and madness are not endings but continuations of a sensory high.

The sound design of *The Texas Chain Saw Massacre* was more innovative and influential than has generally been acknowledged. For example, a gloomy

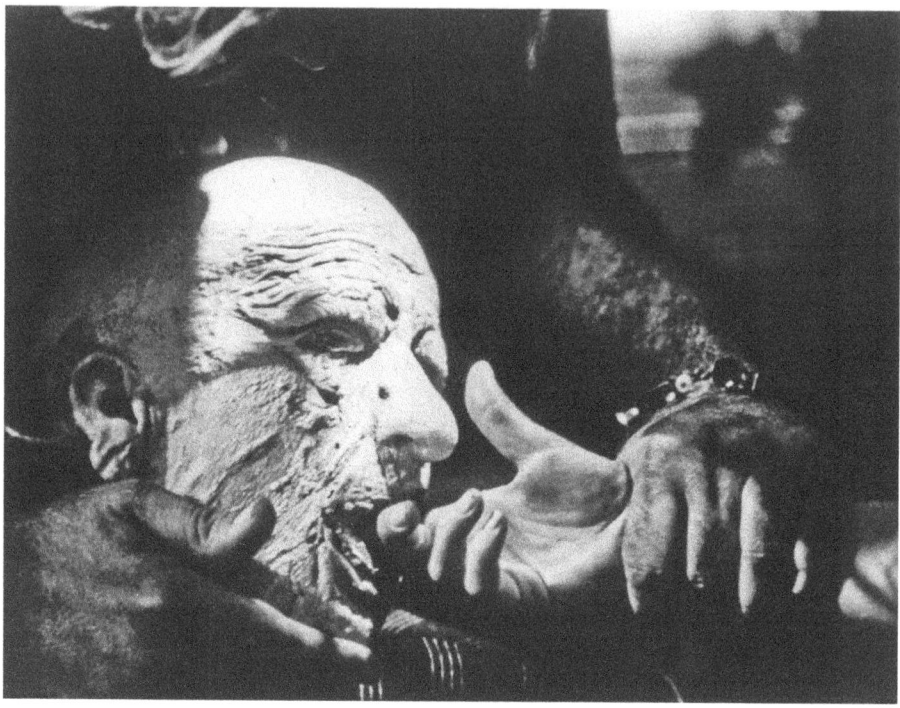

In Tobe Hooper's *The Texas Chain Saw Massacre* (1974), death is not the end, merely the extension of a sensory high. Refn has cited this film as an enormous influence on his own cinematic art. Here, blood is sucked from a young woman's finger by the decrepit grandfather of a cannibalistic clan, like a kind of transgendered fellatio.

newscaster drones unbroken throughout the opening credits and the first two sequences in a non-naturalistic touch that creates a sense of oppressiveness. In fact, many of the scenes feature disorienting background noise that sometimes seems to have no definitive source. Also, there are textures galore: soap bubbles washing over a windshield; a pulsing mass of black filaments that turns out to be a tight close-up on a nest of daddy-long-leg spiders. The sense of detail is like *Night of the Hunter* (1955), in which minutiae, usually small wild animals, enter the foreground of the frame or appear in isolated close-ups to comment implicitly on the characters' fates. But here, the wildlife from *Night of the Hunter* is replaced by images of human detritus and relics of death: a watch impaled on a rusty spike; an empty, sinister yard swing swaying in a breeze; dry chicken bones arranged ritualistically on a nest of plucked feathers. Inserts of dazed, drooling cows in the stockyard are intercut with shots of the vacationing campers in their van, driving to their doom, with neither sentimentality nor irony.

Cinematographer Pearl has said that he shot the daylight scenes "with basically available light," then (accidentally) overexposed the film stock, giving the images a bleached-out look that suggests the sweltering Texas heat.[69] This kind of fortuitous mistake is not something that can be taught in a film school (at least not when this film was made); quite the opposite. Everywhere in *Texas Chain Saw Massacre* we see the triumph of vital instincts bent on finding something new under the sun. One of Hooper's most effective techniques—and proof of his distinctive eye—is the sudden alternations between close-ups and extreme wide-angles that produce a sense of loss, dislocation and vulnerability. We see this strikingly in the scene where the van stops for the Hitchhiker (Edwin Neal), in extreme wide angle where both the Hitchhiker and the van are small against the horizon. The panic of the suddenly opened perspective momentarily takes the viewer out of the thick of the action: it is the revelation of a vast, empty, even agoraphobic space where no one can see or intervene in the unfolding horror. The contrast between close and distant is pushed even farther in the next shot, which is an immediate cut to the deformed face of the Hitchhiker, now ensconced inside the cramped van, leering and invasive of the campers' space.

There is a similar use of distance in the scenes where Leatherface (Gunnar Hanson) first attacks some of the campers; this distance replicates actually being in the room where the slaughters occur more effectively than close-ups, which afford artificial proximity and therefore reinforce the security that someone was "in control" of the events, that the events themselves were pre-selected. At a middle-length distance, one wants to squirm away, and at the same time one leans in to double-check what one is actually seeing. One is left torn, subtly implicated. It is the viewpoint of the witness, the survivor, the one who could have jumped in or run away. This idea found a slightly later expression in the magnificent use of crane shots and dolly shots in George Miller's *Mad Max* (1979), where the camera's swift and sudden pulling up or away from a scene of violence creates the shudder of feeling as though all potential for good, all possible forces of virtue and justice, are swiftly receding from this world that we are watching. In reality, it is us, or our point of view, withdrawing, again subtly complicit in the carnage.

The visual content of *Mad Max* is often as dense as it is in expressionist art. There is one composition from *Mad Max* that seems to have led Refn to craft variations on it in his early films: I am referring to the heightened moment when Miller pulls back from the grotesque hospital bed where Max's brutalized wife is now an amputee in an oxygen tent, until the right side of the screen is filled with a close-up of Max, anguished, staring out toward the camera. Without resorting to cutting to a reaction shot, Miller, with this stylish albeit queasy flourish, manages to include all of the information within a single shot. It is like the framing in a graphic novel; it quivers with an intensity that pushes against the confines of the frame. The audience is given a unique vantage by which to see the horror *and* the character's reaction at once, as if to reinforce the feeling that reality has become nightmare, that there is no refuge from the horror (as might be possible if the director cut away). Both *Pusher* and *Bleeder* contain homages to this Miller composition, early evidence of Refn's interest in building a distinctive visual language. In *Pusher* it is the close-up of a disconsolate girlfriend being ordered into a car by her domineering boyfriend, who can be seen in the background; in *Bleeder* it is the close-up of a distraught boyfriend who has been exiled from his own dinner table by his girlfriend's sinister brother. This kind of deep framing has roots in expressionism, of course, and in Welles, but Refn's claiming of such an aesthetic touch (via Miller, perhaps) for action cinema introduces something fresher, more radical: a consciously theatrical note, disharmonizing and distancing the viewer's reaction by refusing to adopt familiar editing devices such as close-up/reverse close-up. It is not manipulative. The viewer is alone with all the information at once, and with his or her own response.

In Refn's more recent films there are even more complex variations on this apportionment of space within the frame. In *Drive*, for example, there is a shot in a motel room ambush scene where we see a hit man emerging from the bathroom with a shotgun on the left hand of the frame, and Driver (Ryan Gosling) standing behind the bathroom doorway waiting to strike. The tension feels greater for not having cutaways or separate viewpoints; in Refn's films the action itself is always strong enough that his style can be coolly descriptive, even distanced, again without having to be manipulative. There is no fussing around the action, only a preternaturally serene contemplation of it.

In terms of content, the film of Refn's which makes the most references to *Texas Chain Saw Massacre* is *Pusher III: I'm the Angel of Death*. Many of these references are extremely tongue-in-cheek. Headcheese (a dish of choice among the cannibals) is a potential source of ptomaine in *Pusher III*. A restaurant kitchen is conflated with a human slaughterhouse: a man is buried alive in a meat freezer; finally, another man is stripped and hung upside down, where he is bled and then gutted into a slop bucket. The viscera are fed into the garbage disposal in the sink. Even these latter scenes are filmed with a modicum of restraint, with Refn focusing more on the stunned, bewildered reactions of the two men who find themselves having to dispose of bodies in such a manner.

Indeed, in terms of formal artistry, I believe Refn has already gone far beyond his early masters. But we can see how the extreme, visceral filmmaking of Hooper and of Miller (and others) inspired and guided him. Rather than being crude depictions of violence for the sake of violence, grindhouse films had figured out ways of using the camera and editing to uniquely dramatize the adrenalin, suspense, terror and desolation around violent acts. Also, these were films in which direct experience was being expressed and defined—replicated, in some ways, for the viewer—through visual and sound techniques specific to the art of cinema. Put otherwise, this was something only film could do, a sort of Holy Grail which has often been called "pure cinema" and which was expressed once by Godard precisely in terms of how something vivid and raw "exists only in the cinema, [something] which would be nothing in a novel, [on] the stage or anywhere else, but which becomes fantastically beautiful on the screen."[70] This pure cinematic essence, for Refn, exists in the horror film above all else, since horror "deals with visuals and moods and the connection to our subconscious."[71] Of course, sophisticated viewers (and even genre aficionados) widely called films such as *The Texas Chain Saw Massacre* and *Mad Max* "bad," but one's eyes told a different story, and anyway, the films worked even if there was little critical language at the time to account for this.

Much in postmodern aesthetic theory changed after J. Hoberman first published his groundbreaking essay "Bad Movies" in 1980, an impassioned, intellectual defense of why B-movies, or the dizzyingly slipshod works of Oscar Micheaux and Ed Wood, Jr., for example, possess value as subversive art. Hoberman writes, "Many, if not most of the films we admire were once dismissed as inconsequential trash; and that trash itself is not without certain socio-aesthetic charms."[72] He traces several reasons for these charms that mainly have to do with the undermining of realism as a tool to enforce standards of capitalist representation and normativity. "The objectively bad film attempts to reproduce the institutional mode of representation, but its failure to do so deforms the simplest formulae and clichés so absolutely that you barely recognize them. They must be actively decoded." This connects with postmodernism's "death of the author," in which the audience's relation to a text is meant to be a working, critical one. What emerges, in a way that is designed to connote Brechtianism, is "the often poignant, heightened realism induced by such a failure to convince."[73]

It was a daring transvaluation for Hoberman to view low-budget films as "personal, even obsessive works"[74]—made under circumstances that often required some sacrifice and dedication (e.g., a pure love of cinema). And Hoberman does not even really scratch the surface of exploitation cinema from the '60s and '70s, or the deluge of low-budget horror films from the '70s and '80s. Other postmodern intellectuals have taken up a more comprehensive defense of the whole range of exploitation, horror, etc., with reasoning ultimately similar to Hoberman's. Here is a passage from a special issue of *Re/Search* devoted to *Incredibly Strange Films*:

> At issue is the notion of "good taste," which functions as a filter to block out entire areas of experience judged—and damned—as unworthy of investigation.
> The concepts of "good taste" are intricately woven into society's control process and class structure. Aesthetics are not an objective body of laws suspended above us like Plato's supreme "Ideas"; they are rooted in the fundamental mechanics of how to control the population and maintain the status quo.[75]

The hope behind this is the rise (or even just the fitful existence) of something like an anti-culture industry, wherein the imperfections of the world are underscored through an imitative form of imperfection, and wherein the exclusivist imperatives of movie realism—that one spend a great deal of money to create and then exploit a lifelike world which audiences in turn will want to spend a great deal of money consuming, or that one uphold exorbitant standards of physical beauty which become oppressive to everyday people—necessitate "a violent rupture with reality"[76] itself. More to the point, as Hollywood and other centers of mainstream filmmaking become slicker and more trite, the bite of energetic schlock comes to seem vital, even radically avant-garde.

However, as attractive as this logic is, it completely ignores the fact that most exploitation directors—along with their fair claims, in many cases, of possessing artistic vision—hoped to make a lot of money with their films.[77] Most of them had their own production companies, financing their movies with their own money.[78] The fact that they did not always give the viewer a lavish, expensive-looking product can be seen as Robin Hood–esque, perhaps, but who were they really "robbing?" Institutional, traditional ways of seeing—sure. And ostensibly, according to Hoberman et al., a ruling elite who demanded that films always look polished and cohere diegetically. But even if such an elite existed, film had always posed a distinct challenge to such snobbery. Edwin S. Porter's bold decision to end *The Great Train Robbery* (1903) with a bandit firing his gun at the audience was only an early, salutary assault on the confinements of realism. What Refn has called "unreal realism"[79] is the foundational basis of cinema itself. Messy, shoestring experimentation was how the medium had been born, inaugurated and explored ever since cinema started.

Hoberman argues that low-budget grindhouse films "are almost always targeted at the most exploitable or *lumpen* sections of the movie audience (ethnic minorities, teenagers, sub-literates, 42nd Street derelicts)."[80] But the enterprising filmmakers themselves didn't think in such sociological schemas;

they were just happy that there were so many people with an intense appetite for sex and gore.[81] It is markedly different today, when films that hope to make billions must be big and pious, "for the whole family," and must wear their burden of marketing like a dampened, dispiriting shroud. In a way, the drive-in filmmakers were part of the same vast, off-kilter fringe that consumed their work. The actors, too, were sometimes recruited from the streets and the sex trade; it is not uncommon for them to sport bruises, or to appear stoned and strung-out.

For reasons like this, films like *Chain Gang Women*, *Aroused*, *Moonlighting Wives* or *She-Devils on Wheels* actually offer a more accurate image of American extremis than all the vaunted sociology of Kramer, Kubrick or Cassavetes managed during the same decades, right down to the violent sexism and its equally violent opposition (as in the subgenre of rape-revenge films). There is something folkloric about the way such films peep into unreconstructed rural, urban, suburban, and even redneck attitudes that tells a more genuine story. At any rate, rather than something fishy and inferior imposed on an underclass, we can say that exploitation cinema arose from the *desires* of the underclass, and as an expression of what had been generally marginalized within not only capitalism but civilization itself.

Indeed, there was always something suspect if not moralistic and pretentious about the need to "rehabilitate" the artistic fortunes of slasher gore-fests, biker-dyke sagas, or cannibal mockumentaries. The initial attempts to validate Herschell Gordon Lewis, say, or Lee Frost as conscious, Ur-radical artists threatened to drag such cheapjack thrill rides as *Scum of the Earth*, *I Eat Your Skin* and *Let Me Die a Woman* into a realm of vacuous textual piety where they were never meant to go. The always brilliant Gary Indiana has pinpointed the problem: "Critics, quite often, mistake the celebration of the ghastly as an 'indictment of contemporary malaise,' etc.—in other words, they can only like something if it can be bent to reflect their moral certainties."[82]

Likewise, R. H. W. Dillard, writing in praise of low-budget horror films from the late '60s and early '70s, recommends that we avoid "the stock political response"[83] in favor of viewing this genre as "an art, not of absolutes, but of possibilities."[84] Somewhat indirectly, Dillard suggests that such films thrive on the tension between an unerring narrative sensibility (high plot) with crudeness of execution (low form). Here's an amazing new idea for a story, these horror and exploitation films say, but I will tell it to you as if it did not quite matter; as if you (or anyone) could easily fill in all the gaps by yourself while pretending that the teller is equal to his own outrageous tale. The outlandish aspects of the plot will be tempered and made to seem more legitimate by the humble execution. The effect is almost always uncanny and startling, thrusting us into a diegetic world not only shocking but inherently blasé, highly creative but largely shorn of aesthetic self-regard.[85]

Refn's first film, *Pusher*, shows a similar low-budget aesthetic. Only natural lighting seems to have been used: when a character walks into a dim hallway or dark alley, we, too, lose the light—or else the light withdraws into the distant background, making the figures silhouettes. The camera is hand-held even during tracking shots; interiors are drab, extremely lived-in apartments. But even here Refn knows how to make an impact. The film moves, a lot; the frame is always busy, we are always given new things to see (color pops are used effectively in *Pusher*). Refn's visual style is not the locked-down long takes of contemplative cinema, but an adrenalin-driven search for action; at the same time, it has some of the same cool stylization as New Wave or No Wave cinema. There is no "brand" of filmmaking that is alien to Refn.

In this, his films are not unreconstructed exploitation like the cult movies of the '60s and '70s, in which there was nothing disguised about the poverty of means. If anything, the '60s and '70s exploitation directors, themselves from working-class backgrounds and often thrift-driven "children of the Depression," took pride in making films as cheaply as possible. They did not believe in the foolishness of expensive sets or even the workhorse strain of coherent editing. Why shoot take after take? Why create continuity shots when there were always stock footage and scraps of other films lying around? Why laboriously record sound during shooting with expensive microphones that just ended up dropping down into frame, when you could rent a studio for half an hour and post-dub the whole film? The rational use of dialogue is one of the first casualties of this often hypervisual, back-to-basics filmmaking: voices come out of closed mouths; we only see the character who is listening, never the one speaking; whole plot points are exposed through weirdly delivered speeches carpeting silent montages. This was not just an anti-industry of culture, it was closer to a strain of anarchy that would not waste time either bolstering or debunking either "culture" or "industry." It bypassed the exigencies of both, separate and combined. Indeed, something in the ecstatic shortcuts taken by the exploitation directors spoke to people who basically despised the idea of professionalism as the ultimate drain on personal freedom.

What drive-in cinema proves is that culture is a Protean beast that thrives in different forms, even in places where it has been actively discouraged. Certainly, in its ferocious irrationalism, *The Texas Chain Saw Massacre* now seems prophetic, ahead of its time; it has not dated to the same extent that some earnestly highbrow cinema of the '70s has. It has passed into a kind of myth that little else from the same era has attained. It is a more savage account of hippies versus rednecks than *Easy Rider* (1969), a more thorough examination of the Me-Generation decay of the family than *The King of Marvin Gardens* (1972), a more bare-knuckled exposé of the south than *Nashville* (1975), a more successful exercise in primalism and claustrophobia and gender warfare than *A Woman Under the Influence* (1974).

This speaks, again, to the resonance of myth, its instant recognizability in different times and guises. The '70s had a particular knack for creating instantaneous mythology; we can see it now as the most recent decade in which ancient myths were regenerated in the way I traced earlier, as a way of "tribally" coping with widespread societal changes and massive perceived threats to civilization, and with the anxiety of historical awareness catching up to itself. If that sounds vaguely like what we call "backlash," I must admit that it begins in roughly the same reactive place; but myth compensates differently by broadening the stories we tell about ourselves, as well as inventing new ones, in order to position and certify revolutionary change within the filtering of collective understanding. For Mabille, the renewal or invention of mythologies is a kind of overcoming "in favor of exploring unknown territory,"[86] and in which the past is "adapted to the present needs."[87] Unruly "folklore" can upset the stagnation by which "art becomes fixed in an official, classical, academic style."[88]

But it goes beyond art into daily phenomenology and the perception and understanding of the real. This is similar to how Mircea Eliade sees myth as "a hope for a resacralization of humanity and the cosmos through a return to our remembering of mythic (pre-christian) origins which ... give expression to a profound sense of nostalgia for lost origins, a homesickness rooted in the common experience of feeling not-at-home in the modern West."[89] But where Eliade largely dismisses mythmaking as a flawed or regressive approach, "a naively optimistic hope for *renovatio*,"[90] I view it ideally as a successful reaffirming and redirecting of ageless human energies—not a Xerox copy of the past but a new blueprint which shares with our "mythic origins" only their bold force and human outreach.

What is therefore decisive is that myth is not about burying one's head in the sand. It is about asserting that what happens in the present-day modern world can be treated with the same epic power as the most ancient origins of iconography and storytelling. Myth obeys certain constant patterns—good and evil, strength, spiritual values—in order to reassure people that these elements have not been lost along the way of progress. But the progress itself is not denied or suppressed. It is not that we simply dust off *Beowulf*, for instance; we reorient the story to suit a turning of the wheel or two, as John Gardner did with his novel *Grendel*. Some myths are more or less entirely made from whole cloth. Wonder Woman, for example, emerged in the '70s roughly in tandem with the Women's Liberation Movement: the familiar superhero trappings, the glitter, the sex appeal of Lynda Carter (in the TV series) all became mythic paraphrases of the more heady and altogether less familiar (at the time) goals of feminism. Her gold bracelets which deflected bullets became a new myth constructed around a new gender-blind ideal of eternal warrior empowerment, one touched by a certain (female) elegance and artistry. In any event, it is always true that a new or revised myth sells an idea before people are ready for it; at the same time, the rooting of the new myth confirms that the incipient idea itself is worthwhile, genetically related to what we can already recognize and accept.[91]

Myths are not neutral, nor can modern myths all be grouped under the same belief or significatory system. They collide in polymorphous, unprecedented ways in U.S. popular culture. So the original slasher films, with their colorful serial killers (Jason, Michael Myers, Freddy Krueger), operate as conflicted enshrinements of the new social permissiveness *and* its sex-wary opponents; while Rambo and other screen characters mythologized the Vietnam soldier (dead or alive) as a psychotic killing machine *and* the wounded seeker of justice, a man of consummate honor thwarted and perverted by his ordained mission. The uncertainty, the need to have it both ways at once, is the prime cause for the myth, not the other way around.[92]

If myths are symptoms of social uncertainties on their way to being settled within the historical imaginary, then whole regions of the collective U.S. psyche passed into myth during the '70s and early '80s. At its basis myth was, as Roland Barthes affirmed, a form of speech,[93] one uniquely suited to defining and nailing down clouded, anxious memories and future-shocks. Some psychical necessity drove this most recent great burst of Western imaginative powers; when our realities had been converted into myth, the imagination receded. Today we are post-mythic, post-imaginative; art is expected to reenact the real rather than to invent. We have convinced ourselves that we no longer need myths—or we have exhausted our mythmaking capacities. Everything is a remake; the stories, and their auras, grow hazier and less distinct in the retelling. They seem to be more inclusive, but the Frankenstein parts don't fit, they poke out every which way, and the inner blood turns to water.

5. *"I'm a fetish person"*[94]

Refn has often referred to fetishism in relation to his artistic vision. "I don't consider myself a very violent man," he says, "but I have a fetish for violent emotions, violent images."[95] He has also indicated that he fills his films with objects that have a fetishistic power or attraction for him.[96] Refn's use of the word "fetish," particularly to denote that his cinema is driven by the act of making visual contact with objects that obsess and absorb him, seems to run slightly counter to many of the prevailing meanings of that word and its conceptualizations. On the one hand, Refn acknowledges the erotic element of all fetishism by stating, "I approach things very much like a pornographer and it is about what arouses me." On the other hand, while fetishism is often about being neurotically fixated or undeveloped, Refn suggests that his work transcends fetishistic repetition-compulsion, becoming a "way to exorcise certain things in [myself]."[97] Are these postulations compatible?

Let's digress for a moment and try to construct an alternative and potentially productive way of understanding fetishism. At the largest perspective, fetish objects "give reassurance in the face of some anxiety or fear."[98] This aspect of fetishism does not change even if we transvaluate some of the emphases of classic fetishism in order to recast its necessity as psychical defense. In classic fetishism, an inert part of a body, or a token of that body (such as a clipped lock of hair), or even a wholly inorganic object is made to serve as the site of erotic fulfillment in lieu of a more complicated and spontaneous relationship to the living body. It is the finitude of the fetish that bulwarks the terrors of "infinite" intimacy. It is thus thought that fetishism represents a tending toward death or necrophilia, since the cold adoration of lifeless objects suggests the ultimate containment of free-flowing life energies in death. However, the idea that the erotic life of a body can be contained within a definable finite object is essentially one that can have an inherently creative and celebratory quality rather than regressive and moribund. In fact, it comes very close to expressing a central need behind all creativity: to mourn for mortality by investing life in a designated artwork that can potentially survive its own creator.

Giorgio Agamben writes about that piety which anticipates the eventual mortal loss of everything in this world and thus attempts to preserve certain beloved things.[99] This can be related to how we are viewing fetishism, in the sense of the entwined actions of creation and preservation which Agamben defines as "the twin poles of human action."[100] In "an unformed state," one "contemplates ... that which is saved but only insomuch as it will be lost.... And just as a loved one is all of a sudden present in our memory, but only on the condition that he or she is disembodied and turned into an image, so the work of creation is now intimately meshed in every last detail with nonbeing."[101] The artist creates an image which he hopes will survive the inamorata. In an infinitely relaying regress, the conjurations attain form but never permanence: a memory feeds the image (fetish), which in turn acts as memento, which in turn contains the beloved as memory, etc. It might as well be a memento mori, for it will become one any day, no matter what. Agamben cites

Kierkegaard: "'The work of love in recollecting the one who is dead ... is the work of the most disinterested, free, and faithful love.' But it is certainly not the easiest."[102]

This is because memory is more subjective and evanescent than we would like it to be. Something recollected in a bad mood is different from something recollected in contentment; it also takes single-minded devotion to cherish a memory as much as a living being. In some ways the history of our human means of expression as a species has been an attempt to solve this problem. Once there were only oral descriptions of the dead, then crude generic likenesses, then refined paintings which were more lifelike but nonetheless static and unchanging; and now we have moving images, with sound, as weapons in the service of mourning. The fetish has been massaged into modernity and industrialization and digital reproduction in order to satisfy the most primal and unyielding of needs.

In this sense, fetishism is a kind of ritualized mourning *avant la lettre*.[103] Not mourning for what is necessarily dead already but for what will be eventually, inevitably.[104] It is with the preservation of evidence of a living past, or as Mary Kelly has pointed out, *memorabilia*, that fetishism is ultimately most concerned.[105] In its logic of shy displacement, the fetishist's overdeveloped imagination pays tribute to the beloved precisely by his or her ability to meditate on one thing endlessly. The fetishist feels a need for ritual to structure a mind that might otherwise be too discursive and drifting—too much, let us say, like those shifting cycles and patterns of living which always include, and tend toward, mortality. Moreover, because it substitutes an inert object for something that would otherwise freely come and go, fetishism suggests a dislocated voyeurism, a voyeurism which no longer gazes directly at its object, or does not allow itself the luxury of gazing directly. It must earn this blessing of sight; a lifetime is not long enough, but there is the optimistic attempt, again and again, to overcome the barriers, to earn a reprieve all at once, so to speak. Thus, again, a token *against* the inevitable death rather than a capitulation to it.

This is what Walter Benjamin, in *The Origin of German Tragic Drama*, identifies as part of the aesthetics of allegory, in which feelings and thoughts are fetishized as external objects. For Benjamin, it seems to take on an element of primitive and regressive narcissism, the "tenacious self-absorption [which] embraces dead objects in its contemplation, in order to redeem them."[106] However, this "special intensification or progressive deepening" of intention (and attention)[107] does not liberate anything. Benjamin likens it to a hard "stoicism" and states, "The deadening of the emotions, and the ebbing away of the waves of life which are the source of [the] emotions in the body, can increase the distance between the self and the surrounding world to the point of alienation from the body."[108] In this model of fetishistic mourning, life grows less tangible the more it is objectified. Because of this, allegory never thaws out from the melancholy (exemplified by *Melencolia*, Dürer's well-known engraving of a pensive man seated, as if in a diorama, among a cluster of depressing or futile items, a trapped sea, a starving hound, etc.) that wallows in its own inscrutable dismay. The fetish object, as we are considering it, is set free rather than pinned down, and it enters into an active relation with the fetishist, who expands and energizes through contemplation of the object. The fetish is, finally, not a subset or even a synecdoche of the world, but the entire world itself.

At any rate, the fetishist's role is to collect and worship evidence as a higher form of love. Real acts are legible but limited, circumscribed; moreover, they exist only to be witnessed by the fetishist, who prides himself on attending to details normally overlooked in lovers' busy, selfish consummation of pleasure. What is actually a communion of two people becomes, for the fetishist, vulgar and quintessentially one-sided; the fetishist can see only how the truth of love is violated by the endeavor to know it comprehensively. This does not split the fetishist from himself, however, as Benjamin suggests in the case of melancholy. However, austere physical separation is needed, a separation representing the death of the beloved, but mitigating against that finality (and here we might think not only of erotic fetishes but religious ones—crosses, images of saints, chalices). The fetishist removes the idea of separate sides coming together in the work of bliss or fulfillment, since for the fetishist there are no sides, there is only belief, not dissimilar to the belief in an afterlife. In death one might long to have the unruly living body back, with its responses, its growth patterns, its secretions. The fetishist reduces a living body to those traces which are left behind as indications of *having been alive*, as in a kind of aversion therapy, getting used to the idea of inevitable loss in order to find a way to encapsulate and ritualize the psychical dangers of mourning. This renders the body itself sacred, even as it also renders it invisible. Here is where the body remains most present, albeit most "departed"—in the fetishistic imagination, specially salvaged by rapacious and discerning memory.

But the memory does not belong to the fetishist; indeed, it leaps across identification in order to speak for the body-behind-the-fetish, that absent human to whose consciousness it properly belongs. It is much like film-watching: the star remembers having acted the film; the viewer remembers what happened in the film and what occurred to him while watching the star. The fetishized star possesses an "unnecessary" memory of real events, the fetishistic viewer a crucial memory of unreal ones. Actors can be fetishes, bearing allegorically their look, their presence, their history of past performances.

Arguably, the popular Bryan Cranston functions this way in his supporting role in *Drive*, bringing with him the bad-ass mojo of his TV series *Breaking Bad*. The logic goes: we like watching Cranston on TV, we want to see *more* of him, unconsciously to make sure he is present to us.

Therefore, if we connect fetishism to mourning, and also to a celebration of the tangible visualization and coveting of unseen or overlooked or simply past processes, we can see that the same sort of vicariousness does exist, in non-erotic form, in all of cinema—and certainly also in the films of Refn. Cinema is finally the most benign and common form of fetishism. The fetishistic eye of the camera does become an agent for mourning the residual enjoyment contained in certain objects even as they remain fully there, in view. Filming something implies a hoarding of visual contact toward the day when the object might no longer be there, lost to the pervasive anxiety of time and aging. Sorrow always accompanies the attempt to hold back time. Kelly's sense of *memorabilia* as fetishized mourning is centered around a mother's wish to preserve the relics from her children's early lives.[109]

Fetishism in filmmaking can involve certain classic objects, such as cars or trucks. The garage atmosphere in *Drive* (2011) evokes certain scenes in Kenneth Anger's epochal *Scorpio Rising* (1964). Beyond the immediate pleasure of looking at cherished fetishes, there is an aspect of cinematic fetishism that wards off melancholy and celebrates life. Ryan Gosling is pictured.

What should be emerging from this argument is the realization that fetishism, as a condition of living and experiencing the world, is not primarily sexual at all—libidinal if anything, but ultimately a far more generalized *survival instinct*. Fetishism can be said to exist wherever consolation or strength is derived from an inanimate object, that consolation or strength being entirely directed toward the preservation of life against death. Action films, horror films, all of the violent genres which have had such an influence on Refn have always been deeply immersed in fetishism, although this sometimes went unremarked because not only were the fetish objects unaligned with sexual interest or fulfillment, they were also specifically weapons. They did not passively gratify a worshipful lover; they were wielded in the self-defensive fighting against enemies and in the taking of lives.

Leatherface's chainsaw, for example: this functions as a violent, powerful, active and celebratory fetish that has long bypassed any simple substitutional needs. It does not substitute for the phallus, which binds meanings together into an order; it does something else entirely—it disperses, it eviscerates. The cannibal family (in which Leatherface is, as a best guess, one of the brothers) has collapsed so much into dispassionate, end-of-the-line inbreeding that it is no longer centered on the possession of phalli; instead, the men are psychologically aligned with the vaginal wound. Hitchhiker bears a large red birthmark that covers nearly half of his face, and in a key scene he cuts his palm open with a knife; the ancient grandfather passively sucks at a girl's bleeding finger in an act that suggests grotesque transgendered fellatio. Basically there is no conception of an identified sexuality to which these behaviors and markings could stand as either perversion or mode of resistance. Leatherface's chainsaw is simply what he has, the way violence is what he has instead of a sexual orientation. The roar of the chainsaw, drowning out the screams of Leatherface's victims, denotes, again, a joyous, active fetish—indeed, if it substitutes for anything, it is Leatherface's otherwise squealing, clucking, or nonexistent *voice*. Yet we never imagine him ever wanting to say anything else besides that mechanical roar. He is sexless, poised between animal and machine. We could say that Leatherface is not an example of "*failed masculinity*, particularly in terms of [the] inability to speak,"[110] but a complete refutation of sexual categories themselves.

Of course, Refn has wittily deployed classic sexualized weapon-fetishes, almost always with a blatancy that hammers like CPR on the dying chest of cliché. There is Bronson's lower-class sawed-off shotgun, which he rests against his groin and strokes. More intriguingly, there is the bitter Mafioso (played by Albert Brooks) with his collection of oddly shaped, ornate daggers, preserved under glass and reserved for the killing of former friends, in *Drive*.

These examples are markedly more traditional in a psychoanalytic sense. With the phallic shotgun in *Bronson* we are correct to read a blunt fetishization of masculinity; with the knives in *Drive*, a twisted self-loathing that masters itself only in the inflicting of pain. Between these two weapon-fetishes, the one in *Drive* is already much subtler and more sophisticated, suggesting the quickness with which Refn outpaces his own insights and visualizations.

For me, along with Kelly's work,[111] the example that caused me to re-think fetishism specifically as an expiatory or joyous act of mourning occurs in Refn's *Bleeder*, where the camera slides greedily over the spines of stacked and shelved videotapes in the rental store. The tapes are bathed in a strange, otherworldly glow, and the soundtrack blares the chorale "Wir setzen uns mit Tränen" ("We sit down in tears") from Bach's *Matthäus-Passion*. This is the oratorio's final chorale mourning Christ after his crucifixion. Christ's tomb is apotheosized as "the soul's resting place": "In utmost bliss the eyes slumber there."[112] This healing bliss of "the eyes" is transferred over to the secular realm of a video store where one's favorite movies live again and again on videotape. (Instead of the old motto "Please Be Kind—Rewind": "Please Be Correct—Resurrect?") The Bach chorale gives to the tapes a sacred air, in keeping with the worship of movie lore that is expressed and explored throughout *Bleeder*, whose young heroes seek always to be "worthy" of god-like cinema.

I do not want to impute too much grandiosity to Refn when it comes to such a highbrow touch. I cannot say for certain, but it is just as likely that he chose this selection because it has a "Gothic" quality and because Martin Scorsese gave it a certain bad-ass cachet by choreographing a car bombing to it in *Casino* (1995). However, marvelous, serendipitous instincts have been the life's blood of cinema since Méliès turned his first crank, and the effect of the solemn but ecstatically beautiful liturgical music recapitulates both sides of fetishistic mourning: the sorrowful acknowledgment of the life that has been removed from sight, and the hope for resurrection in the form of renewed trace-contacts. Like an omnivorous film addict, Refn's camera wants to see all the movies at once but must content itself with scanning over their external boxes. The memory of pleasures once felt (movies one has seen) merges with the hope of future pleasures (seeing them again or seeing new ones), for fetishism is finally about the unexpected return. The possibility of new films to absorb and love is like the body-behind-the-fetish whose essence remains inside the fetish and who will hopefully at some point come back to update the progress of the fetishist's worship with fresh traces.

Thus, there is no arc to fetishistic courtship: it is a series of moments which relate to an unwitnessed past and a longed-for future (both of which must be taken on "faith"). Similarly, in the jumbled rows of videotapes there is no sense of origin, no alpha or omega, no beginning or end. The litany of movies exists outside of time and temporal structuring principles; again, we are reminded of that paradoxical suspension of disbelief which psychoanalytic theory instructs us about fetishism in the well-known formula "*I know very well, but still ...*" Just as the favored directors in *Bleeder*'s video store are beyond classification by genre, era or nationality, and are permitted to be sui generis, as it were, so the fetish object must be made to transcend the humble category of objects to which it belongs, in order to invest it with the personality required for it to be a substitute for arousal and love.

The lack of a courtship, with its progressive timeline, actually aids in the suspension of disbelief, since it encourages the sense of destiny, of an unalterable *fait accompli*. If the fetishist never has something like a "first date" with the beloved (merely a first point of contact with something that has predated any knowledge of the beloved), then the relation to the beloved, in theory, never has to have an ending. The flipside of mourning is the longing for immortality, which expresses itself in extreme grief at the sight of death, mingled with guilt at the extreme relief to be the one who has been left alive. In *Bleeder*, the camera's plunge into the stacks of movies suggests not only that the beginning of movie-love is impossible to pinpoint (and thus, one hopes, endless, eternal), but a sort of provisional "heaven" or Valhalla in which immortals (movies) can be collected and tended to in perpetuity. Every movie, like every fetish object, is finally a warrior who gives itself on the field of battle—the battle to affirm the symbolic and the real as united allies rather than doomed antagonists.

6. *"If this is going to be my last movie, at least I was able to make it the way I wanted to"*[113]

What cultural production pointedly lacks today, disqualifying it from industry status, is regularity. Part of what made the culture industry insidious was the densely woven texture of its output; one could not escape it, as Adorno reminded us many times. The same funding, the same standards, the same intentionality operated in radio, movies and the emerging television—the same crass commercialism and covert propaganda for the white, straight, sexist American way of life. This is no longer true even with television, which was, in many ways, the last holdout of the traditional culture industry. "Reality" TV is probably the last gasp of the old, hidden mechanisms of control, the idea that something like a regime of popular taste, discourse and imagination could still shape social-behavioral conditioning; could offer up exactly the same overdetermined message to every man, woman and child; could, in a word, present reality itself as a fixed entity with a fixed set of rules.

But even the grip of television (on reality or anything, for that matter) has finally begun to loosen. The very market (of stay-at-home watchers/consumers) which it helped create has forced it to give more freedom of choice, and to invest in that same "lack of positioning" which has always characterized postmodernism's unstable, relative identity-making. In 1962 Godard already described the film-going public as something that could no longer be classified monolithically: "The public is neither stupid nor intelligent. No one knows what it is.... One can't count on it. In one way this is a good thing. In any case it is changing."[114]

Fifty years later it is changing once again. The expanded freedom of choice has morphed radically into the will to create ever more esoteric and individualized choices, ones that are not sanctioned or even assimilable by mass culture. I am thinking of cell-phone footage of concerts, which have completely altered our ideas about bootleg recordings; one step further are fans who create their own videos to accompany a favorite song and then post the results online. For music fans there are marvelous gems from even small-venue live shows on YouTube. We have not yet found the limit of this kind of interactive creativity, which exists for its own sake (the makers of these videos often have fake screen-names and are thus largely anonymous) or for anyone who happens to stumble across it. Not to mention, in a much darker vein, the truly shocking teen trend of filming and posting acts of assault, thereby making the creative use of media entirely coextensive with lawbreaking—dangerously but potent proof that this freedom of "what to watch" is not deceptive, illusory and ultimately conformist, as the most fatalistic theories of co-optation would have it. Instead, this freedom is committed to honesty and the total acceptance of all events, even unacceptable and criminal ones, as public and shareable.

This belief in extreme transparency, this calling for the death of secrecy everywhere, is perhaps the inevitable response of the 9/11 generation that spent their childhoods during the fear-mongering era of George W. Bush, one of the most secretive (and violent) presidencies of modern times. Teen "beating videos," no less than drive-in exploitation cinema from an earlier era but more dangerous, seem to embody what Murray Pomerance has called "the deep, perhaps transgressive, thought that cannot express itself in the sanctora of approved official culture."[115]

Leaving aside the troubling moral implications of "beating videos" (which, it must be said, hardly represent the average in digital culture—at least not yet), the net effect of information-age technology has been a D.I.Y. revolution in the form of amateur, self-produced programming. Refn states, perhaps showing his still-thriving roots in Mette Hjort's good old hebephilic Denmark: "Young people have gotten so good at understanding images that it's us that have the burden of how we can challenge them, because we're the ones that are being slow."[116] And what critic of the "culture industry" would have guessed that people would share their favorite discoveries online *for free*, as part of a collective teleology of cultural advancement? The net is far from being a perfect system, but it is one that is moving and changing, not static, and our ways of analyzing its virtues and its faults must be similarly open.

Today films do not compete only with other films, but with every other kind of recorded and/or digital media. Thus far we have not seen many practical benefits to this free-for-all competition, but I suspect that we will eventually, as filmmakers adjust themselves to these profound changes, the most radical since the coming of sound to silent films. (Compared to the new lowered status of film in the post-digital age, the turning point of television in the '50s seems trivial: movies just got bigger, via Cinemascope, or more novel, via 3-D, but did not fundamentally change in terms of content, style, running time, publicity, etc.) The ideal of theatrical release has become just that: an ideal which no longer represents the actualities of cultural reception. Rather than fighting this trajectory (as David Lynch has famously done), Refn seems accepting of the fact that his films must work on a cell phone as well as a big screen. Refn says in the commentaries for Magnolia Pictures' DVD edition of The *Pusher* Trilogy, "Something we as filmmakers will have to accept for the future [is that] our films are going to be made for a lot of different scenarios ... and we can't just say, 'Our film is made for the big screen' ... because very few people are going to see it that way."

And the idea is to be seen, to connect with large audiences, because this was a way that film—even up through the heyday of foreign cinema in the U.S. in the '50s and '60s—has always had the greatest impact and meaning as an art form. There was always a courting of capitalist co-optation in even the most evolved and artistic cinema, since films, no matter how rarefied, were always meant to be mass objects. I do not deny that real co-optation can and does exist. Co-optation was one of the most important discoveries of Marxist and Frankfurt-school theory. The idea possessed astonishing clarity and rightness: everything that begins as subversive provocation eventually becomes absorbed into mainstream culture if it has any ongoing life at all, even to the extent of becoming boutique items. Money is eventually made from even the weirdest of the weird; punk is a fashion look on sale at the mall, snuff films are presented with commercial endorsements, etc. It is the job of culture to always find fodder for the money machines. This is all true as far as it goes. However, the formula has become an unhelpful and in many ways hypocritical dead end, a way to be cynical about culture even while promoting it. The culture industry as a concept often felt like a rejection of any and all (mass or pop) culture. The pessimistic way of seeing culture is to say that the well is ineluctably poisoned by its link to commerce; another way would be to continue seeking new sources of water. And people, as an artistic species, do manage to find new ways of combating, pushing and interrogating the process of co-optation. As Timothy K. Beal writes, "Entropy is not only the end of the world but also its source. Chaos is both deadly and fecund."[117] Co-optation is driven internally by culture itself as much as externally by the forces that would control and exploit it.

One can become brainwashed in any culture, but in today's world of media access, it is the phenomenon of self-brainwashing that is most dangerous. People who seek infallible, holier-than-thou demagogues to lead them will soon go the way of the dinosaurs, one way or another. They have already marked themselves as outsiders on the widest stages: one cannot display contempt for the global village and try to rule it at the same time. The result is madness and enmity.

The current struggle of culture is to liberate itself from precisely the intellectual tyranny of being a culture that is so relentlessly, and meaninglessly, defined along the ideological grids already in place. The "perfect" work of art, like the perfect ideology, is already receding into obsolescence; for us, it is a sign of being out of touch, of trying to shame people with a would-be seamless continuity of purpose and design that ultimately risks nothing. "It is idiotic," Artaud wrote, "to reproach the masses for having no sense of the sublime, when the sublime is confused with one or more of its formal manifestations, which are moreover always defunct manifestations."[118] "For me," Refn says, "filmmakers who are risktakers suffer the beating but they are also the bravest."[119] In art, as in so much about the current age, bravery (as well as being open to new forms or to utter formlessness) is something of a requirement.

So when Refn states that he directs every film as if it were his last, he is acknowledging not only the powerful changes to culture in our time, the lack of certainty and the hopelessness of achieving real continuity, but also the tendency to anarchy which animates his work, the same anarchy which Godard espoused in one of his most important and impassioned statements: "Such is the nature of dialectic in the cinema: one must live rather than last. It is pointless to kill one's feelings in order to live longer."[120] In Refn's work we find the same exposed, vulnerable, startled emotions that have always formed the basis of the best cinema. And what is anarchy in its purest form but the sharing of emotions beyond what is considered seemly or appropriate, in the hope that a natural identification will spark and spread among people who would otherwise remain strangers?

Indeed, the rather haphazard and entirely subjective portrait of Refn emerging from these introductory notes would seem to be that of a complete anarchist, or at least, as Danny Leigh described him in *The Guardian*, someone who "still likes to frighten the grown-ups."[121] Then again, does it take much anymore to be seen as such? Sometimes all it takes is articulating the nature of the fear that people are made to live under and accept. "Because, you know," Refn has said, "we're always afraid in this industry, what if you can't get your next movie made?" Again, the word "industry" can only be ironic here, since what is denoted is not consistent production but a haphazard, faltering one. Refn goes on: "So I've always made films with the notion, well, if this is going to be my last movie, at least I was able to make it the way I wanted to."[122] And Refn knows what is at stake in this quandary, as well as in any possible solutions to it: "Up to this date, I've been able to survive like that."[123] Certainly, problems of funding and distribution are capitalist problems; the fact that directors have to wait so long now between films, and often cannot get projects off the ground, only confirms the disintegration of cinema as an industry in all but the name. "At least that's the plan," Refn said to an interviewer about beginning pre-production for *Drive*, "but it might all change by Friday."[124] Flexibility is the true companion to bravery, not rigidity. "But you never know in this industry."[125]

And there is, as Refn knows, an anarchist's pleasure in bucking the system from within: "Good or bad, I don't think about it like that. I think more that being able to do what I would like to do, is probably the most pleasurable part of it."[126] This is reminiscent of Ryan Gosling's appreciation of how both Disneyland and *Blue Velvet* found ways of bringing dreams into the world. The main problem with the left's response to capitalism's current phase of rampant and illegal growth is that we are forced into a position of dry, bitter cynicism: we no longer see dreams, only the dollar signs that surround them. Once it was essential to insist on this. But have we killed our love of dreaming (our love of life) in order to punish the mercenary schemes of others? In this land whose denial is so epic, have we blinded ourselves on purpose just to show that our kings have only one eye? That is not how a Cyclops is defeated.

The story of the left's response to millennial capitalism is precisely the story of how we allowed our idealisms to be curdled into cynicisms. We need fewer cynics and more anarchic thinkers today. There are important differences between cynics and anarchists. Contrary to some people's belief, the anarchist is not someone who believes in nothing. The definition of a cynic might well be someone who overly anticipates and dwells upon each little misery, seeming to take comfort in an a priori denial of real suffering; while the anarchist still wants everything to flow with life-supporting energy, even setbacks, even troubles. Cynics will cling to what is left of systemic knowledge and culture, telling themselves that cooperating with business interests is a way of killing the birds of art and commerce with one stone, so to speak, when in reality it is more like an act of robbing Peter to pay Paul. Anarchists will make themselves at home wherever they may be and wait for the rest of the world to catch up; they are happy just to find a reason to survive.

The cynic-director says: *I must ensure that this is not my last film; I can make up for it later when I have acquired more clout.* That "later," of course, never comes, because increased clout only serves to expose the cold-clay feet that held the cynic back in the first place. On the other hand, the anarchist-director says: *Let's go out with a bang*. And as often as not, it's that "bang" that tends to have real staying power.

7. "But what the fuck is an ending, you know?"[127]

Exactly.

– 2 –

The *Pusher* Trilogy

"Maturity and masculinity come together in a confident definition which masks a host of contradictions," asserts John Fiske. Men define themselves in terms of "individualism or power and control," but "society frequently denies males the means to develop these qualities." Because the "material experience" of men does not measure up "to their ideologically produced expectations," the concept of "masculinity ... is socially and psychologically insecure." ... And, given this situation, responsible community appears to be unachievable.—Marilyn C. Wesley[1]

He who cannot put his will into things, puts at least a *meaning* into them: that is, he believes there is a will in them already.— Friedrich Nietzsche[2]

God grant me the serenity to accept the things I cannot change, the courage to change the things I can, and the wisdom to know the difference. —The Serenity Prayer

Frank (Kim Bodnia), a heavy man with a perpetually surly expression, is a heroin dealer in Copenhagen. He is making a deal with a new client and feels uneasy; his best friend and partner Tonny (Mads Mikkelsen) has begged off going along to the drop at the last minute because of a twisted ankle. The new client has picked Frank up in a car, and they are driving through downtown. Frank's suspicion and anxiety are on high alert as he argues about whether he should show the product first or the client should show the money. "It's always the product first," the client says. Once Frank pulls out the package of smack, the car is cut off by another vehicle; it's the police. Frank escapes, brown powder scattering around him like a cloud as he begins to run down the street.

Frank is pursued by two cops on foot. During this chase scene, composed of several lengthy, unbroken takes, the running is real; Bodnia the actor is visibly winded, even pained, as he makes a last sprint toward a lake. Then, regaining his poise for a moment, he tips himself over into the water with a cock-eyed grace that is almost balletic, almost Belushi. The heroin dissolves, making the water murky; Frank stands waist deep, soaking wet, forcing the cops to wade into the lake in order to arrest him: "I've got free donuts," he taunts them.

This propulsive sequence, one of the adrenalin highs of *Pusher*, is a great example of Refn's concise artistry as a director of action: it's a sequence of pure spontaneous nerve, of unembellished craziness which nonetheless feels entirely organic and (miraculously) character-driven. Here is Frank, for the first time in the film out of his element, not in control; unable to leverage this situation he simply reacts. The sequence keeps topping itself, because this is Frank the Pusher (*the* Pusher), and nothing he does is quiet or low-key. So there is the back-and-forth bickering in the car; the abrupt escape; the running; and finally the lake. The entire play of the action has a satisfying arc, like hooking a marlin. There is a long catch, followed by a long release. And through it all we feel as though we know Frank, we recognize him *in action*. "Yes," we think, "this is exactly what Frank would do in this situation, he would go for broke, he would

The buddy relationship between Frank (Kim Bodnia, right) and Tonny (Mads Mikkelsen) in *Pusher* (1996) is affectionate yet classically aggressive, involving frequent jousting about sexual boasts.

lead the cops on a merry chase, he would destroy the evidence and end up soaking wet," etc.

Now this is not as obvious or commonplace as it might seem. In most action films there is a separation of character and event. The characters reveal themselves (if at all) in loaded, often stagy dialogue; when an action scene kicks in, however, they become generic bodies flashing across the screen like avatars in a video game. We aren't really meant to identify with them in action mode, not only because their existence is left tenuous in the first place, but because the violent release which they perform is meant to be ours rather than theirs. The viewer's ultimate identification, now mainly with mechanical objects or special effects, is left empty. In *Pusher*, his first film and also the first chapter in a trilogy completed some ten years later, Refn immediately signals an ability to rethink these elements of action cinema: there is not a lot of expository talk, the characters reveal themselves behaviorally, and when we see them running or fighting or killing someone, it is an extension of their already established, everyday reality, their sometime clumsiness—in a word, their humanity.

"I like my characters," Refn has said, "to develop organically," citing this as the reason why he usually shoots his films in chronological order. This almost verité approach allows that nothing becomes overdetermined about the exposition or the acting in general; we are primed to watch for small behavioral reveals and changes in order to, as Refn says, "fill in the blanks."[3] One feels as though one is among real people, trying to figure out what they are thinking and feeling from moment to moment, wanting to get closer in spite of our dread at their actions.

In fact, the humanity of Refn's characters is wholly earned and is in no way reduced by the moral dubiousness or outright immorality of the violent action itself. This is because, in all of Refn's films, moral issues are always pointedly at stake; they are never concealed or dissembled. The resort to violence is already in some sense a defeat, or rather a debt which a given character will have to repay at some point. Refn's heroes assume a destiny that requires their increasing commitment to, and investment in, a bloody quest that can generally end only in the offering of themselves as sacrifices. Thus, there is also an organic sense of the protagonist in relation to some community which his destruction appeases and strengthens. This is the root of the ancient tragic hero, able to commit violent acts with sovereign freedom but ultimately insignificant, a plaything of the fates and a duty-bound member of the polis. As with the tragedians, Refn insists on a certain ecology at the heart of savage devolutions: they are processes which keep going until they have achieved a lost balance, or a new balance that did not exist before.

Narratively speaking, everything starts to go bad for Frank after his arrest.

He is now on the hook to his boss, drug kingpin Milo (Zlatko Buric), for the monetary value of the lost heroin. He will spend the rest of the film vainly hustling to pay Milo back, failing at every scheme, while impotently watching his debt grow larger and larger by the day. Over and against *Pusher*'s air of squalor and malevolence, Refn achieves a nearly comic absurdism in the way circumstances move inexorably against Frank; nothing in this drug economy is random, although, like any libertarian system, it involves free, unregulated agents. A pusher pushes—his will against the will of his clientele, the addicts. But the pusher's will amounts to an illusion. Because his actions occur within a larger, more or less self-sustaining organization, he can disguise his own individual powerlessness by temporarily borrowing the clout of the organization itself. This is what Nietzsche means when he states that those who cannot exercise their will place their faith in something which gives their life an a priori meaning, even if this meaning is a lie.[4]

In some ways, Milo puts a human, even fatherly face on this borrowed systemic will: a restaurateur, he is often shown cooking and tasting things inside his cozy, domestic kitchen, although this kitchen doubles as a torture chamber for Milo's enemies, as it will also in *Pusher III: I'm the Angel of Death*. But Frank's faith in Milo, such as it is, is misplaced. The zero-sum narcotics trade allows for no setbacks, no stretches of bad luck; indeed, these are fatal. Just like the addicts who come and go, eternally replenishing themselves in new numbers, the street pusher or foot soldier, no matter how good at his job, is essentially replaceable at a moment's notice.

Poverty and the urban struggle to survive ensure that bad choices can only turn into vicious cycles. Although occasionally defiant of Milo, Frank cannot break out of his dependency on Milo's largesse, his born serf role in Milo's fiefdom. Refn has said, "People who grow up in this environment become this environment; very few break away from it."[5] This truth is belied by many gangster films, which depict gangsterism as a successful "breaking away" from hardscrabble, straitened origins (e.g., the gangster at some point becomes wealthy and successful, albeit eternally troubled). Refn plainly maintains that most depictions of criminal underworlds in film are nothing but "fiction": "The world does not need any more gangster films, so these films [the *Pusher* trilogy] would only work if their approach was more negative." Rather than bravado, he tried to acknowledge "sadness" in everything.[6]

The sense of dire limits is palpable. Pushing is all that Frank knows, that and Copenhagen; and if he cannot square things with Milo, he is fatalistic enough to see no future for himself anywhere, not even that of a pusher in some other city's drug market. "What the hell would I do in Spain?" he tells his disconsolate girlfriend Vic (Laura Drasbaek), who had hoped to run away with him. This is Frank's greatest limitation: mobility is nonexistent to this world; all Frank can think to do is attempt to bully and defraud others on his level or below him. Indeed, Frank treats his addict-customers with contempt, unwilling to recognize that he is barely better off, and certainly no freer, than they are.

Again, however, like Nietzsche's sense of a belief so powerful that it can sustain someone's denial of actually being powerless, the hierarchy of the drug business is accepted at face value, even by those at the lower end of the food chain who are basically fair prey. Frank plays out his street cred as badass middleman until there is nothing left, but that cred buys him a week of life—an increasingly desperate week in which he inflicts maximum damage on his cohorts and underlings. He beats his best friend Tonny nearly to death with a bat for talking to the cops. Tonny returns alive in *Pusher II: With Blood on My Hands*, with brain damage and short-term memory loss and deep cranial scars where his head, he says, "had a date with a baseball bat." In *Pusher* Frank also beats up and withholds pay from one of his mules, Rita (Lisbeth Rasmussen), snake-necked and angular like a Eurotrash Klimt. He even attempts, unsuccessfully, to pimp out the hapless Vic.

At the same time, Frank is depicted as less ruthless than Milo and Milo's enforcer, Radovan (Slavko Labovic). In a brutal scene where Frank and Radovan attempt to collect a debt from a sick, frightened, homeless junkie (Thomas Bo Larsen), Frank tries to defend the junkie because he remembers being childhood friends with the junkie's brother. We see that Frank is defiant of Milo at various points, but we also see that he cannot let go of the fantasy of rapprochement with this father-figure who seems to represent an easy life, the keys to some kingdom. Frank, again, believes in the hierarchy of the organization and the way its borrowed meaning can augment his own flagging will. In the end, he pushes Vic away and sets his sights on Milo's offer of forgiveness, which we understand to be a deadly trap.

Pusher, then, is reminiscent of some Fassbinder and Scorsese films: we follow a brutish, unredeemable character while having his limitations and lack of options hammered home again and again. *Pusher* is not a story of change and redemption, but the failure of both at the hands of merciless expediency and ignorant egotism. The situation worsens until the protagonist is finally left alone, remorseless and doomed.

In *Pusher*, drugs stand for commodity-culture, for commodification itself, since there is, in a sense, no more perfect commodity; only food and water rival it, or, on the day that it can be withheld and sold, oxygen. Even beyond the addicts' extreme need for them, however, drugs enjoy a complete lack of regulation or consumer protection. The last semi-humanitarian feint of capitalism is shed: the shibboleth that the customer is always right. Frank need make no concessions to his customers, as we see from the early scene in which he bullies two college kids into paying too much for a tiny amount of nearly worthless dope, knowing that the kids will have no legal recourse. (In fact, legitimate business in global capitalism begins to ape the policies of the drug trade more and more openly; all capitalist agents are dealers whose power stems from being able to operate outside of legal strictures with wild abandon and lack of remorse.)

This is slightly different from what Yvonne Tasker correctly points out about the '80s TV series *Miami Vice*, where the ironic "over-determined figure of drugs ... functions as a 'bad' system of exchange, a metaphor for the evils of capitalism which still allows for the possibility that capitalism can function simultaneously as a 'good' system, exemplified in the other forms of consumption that are celebrated in the series."[7] That chimerical or hypothetical "good" system of exchange is increasingly a nostalgic fiction, as Refn might say, even in relation to crime, its supposed antitype. In cutting-edge films about dealers, this specious notion of white and black markets, of good and bad agents, breaks down ever more decisively. It is difficult to tell, in *Pusher*, for example, where the selling of drugs leaves off and the consumption of them begins. Tonny often snorts little bumps of cocaine behind Frank's back; Vic allows Frank to stash his heroin supply at her apartment and is happy to be remunerated for this service with a larger share of drugs for her personal use. Since drugs are literally currency, there is no reason why actual money should not become a drug, exempting no one from the same destructive dependency. Above-ground or underground, there is seemingly no one in Copenhagen, high or low, to judge the pushers or stand above them. (A similar vision of society bound together through cynical condoning of illegalities appears in Refn's highly individualistic dystopian view of Los Angeles, *Drive*.)

Pusher II: With Blood on My Hands gets even deeper into the dire wages of drug dependency, with many of the female characters chronically abusing the cocaine given to them by their dealer boyfriends or their pimps. Hard drugs are used to control the love and loyalty of these women, who grow mean and crazy under this control, to the point where the men stop wanting to control them and cast them aside. This was the fate of Tonny's own mother, for example. Human disposability, practiced repeatedly by certain males and passed down through generations from father to son, looms as the largest social-emotional problem, of which drugs are merely symptomatic or instrumental rather than causative. Like some kind of germ warfare, the drugs are akin to a heightened technology of the already keen capacity to conquer and do harm. Refn says that "drugs make [my characters] do very dumb things."[8]

In *Pusher II*, not only are unpleasant side effects of cocaine (erectile dysfunction, diarrhea, paranoia, etc.) highlighted to undercut any "glamorous" misconceptions, but there are numerous complex and disturbing scenes in which we cringe at the presence of a six-month-old baby plopped down on the floor in rooms where the women who are supposed to be watching him are snorting lines, getting nosebleeds, fighting and yelling, or wandering around half undressed. It is like a baby born among zombies, and the fact that new life must be forced to come from a type of death or non-life is noted with matter-of-fact horror; motherhood is another war to be survived or not survived, by the children and by the mothers themselves.

"First you try to kill me," one of the women sneers at the disgusted Tonny in *Pusher II*, "and then you ruin our high." The irony in *Pusher III* is that Milo himself has turned into one of his own drug-created zombies. While still maintaining his monopoly on Copenhagen's heroin trade, he has started attending Narcotics Anonymous in order to conquer his habit. It is hilarious to see him saying the Serenity Prayer to himself in the midst of a bloodbath where he has just eliminated two rival dealers by taking a hammer to their skulls. Naturally, Milo's recovery conflicts with his ability to be a capable dealer: early in the film, his abstinence prevents him from trying a hit of "ecstasy," so he ends up buying ten thousand hits without knowing that they are actually gumdrops. Throughout the film, as he falls off the wagon more and more, he regains his former ruthlessness and business acumen; drug use, much as it is for the dealers' various girlfriends, is a means of control, a necessary evil that facilitates the perpetuation of a life that would otherwise be untenable, indefensible and unlikely.

Not that drugs do not provide any thrills at all. The characters in the *Pusher* trilogy chase the elusive high which has formed their most basic sense of every kind of pleasure and fulfillment; everything else in life is understood in relation to the drug high. As if to mimic the exorbitant rush of drugs, the parvenu pleasures indulged in by Frank and Tonny in *Pusher* (whenever they have made a big score) have an unabashed vulgarity. In an early scene they eat at a fancy restaurant. This set is ingenious: direct lights on Frank and Tonny, and on an enormous fish tank behind the table where they sit, allow the surroundings to be dim. This could have been someone's apartment, but Refn's use of Rembrandt-like lighting gives it the perfectly woozy, dramatic feeling of a chi-chi restaurant late at night. Tonny uses a goblet of top-shelf cognac as a fingerbowl, then gargles the stuff because he feels "dirty on the inside." This is as close to any metaphysics as these guys come: what is pleasurable for the body is pleasurable for the inner life as well. Frank tastes the cognac that Tonny's fingers have been in, and in a parody of connoisseurship, tries to guess which woman Tonny was with from the scent she left on his fingers. This is treated as light-hearted, stoned banter, but it is also symptomatic of the fact that there is no dignity in the world of *Pusher*, where consumption in particular is shown to bear the mark of the beast, a divided Id psychotically in thrall to multiple Superegoic voices, haute cuisine cut with raw cunnilingus, everything merely a substitute for something else, cognac reduced to yet another slurpable sensation. Likewise, while shopping in a convenience store, Frank and Tonny openly discuss which female TV personalities they would like to have anal sex with; Tonny offends Frank (by desiring to fuck a black woman news anchor) and ends up having to pay for their purchases. Hardly anything in *Pusher* takes place outside of consumer spaces. Frank tracks down and attacks Tonny in the neighborhood bar where they always go to drink; regular consumption, in this case, makes it easier for your enemies to find you.

Luxury is above all an illusion. In *Pusher II*, a small-time pimp (Kurt Nielsen) refers, mostly sarcastically and bitterly, to his "jet-set lifestyle" while we notice that his house is a trashy amalgam of faded peeling wallpaper, piles of rat poison, dirty dishes, and one or two prestige accouterments like a leather couch or a flat screen TV. In *Pusher III*, Milo admits that his pricey-looking suit is a knockoff, calling it "Chinese Hugo Boss" or "Hugo Buga." But even this nominal vision of clap-trap success might be more than the dealers could expect to get from working at low-wage, unskilled jobs. A certain kind of man will always be willing to take his chances with what can be scrounged outside the law over wasting himself in desultory work. As with a number of Refn's heroes, in later films such as *Bronson*, *Drive*, and *Only God Forgives*, we sense such men's extravagant hopes for their lives most precisely in their failures and constraints.

Thus, unbalanced consumption is akin to reckless gambling, where a fixated, stubborn man cannot walk away from the losing table even though the rewards do not match the investment. Frank spends most of *Pusher* doubling-down on his losses, much like the Harvey Keitel character in Abel Ferrara's *Bad Lieutenant* (1992), because to walk away would be weak somehow, unmanly, an admission of incapability and defeat. Even something as random and external as "luck" becomes intrinsic to phallic self-image; again, this recalls Nietzsche's observation about the individual's largely delusional belief in something that ventriloquizes the will, so to speak, and makes it feel more solid.

In fact, the wan hopes raised by consumption are violently dashed again and again in what Stephen Greenblatt calls "kairotic moments,"[9] decisive turning points which are also points of no return. For example, Milo strips Frank's much-needed car from him in an attempt to recover part of Frank's debt, then humiliates him by saying that the car is worth only a portion of what Frank owes. Likewise, bargaining with Frank and Radovan for his life over a debt, a junkie reluctantly offers his watch, which Radovan heartlessly smacks across the room. In *Pusher III*, the tables turn on Milo and he offers his own watch to Rexho (Ramadan Huseini) to ameliorate a debt; but Rexho hurls the watch across the room, intending to extort something from Milo that is worth more than money: his obedient loyalty.

But if objects that people held dear and thought defined them keep changing back into commodities of blunt, unsentimental worth, then this is true of intimate human relations, too. Vic loses the emotional investment she has made in Frank; the only time Frank weeps in *Pusher* is after he assaults his best friend Tonny, yet we understand that, by the rules of his own game, he had no choice. There is an acknowledgment, in *Pusher*, of that late-capitalist dread which Godard identifies as "the death of friendship" (in *Histoire[s] du Cinéma*). Milo calls Frank "my best friend in Copenhagen" during the very conversation where he makes it clear that he will cut Frank no slack in terms of paying back what he owes. Later, luring Frank into the fatal trap, Milo purrs on the phone, "Frank, my friend ... we have to fix this, yeah?" "Friend" is a strategy for lulling one's enemies, for getting what one wants. Intimacy itself is commodified, to be returned when defective, discarded when valueless.

Moreover, along with the devastating effects of reducing life to dependencies and necessities, the drug economy stimulates and grows itself only through disasters, which crush individuals while enhancing the power of the business structure of the drug economy itself. This is disaster capitalism writ small, occurring secretly within largely hidden lives. The mob might lose money, but it never loses both money and face. The chance to make an example of someone who has double-crossed them has its own value as a guarantee of future loyalties.

This black market on the streets of Copenhagen has its own existence which Frank can never really touch, much less take over. We seem to see more than Frank does throughout the film; Frank often seems "blind." Yet, in *Pusher*'s final somber montage, set to eerie ambient music, it seems as though Frank becomes, as it were, the eyes of the film. Refn alternates tight close-ups of Frank standing on a street corner, looking off in different directions, trying to decide whether to trust Milo's promise of forgiveness. Between these close-ups of Frank gazing, Refn intercuts perfunctory shots of the urban life that is happening, simultaneously and tangentially, around Frank: Milo and Radovan in the sinister kitchen, spreading a plastic drop cloth on the floor in preparation for disposing of Frank's body; two mob enforcers loading a shotgun from the back of a van; Vic riding home in the back of a taxi, her face hidden by shadows, then gone forever. Everything is anchored back to Frank, as if he were imagining or "seeing" all this, putting it together in his mind. The film ends on his uncertainty. Will he embrace his fate? Does he really have a choice?

I view this ending as an homage to the famous montage of synchronous action which climaxes Martin Scorsese's *Mean Streets* (1973). Charlie (Harvey Keitel) has fled Manhattan in a car to escape the wrath of a vindictive loan shark, Michael (Richard Romanus). There is a car crash, and in the ensuing chaos the film fragments into a series of "checking-in" shots with other actors in the film, showing what they are doing at the same time as Charlie kneels, bleeding and bewildered, in the automobile wreckage. As with Frank's montage in *Pusher*, the editing in *Mean Streets*' grand finale frequently returns us to the image of Charlie, looking around, dazed, trying to focus, again as if his point of view was allied with the film's sudden, everywhere-you-turn omniscience. We see sidekick Tony (David Proval) washing his hands after using the bathroom; Giovanni the Mafia chief (Cesare Danova) settling down with a cigarillo and a drink to watch a Glenn Ford noir on late-night TV; the black woman Diane (Jeannie Bell), whom Charlie stood up essentially out of prejudice,[10] sitting in a diner lighting a new cigarette with the butt of another (in slang, "monkey-fucking"); the loan shark in a funk, his quarry slipped away from him again; etc.

Although somewhat anchored to Charlie's viewpoint, there is also a fanciful element to the flights of this closing montage; set to an Italian folk song performed by street singers, the sequence has a hallucinatory element. Everything is up for grabs at the end of *Mean Streets*. As the Glenn Ford clip underscores (the star rescues a girl from a burning car), there is no classic Hollywood resolution here. Neither is there one at the end of *Pusher*. But the chaos of *Mean Streets* really does suggest the isolation of separate agents oblivious to each other's suffering, a definitive atomization that is made all the more corrosive by a quick cut to an old woman pulling down the shade on her apartment window as a radio or TV voice bids everyone goodnight and a big band strikes up the melody to "Be It Ever So Humble, There's No Place Like Home." It's really more like "you can't go home again." It winds up as a weird kind of cinematic theater, an abrupt expulsion from what is homelike or *heimlich*. In *Pusher*, however, we never get away from the sense that there are real bonds being sundered. While Scorsese's Charlie nearly discovers that he never was in control of his hectic, amoral life (but is spared from final crushing self-knowledge by the montage's kitsch elements which reassure and which substitute for overt rescue), Frank seems to begin to really see just how much he has had and squandered: Vic's love; Tonny's friendship; Milo's protection.

At the same time, there is nothing grandiose about Frank's destiny, and we should not misread him as a Faustian figure, although Refn plays with that allusion in the scene where Frank dances with a skull for Vic's stoned amusement. That skull points not only toward Faust, of course, but the elemental "melancholy Dane," Hamlet. Without belaboring a point that Refn himself only suggests very fleetingly, Frank is an heir to those seekers of forbidden knowledge, Hamlet and Faust, who got in over their heads. He shares their misguided sense of mission and perhaps especially the fatal indecision familiar from *Hamlet*. Throughout the film he takes tremendous abuse, registered in the succession of increasingly abject ways in which he appears at Vic's door: swaggering in with Tonny in an early scene, and finally ending up crawling across the threshold, beaten, tortured and vomiting blood. But what is made obvious and cumulative to the viewer is never fully coherent within Frank's obliviousness. It is worth noting what Refn says about Tonny in *Pusher II*, for the same can apply to Frank: "He lives from minute to minute, and he reacts emotionally to every minute, and that is how he survives."[11] "Hand-to-mouth" existence (the constant struggle of not knowing where one's next meal is coming from) has its corollary in the hardcore drug cycles of using and withdrawal, getting high and coming down; and all of it is a kind of job that one tries to hold onto as long as possible. For Frank, it is all more or less part of a day's work—the great hustler chasing goldmines, unable to look back, unable to stop to think. If he had it to do over again, he would have had to do everything the same.

• • •

The gangster, then, both in his violence and his essential conformism to business values, is no longer particularly anomalous or even outside of society. Gangsterism, in current cinema, is depicted as inherently social, everything from a rite of passage to a phase of growing up to a kind of *Bildungsroman*-like apprenticeship, anything but a life definitively outside of society. But this has consequences for society, of course, which is forced to contract around this lowered expectation for its young male members as socialization and sociopathy grow their intertwining roots.

For Marilyn C. Wesley, "inductions into potential violence signal a degenerate social system unable to integrate the young man into a society that can satisfy his need for private identity and public order."[12] The subsequent crisis of masculinity means that either the individual male or else the "public order" will be sacrificed for the sake of the other. In the absence of constructive, meaningful identities, and with their fathers and father-figures acting as strictly negative role models, Frank and Tonny (and all the other gangsters in the *Pusher* trilogy) are somnambulistic, amoral men barely plagued by a distinction between their own inner disorder and what the urban world absorbs and projects back.

We see this masculine insecurity in Frank's relationship with Vic, the closest person to a love interest in *Pusher*. There seems to be genuine tenderness between the couple: in an early scene, he brings her a big stuffed-animal gorilla (it resembles Frank somewhat!), and she smiles, clearly charmed. Vic has nearly the same good-heartedness as Giulietta Masina in *La Strada* (1954), though her fate is less dire. The actress Laura Drasbaek also has a similar child-woman quality in her features that is somewhat reminiscent of Masina, albeit with a pronounced pouty mouth that offers glimpses of a strength and worldliness that Vic usually seems to hide around Frank. The essential tension between them is that they are both hidden from each other, in ways that indict the mercilessness of gender roles in the world of *Pusher*: he rarely shows her his weaknesses, she rarely shows him her independence. Yet, although Vic's relationship with Frank is mainly defined as a business arrangement (she helps stash his drugs), she seems to love him, and he increasingly turns to her as his crisis worsens. She sometimes places Frank in a "boyfriend role," as when she calls him to complain about "the pervert" across the street who likes to peep at her, asking Frank to come and beat the guy up. This is her way of asking for Frank's love; Frank, busy with dealing, puts her off but promises to take care of the nuisance later.

What complicates the obvious bond between Frank and Vic is mainly Frank's male insecurity, particularly in relation to love and sex. As Frank says to Tonny, "I don't want a whore for a girlfriend." Nonetheless, he brags to Tonny that he has sex with Vic whenever he wants. Later, he admits to Tonny: "I've never fucked her ... I can't. I can't deal with paid-for pussy." But this seems to be more of an excuse than a reason, since he also confesses that he followed one of her johns once and beat up the guy in a jealous rage, pointedly insulting the john's manhood as "small" and "ugly." In Frank's broadly emphasized phallic insecurity, we note an anxiety about what the world might think of him. Put otherwise, when it comes to his manhood and what he does with it, this violent drug dealer is desperately worried about respectability, and also about measuring up to other men. Refn's implicit critique of Frank is a measure of the distance between himself and his protagonist, Refn being incipiently anarchic enough to understand that Frank is not so much a true outlaw as a failed businessman. Rather than being a potential source of jouissance, loving a prostitute only exacerbates Frank's anxieties, as if his manhood did not finally belong to him but was something constructed by and promoted for the community around him.

Naturally, this is part of the delusional nature of male homosociality: the men themselves control the territorializations which they sometimes feel that they would like to escape. It's like a staring match that no one dares to concede to the other, no matter how deeply he thinks he has seen into his brother's eyes. Continuously wary of each other's strength, the men spar and compete endlessly. (In a way, this goes along with the idea of criminals who need to protect their status and their turf; weakness could be fatal. But the nature of phallic insecurity is to make any man believe that something like life and death are at stake, even in bland, mainstream, non-criminal arenas.) Tonny brags that he needs "four girls" to service his penis. No amount of female attention is enough. And, of course, violence, as it always does, substitutes for and subsumes phallic empowerment. The only real antidote to Frank's insecurity is to be accepted by the father-figure Milo as a cocky prodigal son, a chip off the old block, so to speak. If he can aggravate and rip off Milo, and still be forgiven and welcomed back as heir apparent, then Frank will have nothing left to prove, seemingly, regarding his potency. This is a sign of how grandiose and impossible Frank's self-succored fantasies of masculinity really are.

In *Pusher II*, it is Tonny who must confront his actual father, a mob boss called the Duke (Leif Sylvester). Fresh out of prison, Tonny approaches the Duke warily, and the Duke greets him with accusatory questions about

In an unsentimental reunion, Tonny (Mads Mikkelsen, left) gets out of prison and goes to see his father, the Duke (Leif Sylvester). The Duke demands that Tonny roll up his sleeve to prove that he is no longer a junkie. *Pusher II: With Blood on My Hands* (2004) revolves around Tonny's belated revenge for his childhood loss of innocence at his gangster father's hands.

whether he owes money to anyone and whether he is hooked on junk. Cinematically, Refn does something poignant and perfect here to illustrate the gap between father and son: he begins by showing them in alternating medium close-ups as they talk, suggesting that they are facing each other within arm's length; but a few minutes later, at the end of the tense, chilly conversation, he cuts to a longer view which shows the father moving wearily toward Tonny across the space of the pier that has actually been standing between them all along.

For the Duke (according to Refn, his name is a reference to John Wayne[13]), being a father is only about making enough money to throw at one's dependents. Refn may have been productively channeling his own anxieties during the writing and shooting of *Pusher II*, since he had recently become a father and was facing financial hardship (more about this in Chapter 4): "My life became a parallel of these [*Pusher*] films."[14] In the process Refn seems to have exorcised his own doubts and come out firmly on the side of seeking something more redemptive than soulless greed. "Use your head," the Duke tells Tonny, "set a good example for your son," meaning that Tonny should apply himself to making, or stealing, a lot of money. "Just like you?" Tonny asks his father leadingly, gaining awareness (as he does throughout the film) of the bad parenting that he was subjected to. In *Pusher III*, Milo's relationship with his daughter Milena (Marinela Dekic) is similarly fraught by Milo's feeling that he needs to make money in order to fulfill not only his paternalistic duty but in some sense his paternalistic rights as Milena's creator: "I was the first person you saw when you were born.... Anything you ever wanted you would get." Unlike Tonny, however, who wishes for real love from the Duke instead of pay-offs, Milena is even more money-driven and ruthless than her dad: she insists that he cut her in on the family business and offers to use her fiancé's cab company as a front.

In *Pusher II* and *Pusher III*, it is frequently the women who are hard and tough, while the young men are needy, abashed, clueless objects of social and psychological humiliation. Refn has said that every scene in *Pusher II* was built so as to end with Tonny being humiliated in some way. Although Tonny spends much of *Pusher II* trying to evade his own responsibilities as father, he seems to instinctively rebel against a cold, unemotional "fatherly love" that feels more like indifference or hate. We are left to imagine Tonny's own upbringing as the son of a hooker in the Duke's stable, who the Duke impregnated then cast aside. In the end Tonny kills Duke rather than letting himself be turned into a heartless hit man for Duke's crew.

Thus, even if these young men's sense of being men always lies somewhere beyond their grasp, the threat that they feel themselves living under is genuine.

Tonny has the word RESPECT tattooed on the back of his shaved head, as if to protect the vulnerable male back from betrayals from behind. Again, there seems to be a conflation between the male's holding of street turf and his ability to protect himself from more direct predations and violations by other males— not only getting bumped off, but getting raped. A number of recent gangster films have literalized the homoerotic tensions which always existed within the genre, in the form of explicit male rapes. Rather than depicting the tensions being deflected onto the abused or neglected or worshipped bodies of female props, these wilder recent films plunge headlong into the idea that the pecking orders of violent sociopathic gangs will work themselves out in the stronger males imposing forcible sodomy upon the weaker. We have seen this a lot in prison films, but the new gangster cinema (of which Refn is a leading light) now suggests that the rules of prison apply in civilian life as well.[15]

A graphic male rape occurs in *Svartur á leik* (*Black's Game*, 2012), a powerhouse gangster film from Iceland, which Refn himself executive-produced. This film, based on "real hardcore shit," as the credits tell us, takes place in 1999 during the first explosion of violent drug activity in the formerly sheltered Iceland. Thus, the film's meta-context is already concerned with loss of innocence on a mass scale. One of the leading dealers (Jóhannes Haukur Jóhannesson) terrifies his mother by snorting meth and head-banging around the house buck-naked. We note that there is a poster for *Pusher* hanging on the wall of the guy's room.

Other gang members in *Black's Game* include the young Stebbi "Psycho" (Thor Kristjansson), savvy but still green around the gills and far too good-natured and trusting. He watches with wide-eyed horror as he is dragged along on a bank robbery. Much of the violence is initiated by Bruno (Damon Younger), a seasoned criminal and sadist who quickly assumes leadership of the gang. Bruno is methodical but crazy, able to beat up guys nearly twice his size. As they get strung out on their own merchandise during the long Icelandic nights, going for days without sleep, their different personalities emerge: Stebbi numbly works hard to gain approval, while Bruno becomes twitchier and more controlling. We are as surprised as Stebbi is when Bruno corners Stebbi at a drug party, beats him, ties him up, and forcibly sodomizes him against his will. This is the shocking centerpiece of the film's exploration of the loss of innocence; needless to say, it is not what Stebbi signed up for, and it isn't long before he is persuaded to help the police break up the gang.

This rape crystallizes all the immorality and destruction wrought by hard drugs and crime. It also makes explicit those hidden male sexual tensions which have been identified as part of the macho gangster-action thriller nearly since the beginning. It heightens the sense of craziness and total chaos, the sense of a world without rules. The rape is not necessarily gay so much as a brutal display of Bruno's power over Stebbi; within the film, it cannot be said to fall within a recognizable sexual orientation, but then again, the male sexual tensions in gangster cinema never did. They arose from the proximity of men who were so tough and wild that they could only relate to each other, but these relations were fraught with the paranoia of competition, territoriality, psychopathology and violence.

There is a less overt and more psychological kind of male rape in *Pusher III*. In a café, Milo, trying to stay on the wagon, encounters a seedy young dealer who offers him a dime bag. At first Milo refuses in no uncertain terms, but the dealer keeps sliding the white packet across the table, telling Milo, "You say no, but you mean yes." This is the verbal form of rape, by which a man bypasses his quarry's objections and in fact categorically redefines them as their opposite. Where no means yes, nothing can be refused. Finally Milo gives up; he goes into a men's room stall (a place of male vulnerability and clandestineness) and immediately smokes the heroin. Milo's capitulation here has the effect of setting him on a downward spiral toward a "lesser-than" status vis-à-vis the younger men who are trying to take over his turf. Refn frames Milo's defeated nodding head through an open slat in the stall's wooden panel, suggestive generally of both glory holes (access between private toilets for anonymous sexual acts) and a steer in a pen waiting for slaughter.

In fact, it is precisely the explicit depiction of actual male rape in some of his films, as well as the sexualized naming of other fantasies and dysfunctions, that frees up the violence in Refn's cinema to be so astoundingly pure and concentrated. The violence is now something more than a sly compensation for unnamable psychic burdens; it is instead a wholly separate reflex, separate from and equal to the psychosexual urge. This also means that any resort to heterosexuality cannot assuage the violence, as a compensatory or civilizing force, since violence is no longer posed as an explicit denial of inter-male sexuality. In fact, with homoerotic tensions now full blown, so to speak, the violence which they usually, in genre terms, prefigure and summon forth can naturally be full blown as well, even orgasmic in a way that we associate more with heady screen violence of the '60s and '70s in the work of Arthur Penn or Sam Peckinpah. It is even somewhat romanticized (in *Bronson*, for example), mainly because the focus on inter-male violence largely gets around the feminist disapproval of violence against women as clichéd sexist abuse. The male-male twists seem to connect with bizarre back-brain quirks—like a ratcheting-up of those hints of perversity which used to infuse and somewhat radicalize the otherwise routine heterosexuality of the early Bond films, for example. Like the work of all great directors, Refn's films springboard from, and are intimately concerned with, a psychosexual aura that is polymorphous and no less decisive for being ambivalent about nearly everything (including the very need and desire for sex itself). Both *Bleeder* and *Drive* will be partly organized around only half-admitted cuckold fantasies, for example, the former grotesque and the latter almost sweetly idealized.

Thus, Refn's characters do not use violence to substitute for inchoate sexual impulses; instead they use violence in parallel with those sexual impulses, as if to register and communicate exactly what has been gained and lost in the pursuit of dim, occluded Eros. It is sex and romance which are furtive in Refn's cinema, taking place in oasis-like apartments, stopped elevators, gated cemeteries; even, in *Bronson,* through a camera lens that has been manually irised, perhaps with Vaseline around the edges (a shot in which we peep on Bronson cringing in bed beneath his wife who is lustily riding him cowgirl-style)— semiotically speaking, one enclosure after another, a series of frames inside other frames. (A series of selves inside other selves?) Whereas violence, in Refn's films, occurs in public, even in broad daylight, with all the preeminence of one person walking up to someone else to shake hands.[16]

This broad daylight has a way of stripping all dream-like or fantasy elements from the violence, which is given its fullest dimension of visible physical reality. Indeed, it is the fate of the average character in Refn's work that he is finally exposed to this harsh, inescapable light at the very moment when he thinks he might have found his escape. "The redemption is not too sentimental," Refn says, "because there is also a sadness to it because we know that it won't last. Reality is going to kick in."[17]

– 3 –

Bleeder

> Well, back to the pyramids. At the top is the sacrificial stone.... This stone bed where the victims were laid was transparent! It was a sacrificial stone chosen and polished in such a way that it was transparent. And the Aztecs inside the pyramid watched the sacrifice as if from within, because as you'll have guessed, the light from above that illuminated the bowels of the pyramids came from an opening just beneath the sacrificial stone, so that at first the light was black or gray, a dim light in which only the inscrutable silhouettes of the Aztecs inside the pyramids could be seen, but then, as the blood of the new victim spread across the skylight of transparent obsidian, the light turned red and black, a very bright red and a very bright black, and then not only were the silhouettes of the Aztecs visible but also their features, features transfigured by the red and black light, as if the light had the power to personalize each man or woman, and that is essentially all, but *that* can last a long time, *that* exists outside time, or in some other time, ruled by other laws. —Roberto Bolaño[1]

> The world, then, is not merely a battlefield where victory and defeat receive their due recompense in a future state. No! the world is itself the Last Judgment on it. Every man carries with him the reward and the disgrace that he deserves. —Arthur Schopenhauer[2]

If *Pusher* was a kind of etching, *Bleeder* is more of a full-scale painting, like the street graffiti mural which it memorably uses as found background decoration. Refn's second feature is an in-depth exploration of the furthest extremes of what it means to be male: dogmatically obsessed with honor and revenge to the point of self-destruction, forced to compete in a pecking order simply because some other guy always has something to prove, wigged-out, scared straight out of his own comfort zone, kept going by the intermittent vision of a statuesque ice-blonde in white, and finally finding a sort of hapless, bitter heroism in sheer, grinding endurance. It is only one aspect of maleness, to be sure, but later Refn characters such as Bronson, as well as the male configurations of *Valhalla Rising* and *Drive*, originate in the bizarre power struggles of *Bleeder*.

Perhaps *Bleeder*'s most significant leap is the almost schizophrenic way that Refn does not depict this idea of maleness in the figure of a single man, but tosses it into a mirrored funhouse of sorts. He wants to show in full what Freud calls "the brother horde,"[3] a seething peer group fighting for dominance, united against filial and societal authority but rifted by their own wary antagonisms. Making compelling surmises about the internal dynamic of prehistoric clans, Freud writes that "the brothers quarreled among themselves for the succession [after the father], which each of them wanted to obtain for himself alone. They came to see that these fights were as dangerous as they were futile. This hard-won understanding ... led at last to a union among them, a sort of social contract."[4] Georges Bataille picks up on this (in a beautiful sentence): "Occasionally the most double-dealing of gangsters has a sense for the rules of his neighborhood."[5]

We have already seen this, in Refn, in the conflict between Frank's violence and his lingering traces of compassion for his victims; his fatal trust in the bad paternal object, Milo, suggests Frank's need to find an unassuming place within an existing communal order. There is no such reservation in *Bleeder*, which is precisely a volcanic eruption among members of a brother horde, what we might call a neighborhood holocaust. Its antiheroes are a trio of testosterone-fueled young-male archetypes—Lenny (Mads Mikkelsen), the scornful, shy, defensive fanboy, a likely candidate for middle-aged virginity; Louis (Levino Jensen), the perverse, sadistic wannabe gangster, making up in meanness what he lacks in stature; and Leo (Kim Bodnia), the hysteric, self-loathing, long-suffering cuckold turned wife-beater. Ultimately, *Bleeder* offers no apologies for any of them, instead insisting that they fight it out among themselves (and let the bodies fall where they may) until all the fear and hatred have been purged, and a possibility for real love emerges—but only for one of them. The reduction of all three to only one, Lenny, is telling of how the men are meant to be viewed as enmeshed, warring instincts, coextensive apportionments of male psychical identity.

In a playfully absurdist touch, the main characters all have somewhat homophonic names beginning with "L." Leo lives with his girlfriend Louise (Rikke Louise Andersson), who has just found out that she is pregnant. But the dominant man in Louise's life is her brother Louis, who runs a nightclub and is a kind of local petty mobster. Although Louis and Leo seem to get along, Louis constantly bullies and mocks Leo, questioning his manhood, his heterosexuality, his potency. "So your equipment works, you're not shooting blanks," Louis says when he comes over to chortle about his beloved sister's pregnancy—the film's first insinuation of problematic sexuality, and also its first moment of (psychologically) violent interaction.

Leo takes this abuse rather numbly, hiding in the bedroom while Louis takes Leo's seat at the kitchenette table with Louise. There is darkness working here, under the skin: Leo has begun to suspect that Louis might be the real father of Louise's unborn baby. In fact, in a key scene (fairly early in the film) in which Louis helps Louise hang a mirror while Leo is out, we find that Leo is not just being paranoid. "You did it," Louise cheers for her brother. "I did that, too," he says in an ownerly way, staring at his sister's stomach; then they embrace. This incest has a quality of setting Louis and Louise apart, a golden couple who hold themselves above the others; it is a kind of prideful escape from real life, and it does not go unpunished by the end of the film.

Leo and Louis are also friends with Lenny, who works in a video store and is obsessed with movies. A new, competing obsession has recently entered Lenny's celluloid world, however, in the person of Lea (Lyn Corfixen), a server at a local diner. Each night he walks past her eatery and watches her through the front window as she closes up. The lighted window replicates the safe distance of a movie or TV screen, one where Lea appears to Lenny as a private star of his imagination, untouchable, perfect, otherworldly.

Later on, Lenny works up the nerve to approach her, but his attempts at making conversation are awkward. The only subject he is really comfortable with is movies, and he seems heartened when she says that she liked *Casino*, the "guy movie" that she came into his store to rent last week. Lea is sweet and down to earth, if somewhat guarded; she seems willing to look past Lenny's social gaucheness and see him for what he essentially is, a childlike innocent. Lenny is still so intimidated by her that even when she accepts a date with him (to go to the movies, naturally), he cannot go through with it: he sees her waiting for him outside the theater and runs away before she has seen him.

Meanwhile, Leo is standing outside Louis' club with Louis when a man comes up and shoots the bouncer. Leo witnesses Louis and his henchmen dragging the shooter inside and beating him. Although Leo does not take part in the physical violence, he is trapped inside the club's locked vestibule and watches in a kind of panic. In general now more suspicious and fearful, Leo is also more and more uncertain that he wants Louise to have her baby. Confrontations between the couple are on a constant simmer. One day Louise is in a laundromat when a small boy bearing a resemblance to her brother catches her eye. The look she gives to this toddler is lingering and loaded, and more than a little creepy. Is she stirred by perverse longing? Is she suddenly worried that her baby will come out looking nothing like Leo but exactly like Louis instead? Whatever her motives, she starts a conversation with the mother, and brings her and her two children back to the apartment. Leo is unnerved to come home and find his place resembling a daycare center; his apprehensions seem to crystallize around the boy who looks like Louis (none of this is spoken; Refn artfully uses only reaction shots that clash with the "normal" flow of these scenes to let us know that something is off). There is a tense moment where the women insist that Leo hold the woman's infant, and we dread that Leo will harm this infant somehow. Instead, Leo chases out these houseguests, then hits Louise.

When Louis finds out, he threatens Leo, pointedly calling him a "faggot." Leo, in turn, acquires a gun for protection. In the middle of a movie night with the guys, Leo pulls out this gun and holds it on Louis, trying to get him to confess. Tension seethes as Louis and Leo lock eyes, neither one yielding. Specifically, Leo, framed against the movie screen, is engaging in a fantasy of phallic power in which he substitutes not only for the masculine hero of the film being screened, but for the object of the other males' attention. While standing in front of the screen holding his gun extended at Louis' face, he is enacting not only an attempt at trumping "superior" images of masculinity, but of asserting that this is a fantasy which the other males will wish to witness and savor in the same way they watch action films. The fact that the other men protest that Leo is, among other things, blocking their view of the screen isolates him even more as the bearer of a flawed or inappropriate masculinity. Indeed, Leo admits that the gun only contains blanks, as if to prove Louis' earlier, loaded insult toward Leo that he "shoots blanks" (infertile sperm) during sex with Louise. One way or another, Leo seems determined to make the truth come out, no matter how terrible. Already beside himself, Leo goes home to find that Louise has put away some of his belongings to make more room for her own. Incensed, Leo knocks her down and kicks her, then flees the apartment. Louise loses the baby.

Louis wastes no time. Later that night his men grab Leo on the street and string him up by his wrists with chains in an abandoned factory. Dangling pathetically, Leo screams for help. An evil scheme is hatched: one of Louis' henchmen knows an AIDS sufferer who sells syringes of his blood. Louis pays for some of this infected blood (in a visibly dirty syringe), which is immediately injected into Leo's bared buttocks. The theme of veiled homoeroticism/homophobia between Leo and Louis suddenly becomes more blatant, more outrageously twisted. Louis is doing something worse to Leo than simply killing him: he is branding him with the ongoing taint of a stigmatized disease. Impugning Leo's manhood and sexuality, the injection is a de-sexualized act of dominance, functionally a male rape.

Louis' act of revenge sends Leo over the edge. Now the gun is loaded, and on the street in broad daylight he shoots Louis twice in the stomach, then shoots himself in the hand and squeezes his now-infected blood into Louis' open wounds. This dirty stigmata is an early indication of how later Refn films will update, play with, and recount elements of the Christ story. Louis writhes on the ground as Leo puts the gun in his own mouth and blows his brains out. No suicide in cinema has ever felt more like auto-crucifixion, particularly with the creation of the freely bleeding stigmata on Leo's palm. Leo wants to punish Louis by making him bear witness to his own suffering, his own nearly religious martyrdom—"dying for the sins" of Louis and Louise, as it were, and for all the acts of random urban violence that have crystallized into this intimate apocalypse, which fulfills the suggestion of theologian Timothy K. Beal that religion needs to be spoken in a "voice of disorientation [and] psychological, political, cosmic horror"[6] rather than a voice of certainty and stability.

Shaken by the tragedy, Lenny searches for meaning, and finally summons the courage to see Lea. His newfound ability to show his feelings and be vulnerable is rewarded. She is kind to him and forgives him for standing her up. The stylized final shot symbolically unites them as a couple, sharing a theatrical spotlight in the middle of the darkened diner as a love song (composed by John Lennon) plays on the soundtrack. Although this happy ending can barely shake off the mood of disturbance ratcheted up by the rest of the film, Refn's obvious artistic sincerity demands that we accept it on its own terms, a kind of exalted heavenly reward after an extended sojourn in hell.

Needless to say, *Bleeder* was not designed to please everybody. As the plot indicates, the characters are mostly unpleasant types and/or walking advertisements for misanthropy. Of the cast members, even the attractive ones mostly schlump around like people who do not seem to belong in a movie and do not necessarily even want to be in this one. Like any deeply personal film, *Bleeder* contains elements that are virtually indefensible. It comes at the psychological problems and behaviors of its male main characters so bluntly that, like Scorsese's *Raging Bull* (1980), it immerses the viewer in a kind of nirvana of sheer aggression that knows very little rationalizing. Indeed, in its depiction of the vengeful violence of free individuals, petty-anarchic gods at play, *Bleeder* joins ranks with the matter-of-fact irrationalism of pure legend or myth. Refn continuously raises the pitch of action to something like a renewal of ancient mythology in a current urban setting. The ultimate subject of *Bleeder* is one drawn straight from ancient mythos, a spectacular sacrifice summoned forth to cleanse inexpiable sin, a blood guilt. In this respect, *Bleeder* has an epic sensibility and unflinching clarity that will be associated with nearly all of Refn's subsequent films.

• • •

Perhaps it would be more accurate to say that the *spirit* of an ancient epic sensibility shows through *Bleeder*'s po-mo dress-down. The actual look of the film is intensely low-budget (in one scene, in the hallway entrance of a nightclub, Refn ingeniously simulates a teeming rave with nothing but flashing lights, a thumping beat, and a few extras near the door, creating the right ambiance without having to decorate a set or stage a crowd scene), and the space of its action is severely circumscribed. We become increasingly aware that *Bleeder* is all taking place within a three- or four-block neighborhood of Copenhagen, filled with graffiti, attack dogs to ward off criminals, abandoned buildings, and other signifiers of urban blight. This shows the claustrophobia of metropolitan experience where one might live, work, shop and go out all within one's immediate vicinity. These characters could not escape each other even if they tried.

One of *Bleeder*'s complex themes is precisely this difficulty of living in a pressurized urban milieu without going insane. Louis and Louise had to fight their way out of the slum where they were born; that damage, and the intense bond which it produced, may have scarred them over the long run. And there is no definitive escape, one is always in danger of being dragged down. At the eatery where she works, Lea is browbeaten by her boss' kvetching litany of complaints and critiques, a continuous stream of negative energy which she must willingly absorb if she wishes to retain her job. Likewise, Louis' club is a site of racial tensions and violence. Lurking at the very heart of everything, of course, is the barely mentioned AIDS virus, which becomes a murder weapon: the presence of an infected man who shows no qualms about spreading his disease (for profit, no less) is the film's harshest and most damning metaphor for urban corruption and decay, the war "of all against all."

A film evoked by *Bleeder*, and one that shares its apprehension of soul-destroying city life, is Abel Ferrara's *The Driller Killer* (1977). Clearly, the accelerating drive toward madness and violence, inspired by a male's perceived inadequacy and the unredeemable tainting of romantic love and sex, appears in both films as the morbid last resort of hipster "lifestyles" (trying to make ends meet on slacker wages; the routine frenzy of what Lou Reed called "all tomorrow's parties"). But the spiritual affinity between these films transcends content, as Refn picks up on the same formal interrogation of the cinematic image which Ferrara practices as well.

A Western city, such as New York or Copenhagen, is essentially composed of images (posters, displays, billboards, fashion styles, etc.), dazzling to tourists but often oppressive and mocking to those who scratch for existence there. Like *The Driller Killer*, and also like much of Godard, *Bleeder* is a densely fabricated visual object made from a deeply unsettling distrust of fabricated visual objects: specifically, numerous images of images (including paintings and movies), sensuous but secondhand traps that catch up the eye and destabilize its claims to truthful witness.

In *The Driller Killer* these meta-images are filmed in such pop–Godardian close-ups that they end up becoming more clarified than the real action; as in the brief club scene where the bright, relentlessly animated mechanical field of a pinball table is paralleled with the growing disintegration of the killer's mind. The amped-up, glowing images cast their judgments and make their demands, almost as if the images are using the killer (played by Ferrara) to commit the murders that they themselves would commit if they only had hands—delusional, paranoid evil posing as clarification or beautification of the world. In fact, the killer crucifies and exsanguinates homeless winos who pointedly do not fit the profile of the streamlined urban image world—living reminders of death and decay, street-corner eyesores usually already covered in vomit and grime.

Images also punctuate and seem to egg on Leo's descent into violent madness in *Bleeder*. At one point we see him posed anxiously in front of a Pop Art mural of action hero Fred Williamson; the larger-than-life image of Williamson seems to implicitly question and critique Leo's fragile grasp on his own masculinity (and sanity), as does, in a way, the offbeat poster classifying various fish species that hangs over the nook where Leo eats cramped meals with Louise. Devolution, the idea of a "fishy" man, bottom feeders—this poster not only points to Leo's problems but to the seeming emptiness in young urban life, driven by compulsive irony and pervasive mediation. Likewise, copies of a horror fanzine named "Trauma" hang beside the sales counter of the video store where Lenny hides to avoid the traumas of the risky real world; and there is also an entire shelf of identical rental boxes bearing the title "Pain." We already feel that the image world must yield to, or become augmented by, something more genuine and human, even as images seem to snare, mock and stare down the tenuous, hapless Leo, or explicitly name Lenny's fears while keeping them contained.

We see some of what Schopenhauer might have meant (in another context) about every day being Judgment Day. We are always surrounded by visual and linguistic signs, identifiers which console or ridicule our innermost emotions; it is part of city life, it is also part of mediated capitalist life. It is, as it were, the tension between the world as *my* representation (where I can delude myself into feeling whole and at one) and the world as *their* or *your* representation (where I feel my own subjective emotions reified, exploited and used against me). The angry graffiti is meant to make you angry, the thoughtful graffiti to make you think, the romantic graffiti to make you feel mushy inside. Regardless, the visual presence of an imposing and ostensibly personal subjectivity is assimilated only as an irritant, since one is forced to identify and match oneself with something alien, and also something that turns out to be not individualized at all but generic, a function of urban planning or overcrowded blight. (A common symptom of schizophrenia is the delusion that random signs have been placed in specific locations in order to send messages to you and you alone—but, of course, as with so much mental illness, the force of the delusion lies within the truth that it cannot stop noticing: signs *have been* put up everywhere in order to work on those who see them.)

The visible world is now invested with the mysticism and superstition that used to accrue only to metaphysical experience. It is not so much that we walk through coffee shops and office spaces as if they were film sets, shallowly revealing ourselves through the cups we hold and the books we read—it is that, in a pinch, we can focus this kind of direct information into snap judgments, judgments which satisfy the lowest level of curiosity while leaving intact the nearly gratuitous essence of why and how things are. Refn's camera is automatic and atavistic in its framings. When Lea, wearing white, walks past anti–Monsanto graffiti, we immediately associate her ingénue beauty with the purity of environmental causes; when Louis, after infecting Leo, pukes against a giant mural of clown faces, we understand him to be a clown. Somewhat in the manner of expressionism, but again in a way that we associate most closely with Godard, Refn adopts this found visual poetry, without baroque or embellishment, to denote judgments about the characters. What is Lea all about? Purity. Who is Louis? An evil clown. We know it when we see it, or *because* we see it: this is the classic "montage" of the cinematic eye, which is now, reflexively, the same eye that walks down the street, collecting random evidentiary materials into patterns and bricolages of meaning, but the meanings themselves remain provisional. Purity is perhaps only the look of purity; clownish is only as clownish appears. As they would be in life, overlapping pieces of unadorned reality are invested with significance simply by being selected and observed, cut off from any deeper philosophical inquiry. Or rather, the inquiry is meant to arise from the way in which bald, plain things, surfaces, can be read as signifiers. That guy's the hero—why?—because he looks like the hero.

Who gets to live, and who does not, within an image world? In *Bleeder*, as it was in *The Driller Killer*, the answer is: "No one who does not fit the

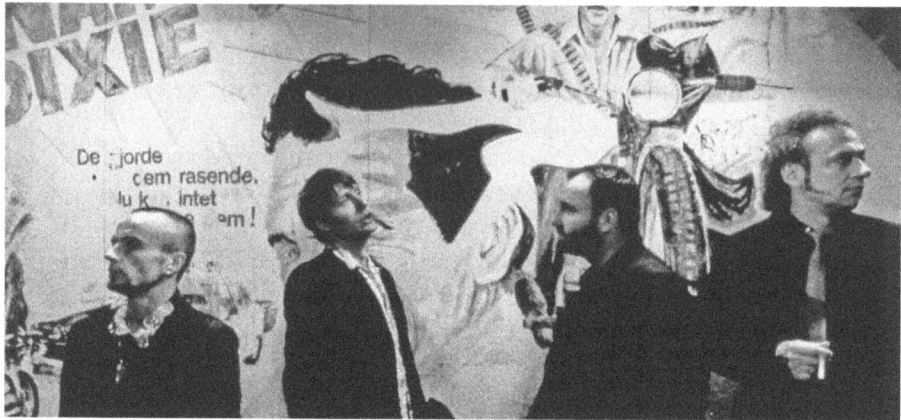

Bleeder (1999) follows a coterie of alienated twenty-somethings in Copenhagen as their pressurized lives reach a violent boiling point. Throughout the film, bright, larger-than-life images, such as wall murals, are contrasted with the characters' drab and moribund existence. Pictured, from left to right: Levino Jensen, Mads Mikkelsen, Kim Bodnia, and Zlatko Buric.

image." Murders are not moral or immoral acts so much as litter removal, exilings of unwanted matter from the optical field. Films about killing always fall into the thought process of a serial killer, whether or not they mean to, and whether or not they end with a symbolic return of justice (which they usually do). This thought process is something like: *this one needs to go; this one's next; that one's pretty, she can stay a little longer; this one's good, maybe she can be allowed to live.* Don't we always just know, in serial killer films, when a character has been used up, has no more to show us, and thus will soon be dead? Don't we feel a kind of guilty relief when a character who has been outstaying his welcome in the film from the beginning is finally brought to slaughter? Most commercial films try to disguise this process and render it subliminal; whereas films like *The Driller Killer* and *Bleeder*—as well as, say, Godard's *Pierrot le Fou* (1965) and *Weekend* (1967)—openly acknowledge that when they kill a character, they are acting in complicity with destructive image worlds: the larger one, linked to capitalism and commodification, and also the sublime aesthetic ones within the films themselves. *Why* is there so much blood? "Not blood," Godard corrected the naïve-sounding interviewer with diabolical serenity, "red." Then added: "At any rate, I find it difficult to talk about the film."[7]

Whodunnit? The images. And they ain't talking.

And if *we* could talk about them, transfer their automatic power to ourselves, we most likely wouldn't need them anymore. *Bleeder* is about needing the images, about doing their dirty work day in and day out, and about reaching the point where one might say, "Enough." It is Refn practicing tough love on his own obsession with cinema, and simultaneously it is his confession (one of the most difficult but also necessary things for a director to execute) of always looking at the world through essentially cinematic eyes. As if to rework Scorsese's and Schrader's ingenious use of the parable of the blind man in the final moments of *Bull*, Refn suggests with *Bleeder* that one finally comes to seeing, and by extension filmmaking, only through first acknowledging that one has been blinded—blinded in part by films and images themselves.[8]

• • •

Toward this end, Lenny is the character who seems to most closely represent Refn, and he belongs to a more passive masculine strain: shy, content with vicariousness, seeking outrageous thrills only at secondhand remove. His appetite for "bad movies," which often display misanthropy in their lurid plots and violent characters (as well as a kind of meta-misanthropy, if you will, in their overall cheapness and lack of polish), is concomitant with his dislike of, and discomfort in, the real world. Lenny's tiny apartment is organized around his armchair and TV; the facing walls are dominated by enormous posters of Mad Max and Bruce Lee (the same ones that hang in Frank's apartment in *Pusher*—no doubt they are from Refn's own extensive collection; more about this in Chapter 4). We learn that Lenny watches four films every day in this space devoted to fan worship, this fantasy space that promotes the idea that the world is bad, dangerous, immoral, probably rigged and corrupt, above all violent. Laugh at it from a distance, shudder at it, but do not entrust it with your heart. The one-dimensional action heroes on the walls, striking iconic poses preparing to do battle, seem more vibrant than the largely inert, possibly depressed Lenny; indeed, they seem to act for him, household gods who intercede with the world on behalf of their owner-worshipper. As long as Bruce Lee is getting ready to land a roundhouse kick, and Mad Max is fingering the trigger of his shotgun, Lenny can feel safe. Of course, the limitations of this worldview become apparent to him when he falls in love with Lea. (The fact that Lea is played by Lyn Corfixen, Refn's wife, suggests a further link between the character of Lenny and Refn.)

Lenny's retreat from life into movies is reinforced by his slacker dream-job, working in the video store owned by fellow movie buff Kitjo (Zlatko Buric), an aging hipster with muttonchops and Three Stooges hair. In a memorable scene, a curious customer asks about the way the movies are shelved; and Lenny launches into a long list, ventriloquized by Kitjo who is feeding him lines Cyrano-style, of who the great, featured directors are, an unorthodox pantheon that includes not only stalwart names like Fritz Lang, Martin Scorsese and David Lynch, but directors of exploitation and horror such as Russ Meyer, George Romero, Jean Rollin (*The Shiver of the Vampires*), William Lustig (*Maniac Cop*), and Joe D'Amato (*Erotic Nights of the Living Dead*). Kitjo also feeds Lenny another series of director names, who have been "chucked out" and relegated to the bottom shelf, including some of the more hallowed art-film directors, including Murnau, Lindsay Anderson, Buñuel, Godard, and—Lars von Trier. After pronouncing this last name, a leading light of his own homeland's cinema, Mikkelsen makes a cute grimace that seems to combine distaste with a slight regret at being "mean" to the fellow Dane.

Voyeurism, and even critiquing, may be mainly passive, but make no mistake: there is a kind of masculinist intellectual violence in this taxonomy of who is good and who is bad, this dismissal of some auteurs and promotion of others: a pecking order wherein some males (directors) symbolically lose face. (There are no female directors in either the beloved or hated camps.) Directors are surrogates for the men who list and follow and argue over them. Brains and combative good taste substitute for other forms of traditionally masculinist strength. Indeed, when Lenny tries to keep his first date with Lea, he sees her waiting for him at the movie theater in front of a poster for von Trier's then-latest, *Idioterne* (*The Idiots*, 1998). He is, of course, intimidated by seeing his two great loves—cinema and Lea—brought together, but more pointedly, Lea throws into question Lenny's comforting certainty that the "idiots," so to speak, are always other people.

But if escapism and aesthetic judgments are brutal enough in *Bleeder*, truly violent acts, for Leo and Louis, overflow the bounds of reason. Actually, for most of *Bleeder*, Leo is in a similar limbo to Lenny's, as a male figure who does not engage directly in violence with other men; he resists entering the fray of the brother horde. In the scene where he witnesses a savage beating at Louis' club, Leo is trapped inside the club's vestibule and has no choice but to watch in wide-eyed horror. At one point, desperate, he asks, "Can I come out now?"—this loaded question trading on popular meanings of "coming out" (centering on latent homosexuality) as well as the helplessness of asking permission. Leo's terrified close-up reminds us that he is, again, losing face, and thus may no longer be "one of the boys" but someone othered, less than.

Louis' energy is allied with his machismo, and also, appropriately to the plot, the idea of potency and the ability to become a father. When Leo asks him if he has any kids, he gives the standard macho response, "Not that I know of." This is, of course, a lie, as Leo himself seems to suspect. (Elsewhere Leo presses Louis significantly on whether he has "ever killed a rabbit," part of the lore of classic laboratory pregnancy tests, and still in coinage in this age of home testing.) The planting of a man's seed, so to speak, is here given the meaning

3. Bleeder

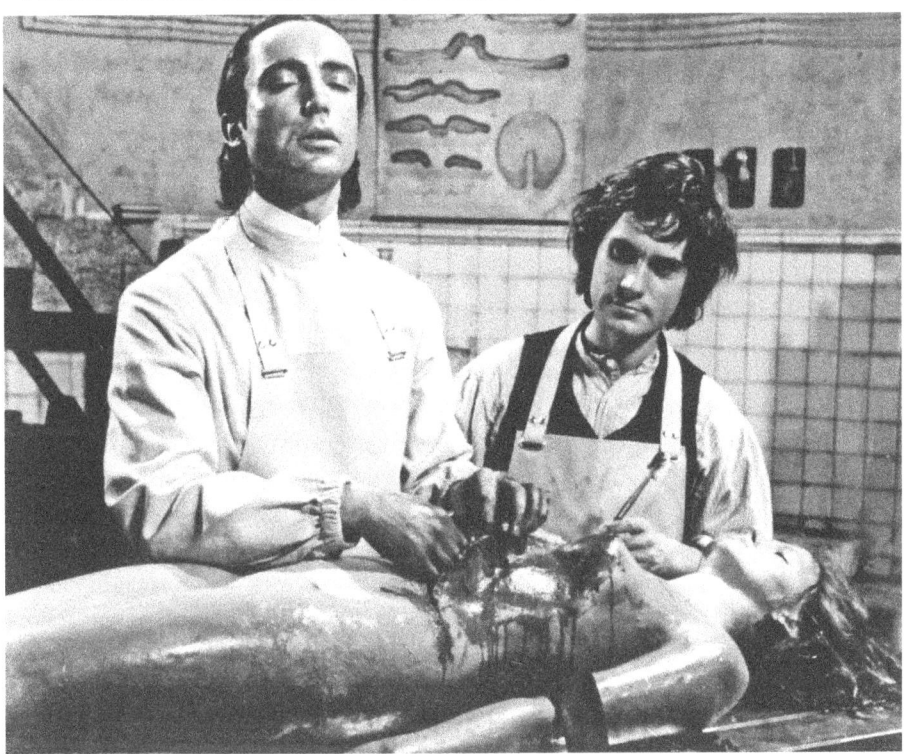

In Paul Morrissey's *Flesh for Frankenstein* (1974), Udo Kier (pictured) plans to "populate and repopulate" the world with dead people whom he has resuscitated. The campy love of movies in *Bleeder* is another kind of fetishistic warding off of melancholy and mourning through the wish for a stabilized world where one knows all the lines by heart and can never be surprised by what will happen next.

of something outside the bounds of paternal and social responsibility; it is a mission of the male ego, and a thinly veiled scenario of conquest. The army of "bastards" substitutes, in the macho mindset, for a spreading of influence and control.

Refn makes this explicit through montage, by cutting directly from Louis' statement to a scene from Paul Morrissey's *Flesh for Frankenstein* (1974), which Lenny is watching on his VCR at home. In the film clip, Dr. Frankenstein (Udo Kier) talks grandiosely about his plan to "populate and repopulate the planet" with resurrected corpses of his own creation. (Lenny, Über-fan, mouths along with this line in perfect timing.) In a more intimate sense, the drive to fatherhood takes on, here, the explicit form of world domination, tied to a different kind of familiar masculine ego, that of the horror genre's "mad scientist." Frankenstein's fathering is pointedly sexless; instead, fathering is inflected with the perversities of overcompensation, will-to-power, and fetishism. "By playing God," theologian Timothy K. Beal asks, "does one inadvertently end up playing monster? ... Is our monstrosity in the image of God?"[9] Traditionally, the mad scientist absorbs our worst animosity toward a God who has power over life and death; he is coded as perverse because of his deliberate blurring of the line between life and its opposite.

This naturally takes in a perversion of pregnancy itself, one of the subthemes of *Bleeder*. Louise is carrying an inbred baby; Leo is increasingly distraught at the idea of this. But this domestic nightmare is not presented as particularly exceptional, as in, say, the satanic pregnancy in *Rosemary's Baby* (1968)—rather, it is somewhat matter-of-fact, like the deformed baby in Lynch's *Eraserhead* (1978), in which pregnancy is yet another intimacy that has become the victim of a jaded, moribund society. In an early scene in Kitjo's video shop, Kitjo enumerates to a customer the wide variety of X-rated tapes starring pregnant women, broken down, esoterically enough for the hardcore connoisseurs, into women in their seventh, eighth, or ninth months. This is an early reference in the film to the turning of the maternal body toward morbid perversity rather than toward life, the self-absorbed orgasm of the consumer usurping any other intimate or societal virtues in bearing children. But the very existence of such "pregnancy porn" begs the ethical questions: what rock-bottom pregnant woman would submit to such truck with pornographers and exploiters, and what kind of person would want to see a woman in advanced pregnancy having sex? And we might also think about what kind of life awaits the fetus, who is a central object in this particular porn-imaginary albeit effaced, disguised as the idea of "pregnancy" itself. Perhaps this type of porn placates the sometime male fear of becoming fathers, the way more normative porn placates more common performance anxieties. Larger societal issues about what it means to have babies are constantly implied in *Bleeder*'s mise-en-scène. "It doesn't bother Leo anymore," Louise says at one point, about the fact that they are having a baby, but the way Refn uses wide-angle shots to isolate Leo in lonely corners of his and Louise's apartment suggests otherwise, even as it exposes their spartan furnishings, unpainted drywall, drill holes and exposed wiring and pipes as an unlikely place for a baby to be.

The mother holds terrifying powers to an insecure, immature male. Louis' and Louise's mother—never actually seen—is a conduit of bad news throughout *Bleeder*, and a special nail in Leo's coffin. The mother is a confounding presence, as a phone-voice already kin to the disembodied-maternal voice of *Psycho* (1960), and while we are on horror, a further clue lies in *Bleeder*'s explicit reference to *Friday the 13th* movies, particularly the third sequel in the franchise, which Kitjo names as his favorite during a friendly argument with Lenny.

3. Bleeder

Friday the 13th III (1982) begins with an extended playing-out of a trope that occurs again and again in the series, around the machete-wielding serial killer Jason and a young woman. As cinema's most mother-fixated serial killer since Norman Bates, Jason is so obsessed by the commanding maternal voice in his head that he sometimes mistakes one of the girls he is about to kill for the mother herself, a mistake which the girl smartly capitalizes on, instinctively making her voice deeper and more domineering, bending Jason to her will and either temporarily or permanently disarming him.

The trope is so transparent as to be completely unambiguous, and so compelling, in a bizarre way, that we never question how these harried, terrified young women suddenly figure out that they can save their own lives by pretending to be the killer's bossy mother. There is something innately disturbing to heternormative sexual paradigms in the way the films feature the face of the deceased mother (always Betsy Palmer, from the original *Friday the 13th*) hovering, superimposed, over the face of the nearly interchangeable nubile teenaged girl du jour. An overbearing woman "created" Jason; the only person who can ever stop him (and then, only until the next sequel, naturally) is a girl who quickly learns to mimic that overbearing maternal personality. The girls who remain giggly and immature are slaughtered in bed with their boyfriends; to save herself, the girl must see beyond the bubbles of ravishment and teen lust to the dire future of having raised an ax-murderer son. In this fatalistic way, ongoing life is affirmed, at the expense of fleeting romance, by allowing for the fact that the youthful inamorata will one day turn into the shrewish mother—a kind of comforting punishment for all, latent in sex's scary, intimidating pleasure. It affirms primal taboos about sexual (and aggressive) urges forced to recede before the presence of the mother, and it seems to represent a kind of socialization for the typically antisocial, or socially backward, fans of slasher movies, since what *Friday the 13th* might teach the fanboys in *Bleeder* is that lone males are killed while mothers and maternal substitutes survive, and that even the most terrifying male (Jason) is no match for the mother. (In fact, this is roughly what occurs in *Bleeder* itself.)

There are other cinematic examples of this nagging need to hide or avoid the mother in fear of a latent overidentification with her, which becomes almost like a suicidal tendency. Returning to early Scorsese, mothers are significant in their absence from the anarchic worlds of both *Mean Streets* and *Taxi Driver* (1976). In the latter, Travis (Robert DeNiro) avoids comforting, maternal women, being drawn instead to the tough cashier at a grind house (Diahann Abbott) and a spoiled, immature debutante-activist (Cybill Shepherd). Iris (Jodie Foster), the female to whom he is most drawn (non-sexually) and whom he kills for, is literally a child and a prostitute, the furthest imaginable female type from a mother. In *Mean Streets*, Charlie tries on a new suit that his mother has left for him with a note, but his ritualized dressing and primping in the mirror are for himself alone; in casting aside the mother's note, he dispels his origins and emerges as a narcissistic, self-created being. Young men might avoid the mother (or the maternal) because of the uncomfortable suspicion that birth awakens thoughts of death; still, death comes anyway. It is in this suit given by his mother that Charlie will later be shot and injured in a car crash. This is like Leo's depressive harping on the fact that he and Louise live between a nursery and a cemetery: brief space in which the mother hovers as both progenitor and angel-of-death. One takes her gifts, as Charlie takes the suit, then concertedly strives to forget that they reinforce a certain existential helplessness and doom, the cycle of life come home to roost.

Also, my intuition about early Scorsese is that the "love stories" paraphrase the director's all-consuming love of cinema, which will admit no rivals. As in cases of mother-fixation, women trigger an obsession that is always already present: they must not resemble (threaten) the mother too much, just as they must come and go, fickle, faithless, unable to replace the central source of the obsession. A pornographic movie literally comes between Travis and the debutante in *Taxi Driver*, with the movie clearly winning in the rivalry. It is only after Travis has destroyed his television in a rejection of its secondhand, flickering images, that he can proceed with his mission, the kamikaze-like orgy of carnage at Iris' whorehouse. It takes this complete rejection of the cinematic womb for Travis to turn, as if in slightly disappointed resignation, to the non-mother, the child prostitute, and even then to seek in her, symbolically, the longed-for consolation of oblivion. (He survives, though.)

Cinema is the real mother, or mother-substitute, in *Bleeder*, too. Kitjo and his movie club are lost boys who repair to a clubhouse-like den in order to feed off images of brutal action, stuck in an endless replay of using movies as a coded form of pre–Oedipal security. In the dark they curl up and listen to the projector's overriding heartbeat, the storytelling voices. After all, when we watch a favorite film often enough that we commit the lines by heart (as Lenny does), we know exactly what will happen next, a way of summoning the stability that one knew in the womb or in early bonding with the mother; a retreat from the spontaneous demands and reactions of adult (male) company. *Bleeder* depicts a kind of cinematic mirror-stage: to "be real," as Leo wants to be, is finally a denial of life rather than an embracing of it, for reality itself forces us often to stake out some barraged place in the middle of all the mayhem—it pushes us toward reflexive, ill-considered, inadequate responses. Finessing reality, as Lenny learns to do, is a survival skill without which there is no time or safe space for emotional coherence, no personal growth. In fact, love of movies is shown to be preparation for real love. We see this fulfilled in the way the romantic ending, with Lea and Lenny in their spotlight, reprises the "Love Me" serenade-scene from Lynch's *Wild at Heart* (1990), referenced as one of Lenny's favorites.

• • •

The violent revenge-plots of both *Pusher* and *Bleeder* seem to have had a direct influence on the directorial debut of Norwegian actor Aksel Hennie, *Uno* (2004). In fact, the body-building best buddies of *Uno*, David (Hennie) and Morten (Nicolai Cleve Broch), have a scene of male bonding while watching *Pusher*, specifically the part in which Frank beats Tonny with a bat. (Their somewhat Tarantino-esque debate about etiquette and protocol—in this case, whether one should turn off one's cell phone during a DVD the way one does in a theater—suggests male intimacy simply because there is enough mutual closeness and respect for the two "tough guys" David and Morten to engage civilly in a difference of opinion.) In *Uno*, a drug deal gone bad (along with several other, more exotic twists) leads to a sort of all-out street war among David, Morten, and several gangsters. The quickly-unraveling downward spiral has a fatalism similar to Refn's, but misses the stoic, deadpan intensity (as well as the feeling for glimpses of transcendence) which elevates *Pusher* and *Bleeder*. More to the point, Refn's knack for leaving his characters slightly unexposed and opaque can be seen as an essential strategy for making their violent behaviors all the more uncanny. Whereas Hennie determinedly drives an element of rationality at the viewer, connecting the emotional and psychological dots of the characters, so to speak, in ways that become too obvious. Hennie's characters live by pro forma rules and their violence appears merely as a cruel extension of those rules. It is earnest and workaday, unlike in Refn's films where, as one comes to see, the violence always seems beyond anyone's control.

What is revealed by Hennie's tribute to *Pusher*, therefore, is something crucial not only to Refn's handling of violent revenge between men, but to the Western Ur-narrative of violent revenge itself, since it helped certify the development of representational realism in narrative forms. This is what philosopher Erich Auerbach postulates, in his still-indispensable *Mimesis*, when he identifies a passage from Gregory of Tours' *A History of the Franks* as being a distinct turning-point in the evolution of narrative structures. The passage itself, the story of Sicharius and Chramnesindus, is an extreme and uncanny tale, unlikely to be forgotten by anyone who has read it. Here is the crux of the story's revenge-plot:

> After slaying Chramnesindus' kinsmen, Sicharius had become very friendly with him, and they loved each other so dearly that they often ate together and slept

together in one bed. ... Chramnesindus ... spoke within his heart: "If I do not avenge the death of my kinsmen, I shall not be worthy of the name of man and ought to be called a weak woman." And immediately he put out the lights and split Sicharius' head with his blade.[10]

In Auerbach's reading of this passage, "an occurrence sufficiently confused in itself is very obscurely narrated." This "imitative form," so to speak, was precisely what made it so important. "Gregory's concern for visual vividness," and for the historical depiction of "unthinking acts" and "brutish souls," is significant in that he does not attempt to make the occurrence conform to some notion of grandeur or even coherence, but rather "the sudden and undisguised brutality which blots out every memory of the past and every thought of the future," Auerbach tells us, "testifies to such an endeavor to imitate the occurrence directly, as Roman historiography never sought to achieve ..."[11] Like Refn, Gregory of Tours stayed true to the violence and also made it more believable and striking by leaving it as an abrupt enigma rather than a fully limned series of causalities and reactions.

Given that "it would seem to have been [the occurrence's] very graphicness which made [Gregory] want to represent it,"[12] Auerbach detects a revolutionary moment in which the language used to depict violence becomes, in itself, "a progressive and terrible brutalization,"[13] one which specifically breaks with the "almost excessively organizing language" of high classical Latin.[14] This is a new kind of verité in Western narrative, minus rhetoric and decorum (also judgment). Auerbach writes:

> Lusts and passions lose every concealing form; they show themselves in the raw and with palpable immediacy. This brutal life becomes a sensible object; to him who would describe it, it presents itself as devoid of order and difficult to order, but tangible, earthy, alive.[15]

Specifically, what is most fascinating today about the irrationalism or partial incoherence of the story of Sicharius and Chramnesindus is the way it is centered around a kind of homoeroticism or queerness, which Gregory renders so plainly and directly that it is impossible to misread it as anything except what it is. Chramnesindus has become Sicharius' lover in the wake of Sicharius massacring his entire family; Chramnesindus' revenge is, then, not only an attenuated response to the massacre itself (at this point, arguably little more than a pretext) but a delayed-homophobic response to the same-sex love he has allowed himself to acquiesce to. Auerbach does not have much to say about this, but what he does say is telling: "It seems indeed that the two had honestly become such close friends that ... it never occurred to them how unnatural and dangerous such a friendship really was."[16] The revenge plot only makes sense, perhaps, in a world that requires sexual desire to be turned away from

3. Bleeder

the same sex and toward the opposite. The dead end reached by Sicharius and Chramnesindus—and I am not holding those two up as a model relationship in any realm of the imagination—is ultimately related to procreation; Sicharius has deprived Chramnesindus of his lineage, his heirs. He has done this twice, first by killing his literal children in the present, and then by becoming his lover, killing off the possibility of children in the future. In any society that places a high premium on procreation, gay sex will usually be in a sort of patrilineal doghouse. For a male to sleep with another male, or to turn him "gay," is to steal his chance at reproducing, or "immortalism." Of course, depriving each other of patrimony is precisely what Louis and Leo do to each other in *Bleeder*. Louis has impregnated Leo's girlfriend, substituting his own progeny for Leo's. In turn, Leo kills the fetus inside Louise, thereby depriving Louis of becoming a father. AIDS becomes emblematic of sterility, the potential withering of a genetic line.

Certainly this is somewhat problematic. But we have become so inured to buddy movies having a ubiquitous homoerotic subtext that it has almost become invisible all over again, hence non-threatening and non-subversive. The angst of *Bleeder* is (to use the most obvious comparison) like a fresh wound, like the nearly sexualized commingling of open wounds between Louis and Leo at the end of the film. One cannot help feeling that one has been watching two men fuck each other in a series of incredibly elaborate, violent and sadistic denials of the impulse to fuck. In Refn's film, men's toleration of each others' displays of strength is already an admission of one's own lesser status, and represents the encroachment of the ultimate act of "weakness," giving to another man that love and understanding which is reserved, in the heterosexual imaginary, for women (and even then, only as potential mothers). And even though Refn seems to understand his male characters' extreme anxieties, he does not condone Louis; he makes it clear that Louis is a misguided hypocrite who projects his own incestuous inbreeding, for example, onto the Arab immigrants whom he despises out of hand. "Black bastard," he says to a shopkeeper who has done nothing to provoke him, "go home and fuck your mother." But it is the Aryan in this film who wallows in incest and corrupted bloodlines. Here the members of what once considered itself a Master Race are depicted as grubby, bloated, demented, dysfunctional, depressive, cowardly.[17]

• • •

With its pack of alienated young males imploding around issues of sexual subjectivity, *Bleeder* bears marked similarities to Gerard Damiano's first feature, *We All Go Down* (1969), an arty skin-flick that is like the cinematic equivalent of the Velvet Underground's *White Light/White Heat*. In *We All Go Down* (available through Seattle's Something Weird Video in a very good digital transfer of what must have been a typically abused grindhouse print), Pete (Bill Doukas) is a speed-freak whose focus on staying high makes him increasingly asocial, asexual and isolated. His heartless using of his friends causes them to call him "a creep" constantly behind his back; he's even willing to sell his girlfriend's body for a score. Even his best friend Rick (Daniel Mogé) has difficulty communicating with Pete: they both speak in numb, resigned phrases like "I don't know what to say," "I don't know, man," or "It's weirding me out." Rick's obnoxious, domineering friend Burt (Bob Shoffuer) tells Rick that Pete "stinks to high heaven" and is "a faggot." Burt tries to intercede in Rick's faltering relationship with blonde ice-queen Judy (Kelly Kurtis), saying, "I'll fix everything up for you." But Burt ends up sleeping with Judy, a betrayal that demonstrates (like Pete's own abuses) the self-serving code within this group.

In fact, for all his womanizing swagger, Burt seems unusually interested in Rick, urging him at one point, "Don't let me down this time." Both Burt and the ultra-smarmy Jay (James Burnette) have wheedling, slightly effeminate voices, which give their constant attempts to seduce Pete's and Rick's girlfriends a somewhat suspicious, dislocated air. Their overweening male interest seems mismatched to its nominal feminine objects. At an orgy, Burt bitches about a couple having sex in full view, suggesting (according to '60s logic, anyway) that he has sexual hang-ups. After sleeping with Judy, Burt tells Rick that he did it just to prove to him that she is "a pig" and not worthy of his love. "You should be grateful to me," he tells the angry Rick. For his part, Rick has a dream in which he is forced to watch Judy make love to another man. We see male-female relations in *We All Go Down* constantly subverted by issues of male-male dominance; in the film, men "rape" each other, so to speak, through the intermediary bodies of each other's female partners. There is an undeniably sleazy aspect to all of this, which Damiano never tries to hide (he later went on to hardcore porn with *Deep Throat*), but the director's main interest is with the way these behaviors ripple outward to affect the characters' psychological and physical being.

Thus, the three main male characters in *We All Go Down* are much the same as the trio in *Bleeder*. Rick is like Lenny, the nice, shy guy in love; Pete is like Leo, the disintegrating time-bomb; and Burt is like Louis, the alpha male and casual destroyer who metes out his own justice to people, and who is obsessed with whether other men are "faggots." Although the female characters in *Bleeder* are not the sneering dominatrixes and resigned, sad-eyed sluts of Damiano's porn-imaginary, the male interactions remain startlingly au courant, especially as *We All Go Down* steers toward crisis point. Pete's sadistic pusher (Jayson Troy) demands sexual favors from Pete in exchange for amphetamine; in the end, he palms off acid on Pete, who suffers a grotesque bad trip centering on his own impotence and sexual confusion. He hallucinates a giant vagina (Damiano blows the orifice up to near Cinemascope dimensions and superimposes it over Pete's consternated face) that vanishes when he tries to touch it; a pair of lesbians who mock his manhood; and an enormous syringe injected into his navel while he hangs from bondage chains, a Christ-figure bleeding from a vampiric hickey. This image of the hanging man waiting to be injected or "shot up" reappears, of course, in *Bleeder*, though it is highly possible that the image itself—archetypally messianic and also related to sado-masochism—is primal enough to have occurred to the two different directors independently. Finally, babbling and in a fetal state, Pete appeals to his "friends," but they refuse to take him to a hospital; Burt smacks the horrified Pete around to try to calm him down. In his drug psychosis Pete chops off one of his own fingers.

In the final scene of *We All Go Down*, there is a kind of emotionally violent showdown between Pete and Rick on a bright street. Pete is clean now, missing a finger, symbolic of the high price he has paid; Rick tries to apologize, but Pete refuses to forgive him. "What did I do?" Rick asks. "You didn't do anything, Rick," Pete says as he walks away, and the blank bad acting of sexploitation cinema becomes aesthetically perfect, since the scene derives all its tension from being acted very flatly and stiffly. It is an awkward, damaged moment, and it is played that way. Self-interest continues to reign supreme, Rick begging absolution to make himself feel better, and Pete being self-righteous and snide. These are less violent precursors of the traumatic and traumatized young men who will reappear as a different generation of twenty-somethings in *Bleeder*. The coldness of the vaguely criminal social milieu, and the failure of relational bonds between men, is indicated by Pete as the source of his addiction problems—just as Leo and Louis vent violence on each other in *Bleeder* as a way of ultimately avoiding responsibility for their own actions.

• • •

In Lynch's *Wild at Heart*, Sailor (Nicolas Cage) declares his ultimate and undying love for Lula (Laura Dern) by changing his song for her from Elvis' "Love Me" to Elvis' "Love Me Tender." The single word makes all the difference, and like *Wild at Heart*, *Bleeder* is about a man's arduous discovery of tenderness after a kind of sojourn in hell. When tenderness is the goal for men, it is depicted as a process of stripping away defenses, the process of a man "getting in touch with his feminine side." Refn has said: "Men who don't have a feminine side are only half masculine because you can't have one without the other."[18] But his films, beginning with *Bleeder*, put an even finer and more disturbing point on things: modern man, we see, is just as vulnerable to forms of rape that go back to Gregory of Tours' ancient clans, if not the swinging Sixties. Whether this vulnerability makes him psychopathic or compassionate is one of the great existential questions of men's issues in our time.

The ultimate message of *Bleeder* is that Lenny learns how to love by watching movies, before he dares to break free of their artificial womb. He recognizes violence and injustice when he sees it in the world because he has seen it in the action movies he watches. At some point he makes the leap from wanting to be the violent hero to finally being able to transcend masculine posturing. The defensiveness (what Wilhelm Reich called "character armor") is voided vicariously, like a long winding auto-therapy which involves years of holing up at home playing the same tapes again and again.

The benefits of this auto-therapy are gradual but ever increasing. Long before the blood starts flowing, Lenny shows his growing tenderness in the scene where the friends harass an Arab shopkeeper. Lenny tries to apologize for his racist friends, an apology which is not accepted by the victim: this is an intuition of how the consequences of real actions must be taken into account before, not just after, the fact. Lenny has been watching the scene of bullying as if it were a movie, and because he knows how it "should" end in the movies (with the victim being validated and restored to dignity), he moves toward this same conclusion in life. Likewise, the final image of Lea and Lenny is one of a pre-destined, instant couple; this, too, is harder to achieve in reality than in films, but the prototype is essentially part of the cinematic-imaginary, what we hope to be brave and good enough to birth from our fantasies into reality.

After Leo's funeral, Lenny is depressed but still up for a movie with Kitjo. In a choice between *If...* (1969) and *Mad Max 2: The Road Warrior* (1981), Kitjo chooses *If....* This is partly Kitjo relenting on his earlier banishment of Lindsay Anderson to the shameful "bottom shelf" (during the video store canon-formation scene) as well as a larger signal that all different kinds of movies exist to teach us things that we might need as we face our lives. Unlike *The Road Warrior*, whose pessimistic post-apocalyptic world leaves little room for growth or change, Anderson's carnage is ultimately idealistic, an anarchic groping toward a better future. Choosing *If...* over *The Road Warrior* is Kitjo's shamanistic, exorcising way of acknowledging that film can be healing as well as gratuitously thrilling, therapeutic as well as escapist. Or rather, perhaps, therapeutically escapist in the way that meditation can be: a humbling of the ego, a submergence in otherness, a controlled absence from the world during which one savors the sight of people who have moved on to somewhere other than the images they left behind.

– 4 –

Fear X

> Men and women are seldom inspired to confront fear merely because they believe it to be evil; without some unswerving vision of positive justice, some ideologically grounded hope for radical change, they have a difficult time identifying fear as an evil to be opposed, and so put up with it. —Corey Robin[1]

> But [Euripides'] Herakles seems a character able to override common sense. He releases Alcestis [from Hades] simply by choosing to do so. As if to say, within every death a life stands waiting to be set free, should anyone have the nerve to do it. As if to say, try looking deep into a house, a marriage, or an idea like Necessity and you will see clear through to the other side. Death, like tragedy, is a game with rules. Why not just break the rules? —Anne Carson[2]

One of the more charming things that we learn about Refn in Phie Ambo's well-made documentary about him, *Gambler* (2006), is his obsession with vintage movie posters. The obsession itself is not all that unique. For the young upwardly-mobile bohemian, movie posters have replaced the museum retrospective art print or the carefully displayed piece of abstract painting as décor of choice. Genuine pop art, and often highly sought-after, valuable collector's items, movie posters do more than display an ironically formal taste for the generally more informal pleasures of movie-watching; they preserve a connection to a film as a vital work in the time of its release, a ceremonial event, taglined, publicized, fetishized, telling a great deal about how given films were first presented to the public. Yet, though vintage posters might have once exemplified the commercial side of a given era of films, today they seem objects of enchantment, advertisements for stylistic grace and nostalgic consolation.

This is partly what makes Refn's poster-collecting such a fascinating theme in *Gambler*, whose main focus is also the commercial side of cinema; but far less graceful and consoling are the horrible disappointment and subsequent bankruptcy issues which Refn faced after the commercial failure of his first American film, *Fear X*. With *Pusher* and *Bleeder*, Refn had become the most successful director in Denmark, a hitmaker with a bankable record of low budget, high art, and massive returns. Then Refn "gambled" on the experimental *Fear X*: "With *Fear X*," Refn says, "I gambled a lot of things. My economy, my house."[3] Refn saw no money from *Fear X* and ended up owing (according to Ambo's film) 5.5 million.

Therefore, much like the canon of cult directors rattled off in *Bleeder*, the posters tease out the questions that seem foremost on Refn's mind. To wit: When will I be immune to setback, safely beyond the need to prove myself in everything I do? When will it be the future already? He spends most of *Gambler* trying to sell producers on financing two *Pusher* sequels, with all the poignant and often desperate hope of someone who would rather sally forth to make movies than have endless sit-downs with accountants and lawyers, potential backers and moneymen.

And also, frankly, it is the hope of someone seemingly rather shy to not have to meet with strangers day in day out, negotiating, butting heads, risking rejection. Much like the way the posters act intercessionally between the films they represent and the world, Refn seems to communicate best via the choosing and displaying of these posters. I collect, therefore I am. In fact, apart from Refn's partner, Liv Corfixen, also featured in *Gambler*, the shopkeeper who frames Refn's posters seems to be his closest friend. Surely this cannot be true; yet Refn brings each new acquisition to the framing shop with a feeling of long-lost reunion and boyish enthusiasm. He explains with pride the history behind a newly acquired poster for the Italian gangster film *Revolver*—like Lenny, the lonely video store clerk in *Bleeder*, not comfortable talking about anything other than the films he loves, yet yearning to connect with someone who isn't made of celluloid.

We see how personal is this theme of Refn's—one of his great themes—the longing for a human understanding so automatic and complete that one need never have to fumble for words or defend one's tastes in wearisome debates. Elsewhere it takes on a dimension of spiritual kinship, even telepathy. In the context of *Gambler* this ideal of love is focused on taste. The beloved, the ideal woman, won't have a compatible star sign but an identical Top Ten list. This motif appears in a number of other recent films—including Arthur

Penn's *Penn and Teller Get Killed* (1988), Stephen Frears' *High Fidelity* (2000), and Monte Hellman's *Road to Nowhere* (2010)—the idea that true love means never having to fight over a remote or a rental. It means finding the soul mate to one's Not-So-Inner Aesthete and never having to switch off that modern World Without End, the marathon playlist, the media feed, the endless stream.

Refn's open, childlike delight in the frame shop appears in marked contrast to his seriousness throughout *Gambler* and the deep anxiety we see him struggling with. Ambo punctuates *Gambler*, wittily, with close-ups of Alka-Seltzers plunked, hissing, into glasses of water. The numerous business meetings are all tense and discouraging. But again, the motif of posters, adorning the walls or stacked against the baseboards of Refn's and Corfixen's apartment, is a constant return to the source, so to speak, the obsession with movies that keeps Refn going, as well as a sort of rotating canon of favorites given physical shape. So we note, at different moments, posters for Lucio Fulci's *Zombie*, Sergio Leone's *Once Upon a Time in the West*, something where the great Eddie Constantine plays "Gangster-Eddie," Russ Meyer's *Supervixens!*, and Anthony Mann's *Winchester 73*—films that are visually bravura and uniquely passionate, and which had the singular good fortune to turn low budget and an inspiration for violent action into commercial and sometimes curious critical success. As representatives of the roots of Refn's own art, the roots which he is literally trying to get back to in *Gambler*, the posters are both an inspirational record of first and enduring loves, and also a kind of mute chorus offering solace for the director's every harried phone call, every brainstorming session, every migraine. Two longtime favorites stand out in particular, co-leaders of the chorus: a poster for the original *Texas Chain Saw Massacre* holds pride of place above the hearth; while an enormous, nearly billboard-sized *Cannibal Holocaust* hangs above the bed in the Refn master bedroom.

In the midst of getting back to his roots with the same kind of inspired, pungent, low-budget action-thrillers (once made, *Pusher II* and *Pusher III* restored his position in international film as a commercial tiger), Refn mourns and curses *Fear X*, "that damn art film" which not only bankrupted his production company but left him brimming over with existential doubt, much like those fizzy bromos he consumes. He is poignantly torn between what he would like to accomplish as an artist and what he needs to accomplish as a businessman, as a family man (he and Corfixen have had their first baby), and finally as someone who aims to stay in cinema and leave his mark upon it. Yet, throughout the angst there is some fleeting satisfaction at having made, with *Fear X*, what is probably a masterpiece. Faced with the prospect of never being able to make another film, he says, "I remember thinking, if I go out, at least I'll go out with *Fear X*."[4]

This ultimate panic, that every film he makes might be his last, is the Damoclean sword dangling over Refn's head. He talks about how his plans for yet-unmade films have been "piling up inside me until I got completely hysterical." Regular production would be good for a director, would keep him at pace with himself—each idea able to be realized while it remains fresh, nothing left inside to fester or boil away. Nothing is as indicative of the manic-depressive state of trying to get films made today than the fact that it took nearly three years to raise the capital for *Fear X*, and a mere six weeks to shoot. A Thalberg, a Lewton, a Goldwyn would grow gray-haired and besotted at the thought of such insane production delays for an ordinary, professional shoot. But these are different, less energized times. And the filmmaker, unlike the writer or the painter, has never had the artistic luxury of just beginning, on his own in a room somewhere; his vision, from the very start, is connected to so many other people and things (and dollar signs). Refn has said: "We as filmmakers are slaves, and we have to buy our freedom."[5]

Thus, making money actually became a spur to Refn's creativity. In any event, the schema that exalts the making of art while denigrating the making of money is a version of the immaculate conception myth, whereby art just appears in the world, by fiat, messy origins effaced in the name of destiny and pseudo–"divine origin." Why do we feel the need to believe this about cultural production, in which art must be forced to substitute for a host of transcendent longings in a world of compromise and necessary evils?

Not that Refn *never* questions the capitalist system which demands the interdependency of art and commerce. Alongside the fear that too much art will spoil the money, there is the fear that too much money (or commercial calculation) will spoil the art. Refn goes back and forth on this question, specifically as it relates to *Fear X*—his "best" film, he says, yet also "a failure." He is defensive about it: "It was my most ambitious film and my best one. It's also the one I've spent the most time making." At one point he says, "The money doesn't matter," but then he looks at his infant daughter and decides that it does (the extremely supportive Liv always urges him to follow his heart and not worry about making them rich). He also says, "I feel like a complete failure artistically," because his art has not been capable of generating financial security.

There is something *au courant* about this belief that if a work of art is as truly great as it pretends to be, it will be recognized as such and remunerated. It won't slip through the obscure cracks of inattention. This is not as fanciful as it might sound. According to this vision, rather than casting mystifications all over the place, the market machinery of culture (which now extends to the internet, of course) serves to *clarify* artistic value; even where it appears as something new and radical, the exalted is no longer rarefied discourse but a common language as fluent as liquid assets. "And I need to re-establish a so-called success," Refn concludes. But even this must be on his own artistic terms: he must make "something artistically satisfying, because if I don't do that, I'll feel empty." There is some negotiability here, though, because "it's the only way to pay my debts." This have-it-both-ways stance would have seemed contradictory to earlier incarnations of the auteur. Watching Refn negotiate his life's work, one cannot help thinking that it already *is* the future, this hot new world of constant adrenalin, DIY multitasking, and casual, carnal genius.

Although it looks like a permanent state of "Goodbye vintage posters; hello, Alka-Seltzer" for most of *Gambler*, Refn's story does have a happy ending. The debts were paid off largely by the *Pusher* sequels. And perhaps the fact that he was not offered a huge Hollywood contract with his third feature was a blessing in disguise, not only because it allowed for the *Pusher* sequels to be made but because, beyond that, his continued work in Europe led him to make two of his most challenging, disturbing and brilliant films, *Bronson* and *Valhalla Rising*. The raw, nerve-jangling fearlessness of both of those works shows an artist in a rapid state of growth and increasing self-confidence, digging deeper, testing himself. Neither is a film that he would have likely been able to make with Hollywood funding. It might be that Refn will need to return periodically to Europe (or elsewhere outside of the U.S.) in order to regain a momentum of creativity that seems all but impossible in Hollywood today, and also to allow himself to experiment productively. "If you stop experimenting, where's the fun?" Refn has asked. "Where's the anxiety of maybe having done something wrong? It can be quite thrilling."[6] Indeed, we may reflect that commercial struggling did unmistakably do something for the film poet in Refn. It turned that poet into an avenging angel.

• • •

Approaching *Fear X*, Refn said he felt ready for Hollywood but was not sure "if Hollywood [was] ready to work with" him.[7] He held out the highest hopes for reaching a wide film audience that was looking for something more sophisticated and profound than the usual blockbuster fare: "I think there's an audience out there that wants to see something different, to see a reality that's imperfect."[8] At the same time, however, he acknowledged that *Fear X* posed a distinct challenge to narrative expectations; people are not "used to a film without an ending."[9] Andrei Tarkovsky has spoken about this dilemma of commercial filmmaking. He said that there are two kinds of directors, imitative-realists and poets. "The poets create their own worlds" instead of merely imitating the world around them, and "have all opposed ... that the taste of the audience should be the deciding factor—not because they want to be obscure but because they want to listen secretly, to give expression to what is deep inside those we call the audience."[10]

"Listening secretly" is a nice phrase that has resonance with *Fear X* in particular, since this film, somewhat but not entirely within the tradition of *Blow-Up* (1966) and *The Conversation* (1972), presents "surveillance" as an intuitive and creative act, rather than merely bureaucratic planning and execution. Although it has often been identified with political and social paranoia, I tend to see this genre as being wrapped up in a sentimental defense of cinema itself as a kind of romantic voyeurism which ends up justifying itself by altering the "real world" into which it peeps. In *Blow-Up* and *The Conversation*, evidence of the real is slowly gathered in a way that undermines the tangibility of day-to-day life; in *Fear X*, the intangible is both commonplace and a supernatural limbo state between different realities, different planes of existence. *Fear X* is the first Refn film that flirts heavily with a kind of psychedelic mysticism within a provocative framework of atmospheric and narrative moves culled from a variety of more mundane genres (thriller, action, horror, melodrama).

Refn assembled an impressive array of talent to work on his American debut. The lead actors are an indie dream-cast: John Turturro, James Remar, Deborah Kara Unger. The film was scored by composers Brian Eno and J. Peter Schwalm. The cinematographer, Larry Smith, cut his teeth running lighting for Kubrick. And the script, which began, proverbially enough, in a cramped L.A. apartment (as Refn recounts[11]), was the brainchild of Refn and novelist Hubert Selby, Jr., the urban fatalist who was an inspirational touchstone for Amiri Baraka, Allen Ginsberg, Lou Reed, Jennifer Jason Leigh, and Morrissey, among other notable artists.

But for a gruelingly long time the apartment was where it remained. It took two-and-a-half years for Refn and Selby to get their script produced.[12] During the tactical nightmares of scrambling for funds and the inevitable changes to the material based on financial concessions, the collaboration between Refn and Selby was sometimes strained. Refn genially reports having quarrels with Selby, who could "get very, very, very angry." But their mutual respect turned into a friendship from sheer proximity over the years.[13] (Refn would later dedicate *Pusher II: With Blood on My Hands* to Selby, "who I miss every single day of my life."[14]) Selby finally said, not ruefully but in acknowledgment of the many pressures that act upon filmmakers' creative processes: "The movie is nothing like what we talked about. We wanted to write an emotional story and Nicolas wanted to go to Rio. We ended up in Winnipeg, Canada, with a very limited budget."[15]

4. Fear X

When asked what *Fear X* is "about," Refn has said, "Basically [it is] about a man who wants to walk across the street. But he digs a tunnel. He goes inwards."[16] In this sense, we could say that *Fear X* is about themes that will preoccupy later Refn films like *Bronson* (in which lashing out against confinement barely disguises the masochistic wish for more and more restrictive confinement) and *Valhalla Rising* (in which an odyssey to "the ends of the earth" becomes a spiritual voyage within).

It would be hopeless to attempt a non-discursive synopsis of *Fear X*; any description of what literally (or figuratively) happens in the film already entails an analytic reading. The film forbids neutrality and objectivity at every turn, an anti-mystery filled with anti-clues that subtract and divide rather than "add up." At the same time, things do happen in the film, but one is often left wondering not only how and why these things happen, but on which plane of existence, and to whom. In addition to surveillance films, *Fear X* is related to an equally esoteric subgenre of the thriller, which treats circuitous and horror-laden narratives as complex metonymies for a purgatory-like afterlife, in which a dead protagonist (who sometimes does not realize that he is dead) moves through a simulacrum-world in which he is allowed to take care of the unfinished business of his life. *Jacob's Ladder* (1990), *Donnie Darko* (2001) and *The Jacket* (2005) are three such films, in which young men who get killed suddenly and seemingly at random find themselves wandering through a disintegrating, menacing world that they cannot quite let go of.

Afterlife films can seem, at times, hokey and contrived, and Refn smartly ups the ante by making the purgatory scenario only one possible interpretation of his film—particularly the last fifteen minutes or so of his movie, since this is where a certain (deliberate) confusion about who or what perishes and who or what survives sets in. "I didn't understand how it was going to end," Refn said. "I had taken out everything that was logical. I kept thinking, what if I've ruined it?"[17] Yet, one reason why *Pusher* and *Bleeder* worked so well was because of what was pointedly left out of them in terms of rational explanation or wholly resolved motivations. Only the strangeness, the extremities, of the characters were displayed; whatever was "normal" about them was assumed as being too familiar or pointless to detail. But even more, this constant worry of *what if*, of nagging doubt and self-blame, is also the emotion that drives *Fear X*'s main character, Harry Caine (John Turturro), so that finally this fear seems to pass from Caine's character to Refn himself behind the camera, and then flow back into the film overall, like a kind of contagious, aesthetic panic attack.

The film opens with a hand parting the curtains of a picture window to reveal a snowy small-town street and a blond woman (Jacqueline Ramel) stopping in the middle of this street to look back as she slowly walks toward a house on the other side. Through the window, Harry watches sadly. The woman turns out to be Claire (played by Jacqueline Ramel), Harry's murdered wife. The film immediately establishes an inside and an outside space, reminiscent of both the intimacy of the birth process and the detachment of voyeuristic spectacle. The window is likened to a television that depicts events without allowing the viewer to intervene. Harry's stricken, trance-like expression will be reprised later when he obsessively watches video surveillance tapes. The idea that all vision has become a form of *tele*vision, an idea which Cronenberg advanced first in *Videodrome* (1983), if not Paddy Chayevsky in *Network* (1976), jibes with the idea that "reality" itself feels ungraspable, unverifiable—or, rather, that one must attempt to break through the veil of a false reality to see the true reality behind it. At a later point Harry crawls toward his actual TV in a way that explicitly evokes the gesture of *Videodrome*'s Max Renn (James Woods) responding to the image of Nicky Brand (Deborah Harry), his lover, who has been murdered; but rather than placing his entire head inside a pulsing, vaginal screen, as Max does, Harry flashes on another hallucination of Claire outside the house. In both *Videodrome* and *Fear X* the image of a beloved woman becomes trapped, in death, within a grid of shifting and distorted TV pixels, spurring the hero's mission to go deeper inside the mystery of his unreal reality.

For Harry it is not explicitly about kinky sex but a longing for a virtual-maternal succor (this Freudian implication plays behind much of *Videodrome*, too); he is like a child-man in need of the Mother, and a parallel is also struck with the little boy in Bergman's *Persona* (1966), naked except for a pair of eyeglasses, reaching out to touch Liv Ullman's face projected on a screen in such enormous close-up that it blurs. The most human part of Caine, the part that feels love (and even Max Renn's libidinal arousal in *Videodrome* is not disconnected from tenderness), has already been hijacked to another world, partly embodied by television but suggestive of a gateway into supernatural dimensions.

In *Videodrome*, Nicky is already dead when Max makes love to her TV image; the image becomes a grim consolation in the face of mortality—in religious terms, the ancient "graven image" which would deflect Moses' followers from the most solemn contemplation of death (or the unknowable, unseeable face of God). A fake immortality that makes an end run around judgment is evoked as a blasphemous gesture; and yet, what is TV if not something like a spirit world (a spiritualist closet of sorts) where even people we imagined dead are suddenly reanimated? In the largest sense, this "TV hallucination" is akin to the feeling that one cannot die in one's dreams, so one seeks refuge by sinking into a waking dream even as one's body still inhabits a vulnerable, worldly, physical space—another Cronenberg theme, from *eXistenZ* (1999). One lives off TV like a space traveler stopping the aging process by stepping outside of time. Finally, the conflation of inside and outside is a prefiguration of death: the reason why interior space no longer feels safe is because a threat hangs over it, an unverifiable security that calls out for testing violation. Exterior space has already been wholly abandoned to the terror of violent ends. The television lie is essentially the same as mortal existence: to be inside is to sense the death that is on its way; to be outside is to be dead already.

There is a cut to Harry waking up, his face on its side perfectly halved by the pillow. His fingers automatically caress the empty space beside him on the bed. The motif of a longed-for symmetry will come to preoccupy *Fear X*, not merely as a stylistic nod to Kubrick's *The Shining*[18] but to something even larger: a classical history in which the public life of the *demos* was ostensibly nobler, more dignified, more purposeful. Almost like the Doric columns of ancient Greek architecture, the mourning for symmetry presents itself as a longing for the very structures that support a free democratic society. Harry is sometimes shown framed by vertical, column-like lines (window frames, elevator doors). Everything in his house is symmetrical, even the palindromic message spoken by his answering machine: "*One message. Message one.*" But that symmetry is ultimately elusive, perhaps even delusional. The loss of the wife, the damage to the *human* symmetry that once prevailed in Harry's life, has unbalanced everything. And there is a further implication to the use of symmetry, the suggestion that Harry is stuck in-between two worlds, that of the living and that of the dead.

In the kitchen, an enormous sunny room whose loneliness is highlighted by its empty space, a radio newscaster chatters. The broadcast turns suddenly from wheat profits and hog futures (although filmed in Canada, *Fear X* takes place in the U.S. Midwest, Wisconsin specifically) to a report that captures Harry's attention, an update about a recent mall shooting: it is now theorized that the man who was killed was "a DEA agent, but not too much is being made of that, as there have been rumors that he was *everything*, from an alien to a Cuban spy." The hysteria implied by a putatively objective news report advancing all of these scenarios, including "alien," with equal seriousness is a reflection on the way the news has become sensationalistic in our time, a ready tool for disseminating mushroom clouds of disinformation. Specifically, by giving the most outlandish theories air-time and therefore implicit credence, the news constantly diverts attention away from the more pressing implications of something that might be an embarrassment to the drug squad, for example, and the system it serves. Perceptual, epistemological chaos is never absent from our news now. Here, too, the constant threat of invaded borders—aliens,

Harry Caine (John Turturro) explores the world of video surveillance in order to track down his wife's killer in *Fear X* (2000). His living room comes to look like a combination police headquarters and mixed-media gallery installation. The omnipresence of security cameras in public spaces is like the yearning for an ever-watchful God who notes every sparrow's falling.

Cubans—recurs as a matter of course, in order to hold the U.S. together through a shared panic around the frayed edges of empire, and to scapegoat an external "enemy" as a way of distracting from incompetence or corruption within the U.S. itself. This shared panic is a token of "the collusion between elites, collaborators, bystanders, and victims," which Corey Robin denotes as characterizing the condition of American political fear.[19]

Harry turns toward one of the walls of his living room, which is covered with news clippings and photos of people from surveillance tapes, digitally blown up and printed out on his computer. The photos are catalogued with as much identifying information as Harry can find about them. We are not sure how much Harry can really tell about these faces from their blurry photos and sketchy backgrounds. At the center of this strange work—it suggests a gallery installation, or a project discovered in the home of a madman, more than an investigative centerpiece in a pseudo-police procedural—is a larger clipping about two people being shot and killed in a mall parking lot by an unidentified gunman, the same story from the news broadcast. One of these was the mysterious DEA agent-alien-Cuban spy from the radio news report; the other was Harry's wife.

Going outside, Harry enters the same liminal, cold, snowy space that his wife inhabited in the opening dream sequence; but Harry seems uneasy, where the wife had been preternaturally calm. *Fear X*'s snowbound rural landscapes are strongly reminiscent of Paul Schrader's *Affliction* (1998), another film where domestic horrors and insecurities have become frozen into a kind of eternal winter. At the mall he guards, Harry spots an elderly man (Victor Cowie) stashing a ladies' cardigan in his shopping bag. Harry runs down this thief. In a disorienting cut which takes us from Harry's "side" of the mall to a long view from the other side, showing him crossing the floor rapidly, around and behind architectural columns, we are aware again of the lost symmetry or balance which began as a visual theme in Harry's house. These two angles on Harry are jarring and incommensurable: the first is a medium close-up, while the second is nearly suspended in open space as he starts to run from afar. This has to do with Harry's own imbalances as much as the imbalances of the world around him, although these will turn out to be more or less the same. This is the mall where his wife was killed; thus, whatever shoplifting "criminals" Harry apprehends in the course of his work will fall far short of the kind of protection he wishes he had been able to provide for his wife, and he will end up protecting only the property of the chi-chi boutiques rather than real human life.

As if to exemplify this, Harry's arrest is made to seem like a violation of life rather than a defense of it. Harry corners the shoplifter in front of the shoplifter's wife (Susan Kelso). They are an elderly couple. After interrogating his suspect in a brutal and humiliating way, Harry roughly handcuffs him while the frightened wife asks, "What's going to happen to us?" There is an "us" there, the kind of fifty-year-plus marriage that has become extremely unlikely in current America, and which specifically represents the lost future that Harry, as a devoted husband, had hoped to find. In the guards' locker room, Harry and his buddy Phil (Stephen Eric McIntyre) make friendly but impersonal small talk with an African American coworker; only after this coworker leaves (with Phil double-checking to make sure he has gone) does Phil hand Harry two more videotapes "for your collection."

We cannot help but note the irony of the arm-patch on Harry's uniform-sleeve, blazoned with the bold word SECURITY, even as he comes to embody more and more a state of anxious uncertainty. (This is much like the word RESPECT tattooed on the back of Tonny's head in *Pusher*, even as we see Tonny losing more and more face throughout the film: to take on a label of any kind is to court the disaster of not being able to satisfy its terms.) Phil tells Harry that he should think about moving on with his life, but Harry does not want to hear this. The emphasis on extended periods of mourning—usually depicted as a female rather than male disposition—is itself already subversive in a society that has cheapened life through economic exploitation and war. In a further tyranny of insisting that everyone's emotions and healing times be somehow standardized, Harry's boss reiterates the cultural refusal of mourning when he reprimands Harry for making customers nervous by staring at them suspiciously: "We all go through things, and we get past them." He adds, "We can't afford to have customers feeling uncomfortable shopping here." Presumably, a recent double-homicide at this mall would not make shoppers "uncomfortable," but having to confront the sight of a sad man in mourning would. Just as U.S. slave masters imposed the policy that slave funerals could be held only in the dark of night,[20] so the suppression of public, visible mourning (and the stigmatization of it as aberrant) renders illegible the deaths which the social order would like to keep shrouded in an incredulous mix of mystique and inevitability.

Back at home, Harry has a vision of his wife standing in their bathroom and holding a home pregnancy test. He relives the moment when they found out they were going to have a child, joyously resting his head against her stomach; then, like Eurydice in Hades shaded by Orpheus' backwards look, she is gone again. In a surreal transition, Harry's hand becomes dark and bony, clawing into a red, pulsing tissue with spidery veins, like a demonic fetus trying to scratch its way out of a womb. And indeed, this fleeting confrontation with death (as well as the overt naming of Harry's need for maternal comfort) marks a kind of progress, since the phone rings almost immediately. The police have uncovered new information about the murder case and want to talk to Harry.

In a further surrealist touch, the meeting takes place not in a normal precinct house but a room in a sleazy hotel. Officers mill in the corridor, gossiping and drinking coffee; construction noises can be heard. Just as Harry's home has been converted into a kind of provisional police station, with its wall of homemade mug shots, so the function of policing has spread into spaces that harbor private, guilty secrets. But as surrealistic as this scene is, Refn is very matter of fact: nothing screams weirdness. One notices it not because it is blatant, but instead almost in spite of the way it is played down; and one wonders at first if one's perceptions are accurate. Finally, one realizes that Refn's surrealist touch is also character-based and integral to the plot: to Harry, who has lost all faith in law enforcement, it makes sense that detectives would interrogate people in the same hotel rooms where prostitutes take their clients. (The full extent of police corruption as a motivator of action in *Fear X* will be revealed later in the film.)

The charming but imposing Agent Lawrence (William Allen Young) takes Harry off-guard by asking probing questions about Claire's background. The agent's interest is piqued by learning that Claire was from San Francisco; he implies that there might be something strange about why she would move "all the way to Wisconsin," and asks pointedly, "Well, nobody can know *all* about someone, can they?" Here, in the way that romantic love itself becomes antagonistic to the necessary suspicion required by a police-state apparatus, Refn's and Selby's script hearkens back to *Touch of Evil* (1958), in which the loveless detective Hank Quinlan (Orson Welles) also tries to cast aspersions on another man's wife in order to cover up, rather than solve, a messy crime. Anyone at all can be shamed in order to shore up the collective order. Having breached Harry's defenses, Agent Lawrence hands him an extremely grainy photo of a man in a cap and tells him that this is the man who killed his wife, saying, "We have it on tape"—supposedly the ultimate and unimpeachable proof of anything (as if this film character had suddenly broken with the factual reality that tapes, anything recorded, can always be *edited*).

Back inside his home-burrow Harry turns his attention to the house across the street, where a light has been turned on, as if to signal something. The next day, armed with his intuitive distrust, Harry goes across and rings the doorbell, which chimes none other than the alien chord progression from *Close Encounters of the Third Kind* (1977). When no one answers, he jimmies the backdoor. Harry uses a flashlight to conduct his search of the dark rooms. He turns up a strip of film, a few undeveloped frames. Obsessive escapism into secondhand, mediated experience spills over from *Bleeder* to *Fear X*. Whether Harry knew it or not, his search for meaningful answers has become a search for undiscovered, unknown, unseen images, as if the cinephile Refn is revealing his own obsessions through Harry. And once again, as in *Bleeder*, the fetish object (film) is linked to mourning for the dead by discovering and preserving something lost. The fan, like the voyeur or like the detective seeking clues, is always searching for something rare and barely traceable, something outside of the network of officially produced and consumed images. He is looking for something that no one else has seen before. (The insecurity of male voyeurism requires an object that is marked as a kind of virgin, untouched by prior claims of hermeneutic description.)

In one of the rooms there is a red-velvet hanging lamp with brocade tassel, suggesting a bordello. So this dwelling, which Harry has also discovered to be rented by a private corporation, is a variety of things: a place of alien encounters; the heart of cinema-worship and voyeuristic fetishism; and, finally, a kind of chilly, voided, inhuman brothel. Like the police interrogation in the sleazy hotel, the corporate-owned house suggests social institutions infected by the "cash and carry" taint of prostitution. Also, it is not a place that can be accessed through the front door, through normal, polite activity; as a cynosure of dishonesty and stealth, and as a permanently unknown quantity (there are reasons why the algebraic "X" is in the movie's title), it can only be broken into or, we might say, "taken from behind."

Harry has the film developed at the mall photo-shop; in this brief scene, the entire conceit of *The Terminal* (2004)—that one is forced to live entirely within the confines of modern commercial spaces, and that a mall is modern man's Ultima Thule—is made immediately apparent without heavy-handedness or cloying sentiment. The images turn out to be: a woman and a little boy; the same boy with a man who covers his face with his hand; and a roadside diner in Montana, in a town called Morristown, the same place where Claire and Harry took a trip to celebrate her pregnancy shortly before her death.

Having lost a mother and child, Harry is now given the clue of a different mother and child, again as if the universe were seeking to regain a lost balance or symmetry. The camera zooms "into" the back of Harry's head, and out of the darkness we see an unknown man's face being pressed like a death-mask into the same red, womb-like tissue that pulsated around Harry's hand in the earlier scene. (This creepy death-mask image will be reprised when Harry finally comes face to face with Claire's killer.) Harry's thoughts are turning more and more toward violent satisfaction and revenge, whether or not he realizes it. He is becoming an angel of death, though it is still unclear whose death he is summoning. However, when he tells Phil that he is going to Morristown to look for the killer, Phil immediately underscores the fact that Harry is entering amateur-vigilante terrain. Referring to Claire's killer, Phil says, "He's not gonna want to sit down and talk to you until you feel better.... You realize you have to be willing to kill this guy." Under what circumstances can—or should—a person kill? And what makes up the emotional difference between justice and revenge? Already implicit in *Pusher* and *Bleeder*, these questions of vigilante vengeance begin to be asked more insistently by Refn with *Fear X*.

Needless to say, these questions do not have easy answers. Historian Robert Muchembled makes the point that in the Middle Ages justice took its cues from revenge in order to establish itself as idea and practice. People trusted the feeling of revenge, which they recognized and understood more readily than they did the more abstract calibrations of "justice," so justice imitated revenge until it had accrued enough cachet to tauten the reins on extra-judicial vigilantism. This is perhaps only to say that in pre–Enlightenment times, revenge was seen as possessing greater honor, due to its greater individual sovereignty, than justice. "Many victims of humble origins," Muchembled writes, "were less interested in ensuring that the offender was punished than in restoring their own position in the eyes of their fellow inhabitants. They appealed to the judges to assure the restoration of their honor by transferring the infamy onto the accused, who was obliged to humiliate himself in turn."[21] Long before justice was a national system or institution, it was profoundly local, having to do with the immediate neighborhoods and towns where victims had lost face. It was what we call today "street justice," concerned with revenge but also with the defense of one's self, one's loved ones, and one's "turf" from future attacks: honor as an unquantifiable status. State justice only implanted itself systemically after it had eventually absorbed "the collective sense of honor and the law of shame."[22] But the transference of infamy to another has not completely died away as a human yearning, especially in cases that seem beyond the scope of justice itself. "I'm not a murderer," Harry says quietly to his fellow mall cop, availing himself of that "law of shame" (against the actual murderer) in order to further assume righteousness of purpose in his mission to avenge Claire.

Here we see that the social power of language to define categories of knowledge and experience is always somewhat religious in essence, since it forces the evidence of the naked eye to be overtaken by pejorative or consoling abstractions. In the urban *Bleeder*, there was no sense of Nature: only a bifurcated Image World in which some images were life-affirming and others death-affirming. *Fear X* seeks to posit some kind of inchoate transcendentalism (in the form of pregnancy, snow, vast landscapes) as an authentic if elusive refuge from duplicitous image and word. The film does not allow Nature to survive, though, demystifying and depopulating it so as to allow the Image World to take over; this is the strength of Refn's critique. Where Nature is wholly supplanted by Word, there we always find residual traces and/or entire bodies of dogmatic religious or nationalistic thought. But, of course, it should be clear by now that *Fear X* is almost entirely about the abstractions, ideological whether or not we understand them as such, that we use *as a matter of faith* to validate what we have seen, and to explain (or explain away) what we cannot or have not been able to see. However, these abstractions have deteriorated and no longer easily share in a consistent communal meaning; thus, there are moments of narrative effacement or blurring in *Fear X*, where coordinates become jumbled, roles turn inside out, and even evidentiary materials themselves become labile. This technique of blurring will grow as the film progresses.

Harry arrives in Morristown and checks into the same hotel where he stayed with Claire. The desk clerk makes a point of telling Harry, "We provide all sorts of entertainment here," a none-too-subtle revisiting of the film's intermittent theme of prostitution simmering beneath the placid surface of "normal" public spaces and institutions. Wasting no time in his investigation, Harry visits the diner from the photo and asks the perky young waitress (Nadia Litz) if she knows the woman in the photo. Seemingly domesticated images are becoming feral entry points for social unease; no matter that Harry's image is pocket-sized, next to nothing compared with the more freighted mural of the U.S. flag which covers the entire back wall of the diner. Some images are more equal than others. A cop, Officer Tim (Mark Houghton), who has been sitting in the back of the diner, immediately steps forward (as if from the middle of this one-dimensional painted flag) and intrudes, commandeering the photo and beginning to interrogate Harry, in a quiet but forceful way, about who he is and why he has come to town looking for the "unknown" woman in the photo.

Actually, Officer Tim knows the woman, though he does not disclose this fact to Harry. He takes down Harry's name and the hotel where he is staying, and we learn, in the next scene, that he immediately phones Lt. Peter Northrup (James Remar) to inform him that Harry is asking questions about Peter's wife, Kate (Deborah Kara Unger). Peter seems worried by this. He is in the courthouse, preparing to receive a commendation at an official ceremony, where Kate is there to support him. (We recognize her from Harry's photo.) Lt. Peter's award is for improving relations of trust between the community and "its authorities." The police chief, played by a nearly unrecognizable Gene Davis, announces, "So this award takes on greater significance in this day of unrest, turmoil and distrust."

Davis might be an example of the actor-as-fetish. He is best known to film cultists for his early role as the nude serial killer of women in *10 to Midnight* (1983), one of the last films directed by J. Lee Thompson, most famous for *Cape Fear* (1962). *10 to Midnight* concerns a twisting game of cat and mouse between the killer and the tough cop (Charles Bronson) who knows he is guilty but cannot find the evidence to nail him legally; the cop finally ends up taking the law into his own hands and shooting the killer dead. In that film, as in so many of the vigilante-themed movies of the '70s and '80s, cops were depicted as beleaguered victims of a permissive justice system, and as morally perfect heroes who needed the license to kill at will in order to get rid of bad guys.[23] It is unique casting finesse that Davis, once indelible as a killer who awakens vigilante fervor, now returns in *Fear X* as a police chief who (it will turn out) orders hush-hush assassinations of alleged criminals.

Peter hurries Kate home after the ceremony, preoccupied with finding out more about this mysterious Caine. In *Fear X*, anything that is external to anyone's familiar comfort zone is mysterious and a nemesis; the film delivers this threatened logic so relentlessly that, although we have been seeing things through Harry's eyes up till now, we suddenly begin to see things through the eyes of Peter and Kate, with little difference in apprehensive anxiety. In their kitchen at home, Kate is suspicious of Peter's secrecy and asks him if he is cheating on her. "I'm not afraid of the truth," she says. Yet, affect is bizarrely muffled: this domestic scene is stiff and un-intimate; Kate and Peter never touch each other, and they speak their lines very flatly and with strange, shivery pauses—an anti-naturalistic stylization to show the *unheimlich* surfacing in an echt-bourgeois, domestic setting. (This kind of offbeat line-reading is familiar in general from art cinema, but this scene marks the start of Refn beginning to adopt it as a trademark of his own style, one which he will develop and refine in later films such as *Drive* and *Only God Forgives*.)

Meanwhile, in a further ironic parody of male-female intimacy, Harry receives a visit from a hooker (Amanda Ooms) in his hotel room. Is she the esoteric "entertainment" promised by the desk clerk, or more likely an undercover spy? She pointedly asks Harry more than once if he is alone (as in traveling alone, staying at the hotel alone). She also comes in and uses the phone, a terse call to a contact in which she confirms something (that Harry is alone?) then hangs up. Again, Refn plays with slowness, time nearly standing still, long pauses between lines, the tension of the unsaid or the not-yet said, which aggravates a dopey-paranoid feeling of "It's being said, Harry is missing cues, he's stepping into the trap." Before she leaves, she leans toward Harry and hesitates for a long time as if about to give him a kind of Judas kiss—either as part of her job/cover or as a spontaneous urge, which, needless to say, can find no fulfillment in the duty-bound trajectory of Harry's quest. Sexuality of any kind (even as flirtatious play-acting) takes a definitive backseat to a sense of life-and-death mission. The ubiquity of random violence in these characters' lives does not turn them into rampant hedonists living for the moment, but instead only seems to enhance their marital bonds, an interesting perception which stands in marked contrast to the way most current directors expose the decay of intimacy as a side effect of social chaos. In fact, *Pusher* and *Bleeder* can be said to be within that "social chaos" tradition. *Fear X* is the first Refn film (aside from *Bleeder*'s hopeful ending) where some idealism is held out and tentatively championed as the way things *ought* to be, even if they are not quite.

Lt. Peter is also on a dutiful quest, and his and Harry's respective missions are about to collide. In a secret meeting, the Police Chief worries that Harry has solved not only his wife's murder but the entire conspiracy within the police department itself. Peter is told to find out what Harry knows and then eliminate him. In spite of his commitment to killing in the name of law and order, Peter is not a born killer and expresses guilt over the accidental murder of Harry's wife: "I killed an innocent woman." The Chief is pragmatic and defends the reasons why Peter had to kill the crooked DEA agent, in whose assassination Claire's death was collateral damage: "Innocent people are hurt and killed every day, that's the way the world is.... We have to keep our focus on our goals, our ideals. Corrupt law enforcement is a cancer. It eats at the heart and moral fabric of society. Without law there is no order."

Harry is summoned to meet Peter in an empty room of the hotel, with the promise that the answers he seeks will be revealed. In the dimly lit room, Peter is unable to make eye contact with Harry. He asks Harry numerous times if other people have seen the photos or helped Harry unravel the mystery thus far. Confused but aware that he is closer to the truth than he has ever been, Harry says, "I need to know why my wife was killed." "Is it worth your life?" Peter asks desperately, tipping his hand, but Harry says, "I'm not living anyway." (The hero in Bausch's novel *Violence* echoes this sentiment after surviving a convenience store massacre: "I feel dead, deep down."[24] There is a kind of mourning for one's own surviving self, specifically its loss of intimate or unthinking safety, which arises in the aftermath of violence.) At this point Peter ushers Harry into the corridor, to his death. However, Peter is shaking and hesitant, and as they stand waiting for the elevator, Harry senses what Peter is hiding and turns toward him. "*You*," he says, taking Peter's face in his hands. "For God's sake, *why*?"

This is Harry's ambiguous moment of triumph, to finally lay his hands on a single guilty party, another flesh and blood person like himself, and thereby make localized and specific a battle that had seemed to be carried out against the world—or existence—itself. An entire society—of random killings, of spurious or corrupt police work, of surveillance systems which do not ameliorate but rather purvey and heighten the climate of fear—seemed to have been guilty in the murder of Harry's wife. But as Hannah Arendt writes, "where all are guilty, no one is; confessions of collective guilt are the best possible safeguard against the discovery of culprits, and the very magnitude of the crime the best defense for doing nothing."[25]

But if Harry regains some purchase on sanity in being able to look his wife's killer in the eye, the moment is short-lived. Peter shoots Harry in the stomach. The elevator opens and, yelling an apology, Peter shoves Harry inside and aims the gun at him, intending to finish him off. But the doors close before Peter fires. Inside the elevator, Harry feels his wound and becomes enraged by the sight of his own blood. He pounds the elevator button and goes back to the floor where Peter is. Fist clenched and raised, he advances into the darkness. Here, Refn opts for abstraction rather than action, an intriguing choice given his skill and affinity for staging scenes of violent action, but the result is in keeping with what Refn recognized in Hooper's *Texas Chain Saw Massacre*, a cinema of pure image and sound: fiery red explosions and electronic crackling give way to red dots, streaks and washes. Finally, the open elevator is shown, flanked by lurid red lights, and we see that the darkened hallway has become a glossy, rippling body of water. Again, like the sleazy hotel that was being used as a police headquarters, this is an image from surrealist cinema: the outdoors invading the indoors, perverse Nature forcing a last-ditch claim on the image world that has supplanted it. It is a place with no locatable coordinates, no longer the drab hallway of a hotel, more like the Slough of Despond or the River Lethe, or the flood in *The Shining*.[26] But this latter reference is telling, since we see that it is only within a constructed, secondhand image world that we can think of Nature possessing *intentionality* when it invades denatured realms. Our anthropomorphism (of water, of blood) is already a sign that Nature as a pure entity is dead.

And then in a flash the image is gone. There is a startling cut to a very bright room in which Harry lies in a hospital bed, in a fetal position, alive and being questioned by policemen. Light streams in through the windows, and there is a cross hanging on the wall. Peter is not there. Harry does not even appear wounded. He admits that he killed the man who murdered his wife, though he says, "I never wanted to hurt him." He has justice, apparently, and also the retention of righteous self-image: the "law of shame" has descended on the truly guilty man.

Officer Tim arrives and calls one of the policemen away; there are unheard words exchanged in the doorway with an unseen figure, and when the policeman returns, he tells Harry he has been cleared of any wrongdoing. "There was no evidence of any crime.... Not even the surveillance tapes show anything." The tapes, once again, are given the last word on guilt and innocence, on reality itself—perhaps not in spite, but because, of the simple fact that they can be doctored any which way to suit any purpose. The image world keeps Nature firmly in place—i.e., as a hermeneutic-dependent abstraction which the image world itself invents and names and frames and scapegoats and pimps out. Harry is bewildered, but when the officer says, "We know what happened to you; you can't change what was, what used to be," Harry breaks down sobbing. But isn't the whole point of the film that "we" (in the audience) do not know what has happened to Harry, we must conjure and swallow our suppositions like a white lie? Is "justice," here, just the hypnosis that revenge needs to believe in order for Harry to be a hero rather than a killer—and, conversely, for their fates ride the same seesaw, for Lt. Peter to be demoted, in death, from hero to unmourned murderer?

In the final scene, just when we are sure that this weird world cannot get any weirder or misplace any more of its coordinates, Officer Tim drives Harry back to his car, which is parked by a stop sign at a crossroads in the middle of a panoramic open flatland. Wordlessly the cop gives Harry his things and nods him on his way. Harry throws away the photos and file cards he has collected, watching as the wind scatters them across the plain. Is this the end of the image world? Has Nature finally won and been restored? There is the queasy sense of a rigged game in which some underdog has been allowed to win, but only temporarily, only in an illusory way. Then Harry gets into his car and drives away into the distance. He seems to be released, no longer stuck between worlds, but which world has he finally come to? Is Harry, in fact, dead now, ferried across some dusty asphalt Styx by kindly-seeming but ultimately stern and murderous cops? Does Nature triumph over Image World only when we have made our ultimate return to Nature—as corpses—and even then most likely still existing in someone else's image world, someone else's conceptual Nature? This coda, in which Caine is forgiven and sent away, could be his tortured soul's compensation for the justice it was denied in life. A justice which seems all the more unreal because it lacks the pointed cathartic satisfactions of revenge.

Even if Harry is alive, what can possibly be waiting for him now that his terrible mission has been "accomplished"? It is hard to imagine him back at the mall, endlessly policing the same space where his wife was killed. But perhaps that is the point, perhaps he has now earned the right to police that space in true security and serenity. As viewers, we want justice for Harry, but we also resist knowing what he knows, learning what he learns. Refn seems to be saying that, in the end, life and death are nothing but a single, unbearable and unconquerable knowledge of the real. In this sense, we need the image world more than we need Nature; only a fool, or a dead man, would be cocky enough to think otherwise.

• • •

Refn presents the murder of Claire as a kind of lost origin, similar to legends and "sacred" texts. Harry's quest has already taken on a life of its own without direct witness of what prompted it in the first place. He is moving according to faith, and does not need to see with his own eyes the founding principle of what he believes. His most primal need (exemplified in his dreams and visions of her) is to imagine her at peace; this is an idea which Refn has struggled with in a number of his films. The ending of *Bleeder*, for example, suggested that there is no simple way of assimilating death, and no single correct one; all that the survivors can do is turn toward the world, toward what they recognize as sources of life and love. Whereas, by contrast, *Valhalla Rising* will assert the more supernatural tendency to want some concept of an afterworld to extend life beyond the reach of death, into immortality.

In this sense, *Fear X* seems to be a turning point in Refn's continuous interest in death and fate, since the film ultimately leaves us wondering if this world is not already, in fact, a kind of afterworld—or rather, more precisely, a place where the knowledge of death hangs over everything so heavily that one must often stop and think about it, preparing oneself for the eventuality, which then becomes permanently fused into present reality. Put otherwise, the objective of making oneself comfortable with the gnawing thought, "I'm going to die someday," is to accept it as though it had already happened—or as Harry tells Peter, "I'm not living anyway."

Surveillance is eerily similar to this kind of living death, a kind of metonymy for the way life is deformed by death. We read, in Christian Parenti's *The Soft Cage*, that modern video surveillance is "a symbolic defense, an expensive mojo that appears to ward off fear while actually summoning it in constant, everyday form."[27] Parenti likens the use of cameras in public spaces to "a cargo cult," in that "essentially imaginary, or magical, forms of agency are acted out in the face of massive and nebulous threats."[28] Someone is watching, thereby ostensibly providing a permanent cover of security predicated on a permanent insecurity "spiraling up into the thin altitudes of political psychosis."[29]

Parenti asserts that we can no longer even count the number of surveillance cameras in our public spaces because they "continue to sprout up" nearly everywhere.[30] But this begs the policy question: if we cannot even count the cameras, how can we possibly *watch* all the evidentiary tapes or live streams that they generate? It would require untold man-hours (or computers that have not yet been developed) simply to scan them all. Possibly more than dozens of people working around the clock would be needed to analyze the data from only one sector of a densely populated city. And as they worked to keep up, more would constantly pour in. Thus, we must conclude that nothing is actually meant to be witnessed or prevented via constant video surveillance. At best, they might be used to gather information on crimes that have already been committed, but this is a cynical and paltry realization incommensurable to the way the tactic has been oversold as a watchdog. If surveillance takes place, as Parenti suggests, within the realm of the "symbolic" only, as a subconscious reinforcement of fear and self-restraint,[31] then we could say that the cameras metaphorize a lost and wished-for sense of omniscience. They are meant to replicate old-fashioned conceptions of God-on-high within a high-tech, scientific and largely secular society. The idea of this omniscience survives as a final consolation against the chaos of meaningless acts. The reassurance that everything is seen and recorded by a monitoring eye recalls the orderly universe in which the fall of every sparrow is noted.

Many reviewers saw *Fear X* as "subtly recalibrating the *Blow-Up/Conversation/Blow Out* the-closer-you-look-the-less-you-really-know conceit for the media-saturated aughts."[32] But although the character name "Harry Caine" is strikingly reminiscent of "Harry Caul," the surveillance expert in *The Conversation*—undermined by his own bad faith, loneliness and paranoia, a classic "man who knew too much"—the name clearly nods, also, to "Dirty" Harry Callahan, the vigilante cop played by Clint Eastwood in a string of action flicks, as well as the biblical figure of Cain, ordinary man turned killer; *The Caine Mutiny*; and, of course, the vaguely homophonic pun "hurricane." (There is also a distant echo of "Herakles," the hero who ventures into the underworld to bring a woman back to the realm of the living in Euripides' play *Alkestis*.) Likewise, Harry is not the "secret listener" (we are reminded of Tarkovsky's definition of the filmmaker-poet: one who surveils the public consciousness not to accuse it of crimes but to liberate it from inwardness and shame) whom we find in *The Conversation*'s Caul, since nearly all of the evidentiary material in *Fear X* is visual. Numerous zooms on seemingly insignificant locations and details suggest spying through telescopic sights; while another frequent visual motif of *Fear X* is blurry distances being brought into focus, as if through binoculars.

But the film's prime medium of surveillance is the rather low-tech VHS. *Fear X* is at least three configurations behind. It is odd to see a film from the 2000s with so many videocassettes in it. The lack of crystal clarity with tape reproduction yields layers of ambiguous distortion, as well as a generally retrograde feel of being stranded in time (like those elements of the '50s which render *Blue Velvet* so time-disordered and resonant). In spite of being heftier than digital discs, the videocassette is yet another emblem of fragile mortality, and the mall cops seem even older and wearier than they already are, handing each other stacks of VHS, widely considered the worst-ever configuration for capturing image clarity (e.g., accuracy). Not to mention the tendency of tapes to "fuzz out" or come unspooled or get chewed up or break outright—no other configuration has made collectors look so foolish when showing off for friends. As Michael Atkinson writes, "Refn makes the most of the chaotic video textures—often, the entire film fragments into a monsoon of unreadable pixels, suggesting the space to be bridged by a potential video-age remake of *Blow-Up*."[33] Indeed, the videotape as fetish object has hardly been used as well since *Videodrome*, and there is also some consolation in the way *Fear X* reminds one, almost with a feeling of satisfaction, that surveillance technology, no matter how widely and sinisterly it is used now, has not developed at the same rate of new configuration as, say, entertainment technology. There is no HD or Blu-Ray equivalent in surveillance tapes, no ability to change the angle of view or download them to a phone. In this, they once again seem to exist in a conceptual idea of the real, while remaining largely cut off from everyday reality, similar to Lesley Stern's characterization of the "totemic object" being restricted to "a context of ritual, of ceremony, of theatre; a context realized in sharp opposition to the everyday."[34] Again, a godlike omniscience that plays out as bluster, as bluff.

Surveillance raises fascinating questions, and Refn is not the only current artist to draw inspiration from "probing the probe," so to speak. New York artist Jill Magid has based a series of installations and conceptual pieces around her fascination with modern international urban surveillance, asserting that in surveillance the basic meaning of images is renewed and reconsolidated: "I wanted to go to the center of power, where the image really meant something." (This was a police headquarters in Amsterdam.)[35] The iconography of classical and modern painting has been a progressive de-investment in the image as representation. Also a de-sacralization, perhaps, in that the consumption of the images becomes easier, less painful, less cathartic. The image has become background, like the wall-size murals in *Bleeder* or the mural of the U.S. flag in the diner in *Fear X*; whereas watching, observing, recording become central to Magid's sense of how video surveillance mirrors the exhibitionistic elements of performance art and environmental art. An ever-watching eye implies that interesting things will happen for its attentive delectation, things whose meaning we might not automatically understand. Everything occurring within the frame of its lens is, by definition, in an image world, a performed or at least deconstructive gesture.

Magid went to Liverpool, "one of the world's most heavily surveilled metropolises," to make *Evidence Locker* (2004), in which she intercut police interrogation footage with images of herself walking through the city and returning the gaze of all its surveillance cameras with her own camera's. As she reports, a certain degree of Stockholm-syndrome neediness set in. "'Many times I saw that the camera wasn't watching, and I became dependent on the system,' Magid says. She became so emotionally invested that at times she would ask, 'It was very emotional—Why aren't they watching me?' They'd call later and say, 'Oh Jill, we're really sorry, but there was a murder and we have to deal with it.'"[36] The desire to have everything under watch and to be constantly watched can have strange consolations, even when you find yourself being momentarily ignored, for at least this means that nothing horrendous is happening to you.

At the same time, the constant activity of watching and being watched throws living into question; one is uncertain of one's very own existence unless it is constantly being witnessed. This is territory that some of Refn's work plays in. For example, one of Bronson's problems is that he is only happy as the singled-out object of an aghast voyeurism, a Christ crucified not on the cross but on the disapproving gaze. More typically, as most filmmakers would, Refn deals with the situation from the voyeur's side. Much like *Bleeder*, *Fear X* explores a somewhat admonitory zone between living and watching, with their incompatible demands, but now from a somewhat different angle. In *Bleeder*, Leo becomes obsessed with the difference between active participation and detached witness; in the scene where he watches a man being assaulted, his own face is "erased" by a wash of video static, which turns out to be Lenny changing videos in his apartment where (we are told) he watches "four films a day." Seeing real violence is shown to be more damaging than watching it in films—a defense, finally, of violent cinema as a harmless outlet for antisocial fantasy. At any rate, we recall that, for Lenny, endless watching eventually gives way to healthier social engagement with others (that is, if he wants his life to be as compelling and romantic as his favorite movies). Similarly, in *Fear X*, Caine's passive absorption of surveillance videos is an attempt, however benumbed and helpless, to be led back into real life, specifically contact with his murdered wife or with her killer. This is fetishism-as-mourning, enacted on objects of worship or longing which are, in fact, recorded images. Caine is not trying to capture a better future (like Lenny) but redeem a horribly mangled past. If Harry ends up indeed seeing less the longer he looks, it is not because the videos themselves have replaced his ability to really see, but rather because the idea of the secondhand (exemplified by surveillance tapes but represented equally, in *Fear X*, by the canned and hypocritical ceremony in which Peter receives his official commendation, or by the numerous desultory, flatlining phone/business conversations in the film) has obscured the ability to comprehend exactly what Caine sees when he looks at the ostensibly real. Everything has an official, surface meaning, and then, when one peers only a little below the surface, a senseless, garbled one; and everyone pretends not to notice that this is the case. Of course, this is often the way in thrillers, but *Fear X* plunges headlong into this vertigo without looking back.

• • •

Surveillance evidence in *Fear X* is not one-hundred-percent visual; there is a deliberate connection on a formal level between sonics and the fearful uncertainty of recorded information. Refn says, "I wanted to allow the sound to convey the abstraction in Caine's mind,"[37] and implies that it was intentional that the word "ear" is embedded within the title, *Fear X*.[38] (Unscrambled, it might read: Ear F/X, or sound effects.)

Here is where the ambient, almost subliminal score by Eno and Schwalm plays a crucial role in Refn's film. *Fear X* partly derives from the myth of Orpheus, the widower venturing into the underworld to retrieve his deceased wife Eurydice. King of musicians, Orpheus alone was granted access to Hades, but in the end he did not trust his own best sense, hearing, and violated the contract by turning around to make certain of Eurydice with his eyes. In a sense, death in general is the revenge of the internalized voice over actual sight; it torments us because it demonstrates that sound—diffuse, incorporeal, deceptive—can never quite be enough, never substitute for the more tangible, un-abstract proofs of sight. Harry wants to poke through that cloudy sonic "abstraction" in his mind into the realm of visual proof. Woven through the darker textures of *Fear X* is a delicate love story, after all, in which the longing simply to see (and touch) the beloved is granted to Harry in the form of periodic visions—silent visions in which the wife never speaks and her appearance alone becomes enough. In the case of love, the eyes must ascertain, must build up visual evidence of the beloved's *thereness*. Merely heard voices run a distant second, they cannot be held onto as comprehensively, they leave out too much presence, too much body language and physical information.

This is because, unlike sightlessness, which has an abject quality of lack, silence often manifests itself as an irreducible whole that is nobler, in theory, than any kind of noise, even the most exalted or exquisite or heartfelt speech. "Noise" disturbs contented silence far more often than the sight of something "offends" against darkness or blindness; we usually want to see when we cannot, especially when we cannot, but we often can appreciate silence for its calming, restorative, or even semi-telepathic powers. Also, the most common human sound, spoken language, is already a mediation whose meaning can be ambiguous at best. According to Maurice Blanchot, "To converse is also to turn language away from itself, maintaining it outside of all unity."[39] Such "maintaining" is meant to denote an artificial life-support. Silence is the true guardian of linguistic purity; the idea that language can begin and end anywhere, or randomly, as in passing conversations, reduces language itself to something finite and merely *usable*. This naturally correlates to issues of purity and wholeness in the context of romantic love. Blanchot: "And such is the fate of lovers who touch each other with words ... because their speech is not a language but an idiom they share with no other, and because each gazes at himself in the other's gaze in a redoubling which goes from mirage to admiration."[40] Love would prefer to be deaf-mute and sighted, if it had to choose; whereas hatred is already a blindness that speaks too loudly and listens too harshly. Needless to say, then, the perfect lovers' speech is shared silence, that profound harmony of two souls which serves to reveal the banality of quotidian, loveless speech and even the desperate compensation of garrulous, speechifying love. One thinks of the wordless traveling shot that follows Lyn Corfixen through a quaint used bookstore in *Bleeder* or the later use of silence to denote a romantic bond in *Drive*.

"For a distance is necessary," Blanchot writes, "if desire is to be born of not being immediately satisfied."[41] This empathic distance keeps the bloom on attraction rather than hurtling toward a premature fulfillment before the desire can become more significant than merely the satisfaction of an immediate need. *Bleeder* postulated that, ultimately, love requires not only distance but a certain cultivated vicariousness in order to develop. One must approach the reality of another always from an outside place that draws nearer and nearer; and the watching of films (or reading of books) becomes a testing ground for this patient buffering zone, this slow empathy. Loving real violence stunts male development and isolates pathological men in a death-tango that leads inexorably away from life and the future; whereas loving violent films is a way of tempering the impulses themselves and being able to be satisfied with purely symbolic violations of taboos.

Fear X picks up on this idea by indicating that real death is the ultimate challenge to this process of learning-to-love through vicarious emotional experience: not only does the death of the beloved force the bereaved to "unlearn" everything that he once had daily epiphenomenological access to, it places the beloved in a new realm of "experience" which cannot be approached at all via life, not even vicariously, since there "is no knowing death, no experiencing it and then returning to write about it, no intrinsic grounds for authority in the discourse surrounding it."[42] The dead beloved has definitively eluded the pattern of didactic vicariousness by which discrete subjective emotions are allowed to evolve into shared and shareable reality. She has moved on in a way that not even a demigod like Orpheus can follow.

• • •

Although murders are committed in *Fear X*, no one in the film really "is" a criminal. Again, Harry does not wish to be a "murderer," although he ostensibly murders; the same with Lt. Peter. In fact, by the logic of the film, crimes such as murder do not make someone a criminal, but rather one's criminality comes from a state of having fallen from some grace, which could happen to anyone. Conversely, there is a positive state of grace which allows for the worst crimes to be committed in something like self-righteous impunity. Indeed, Refn depicts Americans as hardworking and family-oriented even where they are also blatantly murderous. Lt. Peter, who has killed Harry's wife, asserts that he would kill again to protect his own wife, Kate. The realm of order and protection becomes smaller and smaller, and more and more captioned by artificial props. All of the male characters either wear uniforms (the police, the mall guards) or occupy positions of authority (the plainclothes detectives, the police chief).

4. Fear X

The idea of the criminal is, of course, inscribed within the very heart of the vast surveillance state mobilized only in order to bring the criminal into the realm of visibility. Of course, even the one character identified as a criminal—the corrupt DEA agent, already dead when the film begins—is nominally a representative of law and order, of authority. The ascribing of guilt is tendentious and a mark of total power which transcends any localized judgments against it. Indeed, Lt. Peter and Caine, the actual killers or trigger-men, so to speak, are less given to hard-edged, judgmental certainty than their strange leaders are; neither Peter nor Caine is comfortable as a self-mythologizing "hero," and both long for the stability which troublesome crusading has undermined in their lives. Caine's and Peter's firm insistence that they do not want to kill is belied not so much by the eventual fact that both do it, but more by the inevitability with which they rationalize it as unavoidable. "I'm not a murderer" is shown as *the* ultimate cry of the American killer.

This echoes with the character of Martha (Debbie Doebereiner) in Steven Soderbergh's *Bubble* (2005), as much a work of deranged Americana as *Fear X*. Early in *Bubble* we see Martha sitting in church. A heavy, middle-aged woman, she has a vision of the church getting dark, except for a kind of celestial spotlight highlighting her, as if the light of God were shining on her alone. Her need to feel special is understandable, given her extremely mundane life as factory worker and caretaker to her elderly father (Omar Cowan). The closest thing to love in Martha's life is the way she allows herself to be used for her car by a younger coworker named Kyle (Dustin James Ashley), who, from a mixture of pot-induced apathy and selfishness, blinds himself to the fact that Martha is desperately and totally in love with him.

Not that Martha would ever be forward enough to declare this love and risk rejection. Already seething with pent-up, unexpressed feelings, Martha is immediately defensive when young single-mother Rose (Misty Wilkins) comes to work at the factory; she worries about the obvious chemistry that clicks between Rose and Kyle. She tells Kyle she is scared by Rose's spontaneity and free-spiritedness. This obvious smear campaign is ineffective, however, and eventually Martha ends up strangling Rose in a jealous crime of passion. She swears her innocence to Kyle from behind bars: "You know me. I could not have done that.... You know that I would never do anything like this."

I'm not a murderer. Martha is coded as the "good woman" in this symbolic order, while Rose is thieving and ostensibly promiscuous. But with Martha's fingerprints around Rose's throat—the Lacanian "answer of the real" which defeats the symbolic—respectable justice is denounced for being what it really is: ugly revenge. And then the rest of the world takes its revenge on the disgraced Martha. As in a bursting economic bubble, targeting outcasts and throwing them to the wolves, as a plan of action, creates some short-term credit but destroys credibility in the long run, as what goes around makes its way back around again. Indeed, all the comfort that the barely interested Kyle can give her is to shrug, "I don't know, Martha."

Or, as it sounds to the ear: *I don't know Martha*. I don't—didn't—know what someone else, friend or stranger, was capable of. But naturally this is tantamount to Kyle trying to get himself off the hook for his own lack of foresight, or self-insight perhaps. Indeed, social ostracism of undesirable types is always a defense against acknowledging one's own potential stigma. The need to feel special is ubiquitous: it causes Martha to lash out, it causes Kyle to deny and repudiate Martha. In her jail cell, Martha has another vision of herself, again haloed by a special light, but now the telltale light of guilt. Guilt and grace are, finally, the same thing, both marked by a shameless sense of unique privilege and by an utter lack of nuance. The fall from grace partakes of the same pride that accompanied the idea of grace in the first place. Lt. Peter in *Fear X*, we infer, would not be so broken up by having murdered an innocent woman if he did not believe in the grandiose responsibility of authority to be kindly and humane. But conceiving of a world entirely without any controlling and omniscient authority, and therefore without any privilege, is a revolutionary moment quite beyond the hapless, delusional "good murderers" in *Fear X* and *Bubble*.

"Those with the darkest nightmares became the most powerful," Adam Curtis states in his trenchant BBC series on neoconservatism.[43] There is a sort of passive-aggressive competition among the three main characters of *Fear X*, a competition to demonstrate who among them is most damaged and terrorized. Peter has a stooped posture, shivering fits, and an inability to maintain eye contact; his wife repeats things that are said to her as if she were listening from deep underwater, and she rotely suspects Peter of adultery—but not in a display of angry passion, rather as a badge of numb, resigned suffering, a single diamantine tear trickling down her cheek. Caine, arguably the most haunted, is faced with a comprehensive loss of meaning that trumps everyone else, shrouded in bewilderment and disillusion; in common parlance, Caine has "lost the plot," a fatal state for any protagonist.

Likewise, this passive-aggressive competition for a monopoly on fear and damage is the main element behind the characters in *Bubble*. Martha expresses her disapproval of Rose by playing the terrorized, potential victim: "she scares me a little"; Kyle's life has been crippled by severe anxiety disorder, also the perfect license for (or inevitable result of?) his constant stoned apathy; Rose presents herself as the born victim of men and her own chronically bad decision-making. In a climate of orchestrated paranoia, not to be one of the terminally frightened becomes tantamount to being one of the bogeymen, who tip their rough hands to oversensitive observers by failing to out-polite or out-worry them. This is notwithstanding the fact that it's the frightened one who ends up lashing out and taking a life. People who flash their normal, dirty, human faults become scapegoats of a collective desperate to prove itself above suspicion. Once the Talking Heads could indicate intense hatred of rudeness as a sure sign of being a "Psycho Killer"; today, it is merely the sign of being the good citizen, the whistle-blower, the concerned busybody, part of the long arm of the law and the psycho-pharmaceutical diagnosticians. The American unconscious is, finally, the deepest and most far-reaching conspiracy theory of all: the conspiracy that one is all alone, holding at bay the chaos that threatens perfect order and discipline, and that one is also simultaneously, deep down, a born agent of that same chaos.

This is why Refn's ending, in which Caine scatters his clutch of surveillance images to the wind, is bold but somehow unconvincing. Or, rather, it incorporates an element of bad faith. It is formally related to the famous final scene of Don Siegel's *Dirty Harry* (1971), in which the disillusioned cop played by Clint Eastwood throws his badge into a landfill. But that cathartic moment of Eastwood's was finally only a showy, theatrical, ultimately phony break with the structured authority of government (something that would emerge a decade later as a central rhetorical trope of the neoconservatives). It was not the gesture of an anarchist but of someone for whom the law is too lawful and order no longer orderly enough. Caine's throwing away of the images that he has lived with, and through, could be meant as a gesture of breaking from the media-determined hall of mirrors of the post–9/11 U.S. But to forfeit a symbol of authority (the police badge in *Dirty Harry*) is far easier than forfeiting one's membership in the entire realm of the symbolic, no matter how necessary this might be to our ultimate survival.

Thus, Refn allows the surveillance cameras to have the last word, accompanying the end credits, as they have had the "last word" at several other occasions in the film where what would be called "plot points" in a different kind of narrative are resolved by reference to surveillance tapes (the moment when Caine finally watches the tape that shows the murder of his wife, which prompts him to overcome his fear and scruples enough to break into the mysterious house across the street; the scene in the hospital where the police officer informs Caine that he is completely exonerated even on "the surveillance tapes" of the hotel). No matter what presence or absence has been inscribed on the tapes in question, the death of symbology can only be registered via a new symbolic order. The desert crossroads where *Fear X* ends point to an abandonment of symbols, but at the same time an implicit need to recreate them, to repopulate—obsessively "populate and repopulate," as we recall from the inanimate births of *Flesh for Frankenstein*, quoted in *Bleeder*—the barren space in something like a Manifest Destiny of symbolic consciousness. Even if "what always comes back to the same place is the real," and if "what repeatedly returns in ever the same guise—or what the subject seeks to return to—is the facticity beneath or beyond images and symbols,"[44] we generally come to recognize the real only as something which doubles as a unit of symbolic meaning. Put otherwise: Harry has become his own Frankenstein monster.

Cinema has long been a battleground for the redemption of the image, or the interrogation of the image's authenticity and honesty. Godard's and Gorin's filmic essay *Letter to Jane* (1974) turns on the revelatory insight that wherever two human images from radically different contexts end up looking the same, one or both of them must be lying. What is problematic is that the instant it assumes a visible, external form, subjectivity itself becomes an object and can only claim *noblesse oblige* at the risk of insincerity. The bad faith lies in the fact that films that attempt to betoken the end of the image often wind up seeming ridiculous, since the image-making is patently meant to continue; it is like some addict vowing to get clean even as he shoots up.

The fact that the end credits of *Fear X* feature a sinister array of multiplying surveillance cameras suggests that the existence of the Image World will continue to grow and thrive with or without one Harry Caine (just as Harry Caul in *The Conversation* knew that his own mission of surveillance would not be complete until he, too, was paranoiacally under it). The spectral shadow puppets trundling and whirling through the grainy surveillance views reveal how cinema has always been a faulty (albeit brave) critic of the Image World, predicated as it is upon our collective and individual love of images themselves, our ability to become easily entranced by whatever lives and moves and has its being. But perhaps that is also why so many of the greatest filmmakers have found themselves in the schizophrenic position of critiquing images for the sake of reality, even as their reality (as filmmakers) is one long defense of the fabricated image. Refn seems to be the most recent director committed to trying such a critique, or at least exploring the fault line which such a critique opens up.

About the filming of *Fear X*, Refn has said, "I felt like a blind man shooting a movie.... But each time I was depressed, the one thing that always kept me going was, well what happens when Harry walks into the darkness?"[45] The idea of winning cinema back from the threat of an encroaching blindness might seem like hyperbole, but let us recall that we never do learn what happens when Caine takes that walk into the darkness. *Fear X* is like a film with intermittent vision, a series of sights and scenes collected by a man who can only see for a few minutes at a time and therefore is always running behind his own image-inventory, unable to make it cohere. But there might be no more potent metaphor for the strange life of consciousness today, especially in the media-saturated West, given over to messianic fervors and the politics of fear. We are all like Penelopes, waiting for preeminent reason to return to us, to our society as well as to the intimate spaces where we live, and unweaving during the unsettled, dream-blind hours of the night the conscious lies which we have woven together in the limbic light of day.

– 5 –

Nemesis

The female characters in Refn's first three films—*Pusher*, *Bleeder* and *Fear X*—were for the most part abstract and muffled. There was the archetypal dynamic of the one virtuous woman set off by one or more bad women. In *Pusher*, Vic's passive, loving loyalty to Frank is contrasted with the drug mule Rita who tries to rip Frank off. In *Bleeder*, Lea is a goddess who moves through the streets of Copenhagen like a vision of purity; she reads books and is kind to the socially awkward Lenny. Whereas Leo's girlfriend Louise is damaged goods, her wary eyes narrow whenever she begins to conceive some strange, sinister temptation. It is almost as if the worthy woman is known only in contrast to the untrustworthy one, or, in *Fear X*, by the saint-like condition of martyrdom, the ultimate purity. Harry Caine's murdered wife, removed from the world, exists only in flawless, inviolable memory. The detectives' attempts to impugn her character before she met Harry strike him (and us, so skillful is Refn is constructing her nearly allegorical purity in a few brief wordless moments) as unlikely overreaching; a "past," euphemism for someone's lurid sexual reputation, is precisely what cannot be tarnished in Harry's wife, for that is all Harry has left of her. The past devours any future uncertainty, for she is not only the woman who never fell but the woman who shall never fall again—unlike the cop's wife, loving her flawed, murderous husband, or the "hooker" who spies on Harry in his hotel room.

We believe what Refn wants us to believe about these women, but not of their possible lives beyond the borders of the frame. All of these female characters are expedient to one degree or another. If the bad ones exist simply to prove the virtue of the good ones, then we know even less about why the good ones exist, or how. Vic's toleration of Frank's judgmental stubbornness, egotism and emotional neglect verges on classic masochism; yet we infer this more than see it proven, since she is also capable of acting in her own self-interest at times, as well as being more than a little childlike and even simple-minded in her reactions to the world. Her fragile side, indeed her lovingness in general, is mainly meant to show Frank's inability to love and be loved, his studious wasting of his own and others' emotional potential. Lea in *Bleeder* is even more of an unknown quantity, defined solely through how Lenny—and, by extension, Refn—would like to see her behaving. She is passive and agreeable even when Lenny is not present or when she is not particularly the center of the camera's attention. So she merely listens to her overbearing boss, performing kitchen chores at the café while slinking past his badgering advice. On her day off she goes to a bookstore alone. She always wears white, and is so good-natured that even when Lenny stands her up for their first date (he chickens out at the last moment), she forgives him without any anger. She is nearly as much a child-woman as Louise, although Louise is literally performing an ultimate regression into incestuous sex with her brother Louis and a disturbing fixation on a little boy in a laundromat. Whether light or dark, however, the women share a need for guidance, which places the males in an essentially paternalistic relation to them. The women exist to bring about certain reactions and behaviors in their significant male others: Lea awakening real tenderness in Lenny; Louise driving Leo to abuse and punish her.

Fear X begins to explore the negative side of this pseudo-infantilization in more depth. The dead wife, as she appears to Harry in his visions, never speaks. She is defined by her pregnancy; thus she is as much mother as wife, and Harry seeks succor from her "ghost," cradling his head against her breasts. Rather than begin to accept his loss of her and try to rediscover in a living woman what he felt for his dead wife, Harry sinks deeper and deeper into an idealization: the wife's perfection whenever she appears at Harry's hallucinatory beck and call starts to get creepy. She is frozen at their moment of greatest love, her pregnancy test. She is eternally becoming-pregnant, without the more serious demands and side-effects of pregnancy—indeed, without ever giving birth to an actual child.

What Harry seems unwilling to grasp is that he is comforted by this immaculate state of his wife eternally becoming-pregnant, never actually fully at term or holding a real baby. This early period of pregnancy is more about the male's potency than it is about any activity on the woman's part; she is never more a vessel than at this stage where nothing shows yet, where the baby has not taken on any presence of its own, and where her body has not yet transformed. It is the honeymoon of pregnancy, so to speak. Babymaking burns like a slogan in subliminal proximity. Harry's daydreams of wallowing against her breasts clearly suggest a maternal quality that is still more for him than for the unborn. Likewise, the palm of a hand pushing through a blood-red, veiny tissue-wall, which reoccurs in *Fear X*, suggests the stopping of a pregnancy— a reference to the murder of the wife, certainly, but more ambiguous, since we do not know whose hand is pressing away the membranous wall. This pushing outward of a womblike space seems almost like a deus ex machina whose purpose is never resolved because Harry cannot bring himself to admit that the child frightened him and awakened his own longing to go back to the womb. The photo of a different mother and child which turns up among Harry's evidence of conspiracy in his wife's death adds a further sinister turn to the whole idea of motherhood; it is part of the conspiracy that "murders" the love of the woman which the male needs entirely for himself. (Thus, also, the obnoxious connoisseurship of "pregnancy porn" in *Bleeder*, further proof that the maternal figure of woman, even in advanced states of pregnancy, is still primarily there for the intimacy needs of her male partner.)

Something switches up in *Pusher II*, where Refn begins to question the nearly allegorical roles in which he has slotted his female characters: the giving, passive lover-victim, the hypersexual mother, the betraying worm inside a strong man's apple, etc. Suddenly gone is the macho sexual bravado of Tonny, who had boasted in *Pusher* that he needed four girls to service him in bed; instead Refn chooses to depict "the failure of sex and how [Tonny] is humiliated."[1] This failure crystallizes early on in the film, in a scene that is both uncomfortable and amusing. In a brothel room bathed in lurid red light, Tonny, who has just gotten out of prison, is trying to become erect in order to have sex with two prostitutes. Rather than help him, the women scathe his insufficient manhood. "What's with the Hobbit dick?" one cracks wise as Tonny frantically snorts coke and strokes himself. "Get up, super cock," he tells his flaccid member. He gets half hard, then the girls insist that he put on a condom, and he goes soft again. One girl performs fellatio on him for a few seconds then gives up, saying, "I can't do it, it's too limp." The girls snicker at Tonny as he begins to get angry, reminding them, "I'm fucking paying for this." But the joke on Tonny escalates as they pull out an enormous black dildo and offer it to him. This enrages Tonny even more, but there is no violence on his part; the emotional-sexual violence is all on the part of the prostitutes, somewhat like the eerie scene in Bergman's *The Serpent's Egg* (1978) where two German hookers mock the impotence of their dark-skinned pimp, who has presumably gone into hiding because of the rise of the S.S. Refn's scene is much more subtle and seemingly truer to life in that it is not meant to suggest total social apocalypse so much as an early skirmish in the battles over sexual rights which women and men engage in throughout *Pusher II*.

5. Nemesis   123

• • •

The most independent and sexually antagonistic woman in *Pusher II* is Charlotte (Anne Sørensen), who has had a baby while Tonny was in prison and now insists that it is his. Charlotte's friend Gry (Maria Erwolter) joins with Charlotte in female solidarity (we are reminded of the two prostitutes, who do not fight for or over Tonny but rather present a unified front of mockery and disdain): "She says you didn't pull out when she told you to." While the men distort, embellish and outright lie about their escapades with each other, women, among themselves, share their disappointments, their fiascos, and reach a weary consensus about the various local men in their lives. The women also overcome among each other the shame that the men often label them with. Gry says supportively about Charlotte, "I know half the town's fucked her, but she says it's your fault."

Charlotte does not love Tonny. She admits this openly to him; she simply wants him to give her money for her baby. Unlike Vic in *Pusher*, Charlotte is not a creature of lovelorn angst but rather of steely anger. In one memorable

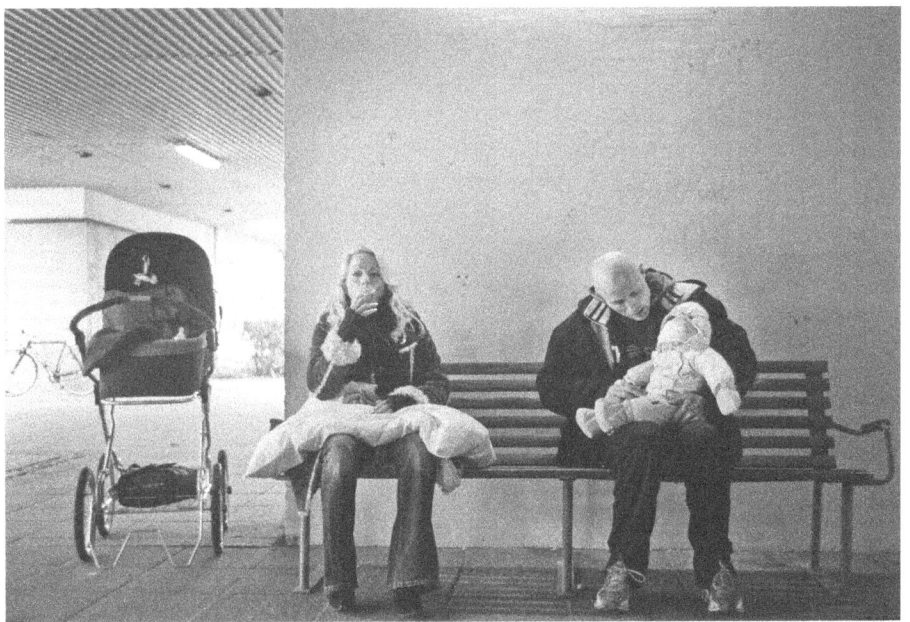

Pusher II offers complex female roles in which the women are not submissive to their gangster boyfriends and resent being tied down by motherhood. At the same time, the film shows poverty and drug addiction as factors more or less engineered by males to limit women's freedom. Here, Tonny (Mads Mikkelsen) holds the infant who might be his son, while the mother, Charlotte (Anne Sørensen), catches a smoke break.

shot we see her breastfeeding the baby while taking a hit off a spliff sticking out of the corner of her mouth. She displays no false sentimentality about being a mother: "This guy is like a leech, making my tits saggy. I just want him to sleep." It isn't that we cheer for Charlotte's harshness and lack of love; she is bracing, though, and she attains a screen presence equal to Refn's strong male characters.

We come to see that Charlotte, like Gry and the other women in *Pusher II*, has been fed drugs by the dealers in order to become an object of sexual control. With turnabout as fair play, she is now using her biology, her baby, as a bargaining chip in a war with men who only understand such leveraging and selfishness. The baby is her commodity, her endless shipment, so to speak, and she will get due market price. She now has something to hold over men's heads the way they have held cocaine over hers.

Naturally Tonny is bemused by this at best; his instinct is to deny Charlotte's threats and run away. At the same time, the longer he is around the baby, the more nurturing he becomes. In one scene, with the women fussing about not wanting to get themselves dirty, they foist off a diaper change on Tonny, who gamely and somewhat surprisingly rises to the challenge. Tonny and another tough gangster talk themselves through the unfamiliar process, and Tonny emerges on the other side with something like fatherly pride.

Tonny's painful journey must allow him to get past a resentment toward mothers in general in order to forgive his own deceased mother (also a drug-addicted prostitute) and thereby learn how to love. The "mommy" issues have been omnipresent in the film. In the brothel scene with the two prostitutes, Tonny asks them to perform sexually with each other ("like lesbians," he says naively) in order to arouse him; the women begin to kiss and fondle each other lustily, one of them calling the other "Mommy." This irritates Tonny immediately, but the girl keeps saying "Mommy" again and again until Tonny finally turns away.

This male fear of looking into the face of an attractive female and seeing "Mommy" is, of course, something we have noted in relation to *Bleeder*, with its reference to the trope from *Friday the 13th* movies in which the serial killer Jason can be deluded and defeated by a girl who convinces him that she is really his stern, domineering mother. The fear is reflexively transverse: on the one hand, the fear that the beautiful nubile girl of today will sooner or later become the "saggy-titted" shrew of tomorrow; and on the other hand, that one's own mother is a desirable sexual object (claimed by the father). This ongoing crisis reaches a head in *Pusher II* when Tonny's father, the Duke, asks him to kill a prostitute from the Duke's personal stable, also the mother of Tonny's young half-brother Valdemar. Tonny knocks on her door, she greets him with a smile and lets him in. "Did someone recommend me?" she asks. Her kindness to Tonny sways him; for the first time he understands the situation of women in this world, which he has been trying to deny, even in relation to his own mother. The drug-lord fathers want sons; but they don't want these sons tenderized and humanized by motherly care, for they will need the sons to do the dirty work. So they keep the mothers strung-out and working and always dying young, and they raise the young men to view their mothers with contempt. In this way, emotional and sexual dysfunction, passed along generationally, combine with perilous economic conditions to cement the son's descent into sociopathic criminality. In any event, with Tonny's embracing of his mother's limited options and even of a somewhat "feminized" and nurturing role (relative to the gangsters' macho culture) vis-à-vis the baby, the viewpoints of women grow to be as strong as men's in *Pusher II*.

• • •

British actor Richard E. Grant is Raymond, an avuncular playboy, somewhat like a warmer, less disturbing George Sanders; in silk bathrobe he is having a mid-morning tiff with an international supermodel-type. Offended, she huffs out of the room and a door slams. Then the doorbell rings a moment later and Raymond goes roaring toward the door, swinging the tasseled belt of his robe and saying, "I knew you'd be back." He opens the door with a smug and randy look on his face—and he finds, standing there, a little old lady, his aunt, Jane Marple (Geraldine McEwan). He quickly shifts emotional gears and kisses her on both cheeks, welcoming her, "My favorite aunt!" "Your *only* aunt, Raymond," Miss Marple corrects him.

It is a small moment early on in Refn's *Nemesis*, but one that is pregnant with what we might as well call "psychology." The psychosexual crisis occasioned by the intrusion of mothers and maternal figures into male-female relationships has popped up before in Refn's work, mainly *Bleeder*; but unlike in that film, Miss Marple is not so schematically taboo and unsettling. Or, rather, she occupies a realm that is on a par with that of Eros in terms of titillation: as a world-class detective, she brings mystery with her, murders most foul, a kind of telepathy with the dark side beneath her gentle and slightly dowdy exterior. Above all, she stands for no nonsense. This is why she quickly tames the "beast" in Raymond, whose errant passion for the supermodel type is suddenly swept away, displaced from him, as if this smart, shrewd, dignified old lady is really the woman he has been hoping to "meet" all along.

In general, in *Nemesis* (based on Agatha Christie[2]), male passions are dwarfed by female ones. Continuing the complexity and toughness of the women in *Pusher II* and *Pusher III*, *Nemesis* presents women as beings, active rather than merely reactive, capable of nuance and key-change, unapologetic for being difficult or harsh or sad, and usually all the more genuine in their compassionate moments for having visible flaws.

The story concerns a tour organized by a dead man for the benefit of bringing together a group of survivors who hold, among them, some sinister secrets. The sheer number of female characters is noteworthy: Jane Marple herself, termed a "goddess of retribution and righteous anger"; wealthy Amanda Dalrymple (Ronni Ancona), strident and sarcastic, popping amphetamine tablets; Margaret Lumley (Laura-Michelle Kelly), glamorous but quiet and high-strung; Rowena (Emily Woof), the anxious, smothering caretaker of a shellshocked, amnesiac husband (Will Mellor); Georgina (Ruth Wilson), the brisk, efficient Daffodil tour guide who becomes juicier out of her uniform; and a pair of nuns, the Mother Superior Agnes (Anne Reid) and Sister Clotilde (Amanda Burton). And behind all of these women is the legendary Verity Hunt (Kelly, in a dual role), long missing but never forgotten, animating the living characters with still-raw emotions of love, jealousy and foreboding.

The archetypal mystery convention of a group of strangers gathered together in one place because they share a (sometimes secret) connection becomes, in *Nemesis*, something more than conventional. We grasp in it the outline of something nearly karmic: proof of the intertwining of human existences and consciousnesses. *Nemesis* is an odd forebear to Refn's later masterpiece, *Only God Forgives*, which defines and explores this idea (specifically in terms of the Vedantic-Emersonian Oversoul) much more deeply.

Design-wise, the two films also share a fetish for elaborate indoor lighting. Nearly every scene contains lamps, often matching pairs, of every size, shape and style: brass lamps, lanterns, tall standards and small table lights, lamps with brocaded shades, lamps with flowered or ruched shades, pink shades, green shades, red and gold and wide and round. So many domesticated sources of light, representing the lies and deceptions which are already entangled around Verity's mysterious disappearance and which thicken further with the murder of Rowena. To truly see, as Miss Marple must endeavor to see through the murder suspects, something stronger and more natural is needed—natural outdoor lighting, which contrasts with the effete, perfectly placed lamps.

Nemesis makes good use of another archetypal mystery convention: the red-herring suspects so obviously suspicious that, of course, they weren't the ones who "dunnit," although they still keep us guessing. Even here we find that the women generally have more intriguing character arcs than the men. The speed-freaking man-eater Amanda alarms everyone with her snooty, paranoid tantrums; but by the end of the film she has relaxed and shown a softer side (she is lonely and pining for love—of Raymond). Margaret had seemed amoral and shady; but again the film finally reveals her as a woman in the shadow of her overbearing older mate (Johnny Briggs) and striving to please him. In *Nemesis*, wherever women are edgy, needy, contemptuous and contemptible— but above all *manipulative*—it is because they have been scarred by a lifetime of bad communication with the men in their world. This is like a more refined drawing-room version of the women whose men have hooked them on drugs and then pimped them out in *Pusher II*. Only Verity, the ageless, vanished paragon, seems a model of healthy and steady womanliness—and she is preserved in an impossible purity, gone missing while attempting to serve Saint Elspeth, patron saint of women who are stalked and killed by men whom they have rejected sexually.

Thus, at heart, female manipulativeness is a survival skill honed in self-protection. Miss Marple, too, is knowingly manipulative: when she wants to probe a suspect, she approaches him or her with a complimentary or concerned demeanor, winning trust. The film notes this with obvious awe of the elderly sleuth, allowing her to overpower everyone in turn in that nimble, kindly way that melts over them like the coolest of candlewax.

Nemesis is an exquisite gem with memorable images that are startling in their Hitchcockian clarity. In the nearly wordless prologue, a beautiful young woman cradles the head of a wounded pilot near a field of wildflowers, his parachute billowing in the breeze. A nun's habit draped around the straw face of a crude scarecrow is a succinct witticism that gives us pause. Rowena's husband walking in his sleep is Refn's most overt visual reference to the Frankenstein monster, limping heavily and stiffly down a shadowy hall, the scars of stitches visibly crisscrossing his reconstructed face. The lovers Michael (Dan Stevens) and Verity, firm in their resolve to run away together, are lit by a beam from a high, cross-shaped window, a touch worthy of the Old Masters.[3] Finally, there is the statue of Saint Elspeth, impaled by the rejected lover's spear, rising distracted and sordid above the dim cobwebbed altar of her abandoned church: the uncanny active embodiment of passive woman, acted upon, martyred, but summoning ever more martyrs in the name of unrequited passion, which does not need male ego or testosterone to incite the broken heart to crimes of vengeance.

– 6 –

Bronson

> *Interviewer*: And what about men of violence? You do follow very violent characters.
> *Refn*: Yeah, I know. That's what my mother always says.[1]
>
> It's like *Bronson* became an autobiography of my own life. — Refn[2]

We do not need to know much about "the real Charlie Bronson," the man accorded the notoriety of being Britain's most violent prison inmate, in order to appreciate Refn's excellent film about him; furthermore, one of Refn's achievements is to finally place this professional convict and brawler beyond our capacity to judge him. Unlike, say, Andrew Dominik's *Chopper* (2000), about Australia's most violent inmate, there is no attempt on Refn's part to ingratiate his film with "reality" of one kind or another. Dominik allows for long passages of dialogue in which Chopper's motivations and sense of self are fully talked out until they achieve a sadly mundane, even normalized quality. This kind of normalization process never occurs in *Bronson*. As wily and affecting as Chopper (Eric Bana) often is, he remains earthbound, a big, painfully straight lug, reckless and quirky but basically an average guy with modest ideas and ambitions. Indeed, the character of Chopper seems to step right out of the TV-doc mock-up that is his highest aspiration of success.

By contrast, Bronson could almost be Nosferatu, cut with Dorothy from *The Wizard of Oz*. He occupies a denser hieratic order. He emerges in Refn's film as pure phenomenon, a nightmare, a sprite; there is no ultimate bedrock reality to the character. This failure to cohere occurs at all levels of our identification with him: he is a failed petty criminal; he takes the name of a famous movie star; he serves time mainly for crimes committed inside prison, not against society per se; he is a masculine man who sometimes seems to think he is a woman; he is not reality TV but epic, expressionist theater. The film's symphonic construction artfully disguises the fact that Bronson is a protagonist with no arc, no timeline; he is no different in the end than he was at the beginning, and no less opaque.

Various misbegotten figures circle through Bronson's aura, but not one of these manages to settle him in our minds. At different times we think of Jake La Motta (Robert De Niro) in *Raging Bull*, David Merrick (John Hurt) in *The Elephant Man* (1980), Franz Biberkopf (Günter Lamprecht) in *Berlin Alexanderplatz* (1980), Rupert Pupkin (De Niro) in *King of Comedy* (1983), Mickey (Woody Harrelson) in *Natural Born Killers* (1994), even (as has been pointed out by reviewers) Ophüls' Lola Montès (Martine Carol). Refn's "Bronson"—and here we might pay an initial compliment to star Tom Hardy's spellbinding inhabiting of the role—knows that he is all of those people and others too; he winks at all of them in turn, impersonates them deadpan or with laughter, then freezes once again into that impenetrable, self-contained enigma, much like the way novelist Roberto Bolaño once described how a "mask of ice clamped itself over" a character's formerly friendly face.[3] Mask of ice, indeed, for Hardy is beautifully minimalist, and *Bronson* might be the first film ever made about a statue—but a statue that we come to recognize, fear and even love.

Appropriately, since we are asked to fall in love with a statue, or at least pay close attention to one, the film makes us simply stare at Bronson for long moments, watching for minute changes in his facial expression or posture. It is the rapt gaze of Warhol's *Blow Job* (1964), trained on a man leaning back against a wall—a gaze focused on reaction rather than action. So for the film's nearly two hour running time we are shown Bronson going into rages, foaming at the mouth, beating people and getting beaten down by groups of prison guards in riot gear. Furthermore, Bronson is frequently naked, physically exposed, where other characters, including the guards he fights, remain clothed. Yet there is a distance between the chronically violent Bronson and us, his audience, that is never quite closed. He is fixed, a fact that we must wholly accept without holding out hope that he will "change" somehow. If, as Schopenhauer maintained, even a stone possesses will,[4] then Bronson is that stone, teaching us a Zen-like appreciation of its obdurateness, drawing us into his mission to remain uniquely true to himself.

Schopenhauer wrote: "It amounts to this, that by what we do, we know what we are, and by what we suffer we know what we deserve."[5] Quoting Seneca's dictum, "Will cannot be learned,"[6] Schopenhauer asserts that individuality exists all at once, a priori, in and through the will, a thing-in-itself rather than something which accretes gradually through learned phenomenological experience: "Hence it is that every man achieves only that which is irrevocably established in his nature, or is born with him."[7] Thus, to the extent that will defines a man's character, character is revealed, known, all at once and is unalterable.

In his monomaniacal commitment to lashing out at everyone around him, Bronson reveals himself as Schopenhauerian Man—stuck with a will he cannot change or control, at the brute level, spiritually undeveloped. He is not merely unwilling but constitutionally unable to alter the direction of his own will. Not even Bronson can explain his own violence; it would be like asking someone to explain the color of his eyes. We might say that Bronson's own violent nature is all he has to believe in. The world he comes from might be, as he tells us in voiceover, "nothing wonky" (meaning he did not grow up abused); his background is certainly nothing special, an undistinguished middle-class life. In the film's opening shots, where we see Bronson as a child at school, we are not even certain which child he is among others in a crowded hallway until the scene where he stands up in class and assaults his teacher. An act of violence makes him stand out, *identifies* Bronson to us—and to himself.

So violence becomes a constant Protean touchstone in the film; through violence Bronson puts together—strings out—a fragile identity. The stone does not move, it remains a stone. That is its contribution to the world, its reputation, its energy.

• • •

The violence in *Bronson* is male on male, and often falls into recognizable patterns: the boxing match, the fist fight, etc., acts of what we might call consensual violence, which can even be considered by some as rites of passage or examples of homosociality. Then there are less recognizable patterns: Bronson alone, taking on a phalanx of armed prison guards in riot gear; Bronson held down by a battery of orderlies and given an unwanted intravenous sedation in his buttocks; Bronson taking his prison art-therapy teacher hostage. This can be characterized as nonconsensual violence: one-sided assaults, some of which (like the sedation scene) are staged so as to remind us of rapes or gang rapes. This type of nonconsensual violence is at the outer limits of homosociality, yet it is so fearsome that it defines the terms of all inter-male relations (in which males appropriate the right to keep each other in line, teach each other lessons, etc.) so as not to come within striking distance of this darker side of homosociality.

However, there is an ordering principle behind this radical mix of seething honor code and obsessional madness, a testosterone anarchy which overruns and overturns the homosocial sphere. This kind of nonconsensual violence (as well as a good bit of the consensual type) is, in fact, a way in which males undertake to give birth to each other outside of natural matrilineal biology. It is a deconstruction and re-authorship of the external and internal body of another male, a destruction meant on some level to be regenerative if not distinctly pedagogical. The terror at the heart of this is not simply getting beaten or losing, but of one man being forced to think of another man as his father-and-mother, so to speak, with that supreme power over him. It is like a fetus minus the womb, a child-development without a stage of nurture-bonding and affection. This male birthing process, devoid of maternal tenderness but constantly circling authoritarian concepts of *love*, is one of the subjects of the novel and movie *Fight Club*, for example, in which a fight between two men is always an exchange in which one man determines or influences the course of the other man's life. At the heart of this is the idea that surviving a beating will reawaken in a man that humbling gratitude for life which the newborn baby cannot feel vis-à-vis his mother, having a still undeveloped consciousness of life and no past history of regrets to overcome. The lucky baby forgets the birth trauma and can take for granted that he is regularly given what he needs, primarily by the mother. The fight, on the other hand, is like a secondary trauma (secondary to the birth trauma) which only men, ostensibly, know when and how to administer.

We would not be wrong to think of the excoriating severity of some religious attempts to be "born again," particularly in ceremonies where the seeker is physically hit, beaten or held underwater by the religious leader. To force the male body to stop in its tracks and acknowledge the presence of something outside of itself, and stronger than itself, truly is an act commensurate with religious conversion at its most aggressive—and presumably demonstrative that the soul is real, hidden inside there somewhere, waiting to be tested. Something is "saved" within the body even as the body itself gets damaged or even destroyed; power accrues to the glory of the violent one who inflicts the scourging and "cleansing" through direct physical means, and only belatedly to the assaulted one who, by forgiving and somehow changing, acknowledges his "place" within the shared meaning of the ordained symbolic social order.

Indeed, given the fact that fighting is brutal and destructive, its regenerative aspect is obscure and essentially driven by the same kind of imaginative faith as all metaphysics are, as when Deepak Mehta says of religious circumcision, "the wound constitutes the metaphysical body."[8] The wound, localized in circumcision but potentially anywhere in cases of male-against-male fighting and assault, designates the body as more than a body, or as the zone of invisible energies where spiritual lessons can be imparted. One batters the outside of the male body in hopes that there is something extra-physical which is reachable within that body. Slang names for beating someone indicate precisely this: "to teach someone a lesson"; "to put the fear of God in someone"; "to put someone in his place"; "to do what his Daddy should have done long ago." Again, these are symbolic, not material, hierarchies, and the entire idea of the fight is a perversion of Schopenhauer's idea of overcoming self-will through the shedding of ego. True, it all comes down to matched wills, but it only serves to place man on the helpless level of the stone again, devoid of the ability to rise.

Suddenly we understand that Bronson's dreary middle-class life is by no means irrelevant or inexplicable in terms of his relentless crusade (largely futile and pathetic) of trying to break and change other men. Beyond brute physical domination, these are not fights that can be decisively won by anyone within the film. Rarely have we seen such epic fight scenes with so little rooting interest or tension. Yet they do afford a certain spectacle, and Refn makes them cinematic to a heightened degree. Sometimes he films them in wide angle and slow motion as if they were battles from *The Iliad*; one brawl is magnificently edited to the crystalline strains of Scott Walker's sepulchral and lyrical song "The Electrician." These effects help us to see that the fights are not strictly physical but again metaphysical, a groping for sacred space (the Walker song refers to a protagonist traversing through a sanctified realm) in the midst of grubby reality. Just as there is no victory or reward at the end of these fights, so they are primarily leavings of the body rather than regroundings or reaffirmations of it in pseudo-spiritual awakening. Redemption may be sullenly, stubbornly pursued by Bronson, but the result is more like the Keystone Kops, a ludicrous stripping away of dignities.

Indeed, everything physical in *Bronson* has an aura of disgust, drool pouring down a chin, a kick to the crotch, even the unlikely tinkling teacups which Bronson serves up to guards and fellow inmates; whereas everything that is filtered through nonrealist or extradiegetic approaches (the running conceit that Bronson is telling his story as a kind of Master of Ceremonies to an attentive full house in formal dress; the faux documentary footage of prison riots; the highly theatrical use of music such as the Walker song and the Pet Shop Boys' "It's a Sin," as well as a number of bel canto arias) has the effect of proclaiming: This is life, this is vindication, legacy, the great reward.

Bronson, then, is more a mental than a physical being, and his ubiquitous muscular body mediates between a suspect realism and overwhelming, rapturous non-realism. Only Bronson seems to possess a real body and a face; the guards are not only clothed in uniforms but masked with riot helmets, or else grouped so closely that they seem to have no identities. This only serves to heighten Bronson's already exaggerated, kaleidoscopic emotional life. (It must be said that a lot of focus is placed on Hardy's expressive eyes, often staring soulfully into the camera in lingering close-ups which pointedly exist outside of the film's action: Bronson watching us, so to speak, as part of the world that has excluded and bypassed him.) This is the male body as grand opera, rippling, glowing, bursting with formal meanings (muscles) that are as overdetermined and estranging as someone bursting into song. It is overdeveloped form, efficient only in the service of esoteric pursuits. In a word, it is *beautiful*. In its chilly, lonely splendor, Bronson's body leads more naturally to thoughts of Baroque refinement than to, say, the World Wrestling Federation.

The muscular male body in action cinema has become a subject of recent academic interest. Often it is seen as a synecdoche of white male cultural insecurity in the wake of civil rights and feminism. Yvonne Tasker writes: "When all else fails, then, it is the body of the hero ... that is the place of last resort.... [T]he body of the hero is the sole space that is safe, and even this space is constantly under attack."[9] To possess a male body, in Tasker's analysis, is to have a refuge, as well as to draw the supposed fire that white males can use to feed reactionary fantasies of being hunted and disenfranchised.

Of course, extreme muscularity itself *is* usually overdetermined. Yet Bronson represents an idea of power that would not seem powerful to most sane people; his extended confinement is hardly mitigated by the fact that he physically attacks his warders and guards. He does not take refuge in his body like a defended citadel but instead exposes himself to greater and greater threat, for which he gains no compensatory satisfactions. His enemies are provisional, random in a way; and he goes to excessive lengths to ensure that he remains definitively restrained. He may strive to win this or that battle, but his ultimate aim seems to be to lose whatever "war" his life has become. Increasingly throughout the film, the moment of defeat crystallizes Bronson for us, reveals him more and more in ways too bleakly fatalistic to qualify as fodder for reactionary fantasy.

Bronson deliberately makes his body a site of weakness rather than power. Its musculature is nearly vestigial. Something larger than the body is already experienced as unfree. This unfree state means that prison is arbitrary; for Bronson, it is no different from a "hotel room." Bronson rebels against what Nietzsche called the degenerate position of having "to extort one's rights" rather than be granted them as natural, or rather than fighting for them openly.[10] Again and again, guards square off with Bronson in these alienated, generic prison spaces—this is the "calling" which Bronson claims he was "made for," a sacred calling as in the manner of saints and of classical artists. He will somatize and give real shape to the inchoate weakness which he already feels, the special disorder of the one who follows his destiny, who must live by learning how to be himself, inventing and testing everything, unable to take any part of himself for granted. Will may be innate and reflexive, but for anything to become this focused and single-minded, there must be a continued overcoming of that force of consciousness which is manifested for us all in ordinary doubt—doubt which can be nothing more than a reflex of the social animal who feels bad about refusing to stay in line. This social-animal reflex must be overcome in order to return to and embrace the innate—innate will, innate identity and being.

In *Bronson*, then, the male body is an uneasy subject, chronically complicit in letting itself be reduced to object-status in order to nudge it up over the barrier of doubt. The convict is perhaps the perfect emblem of this kind of body, one which becomes more enclosed and invisible the more it is revealed and watched; and one which achieves cock-eyed "freedom" through courting the absolute repression of its jailers (this is the central motif of *Cool Hand Luke*, for example). Tasker asserts that the prison drama, as a genre, "has repeatedly been used to provide a narrative excuse for the hero's nakedness.... The prison is also, crucially, a site of punishment, a place designed to separate off those elements perceived as specially undesirable or dangerous."[11] It has become a rather cheap thrill, in prison movies, to see the obligatory scene in which the new inmate is brought before his captors and made to strip completely nude. The prisoner's nudity in relation to the dressed captors and guards creates a sense of vulnerability and shame (we are almost always reminded of the prisoner's anal cavity in these scenes, which must be checked for contraband and which thus becomes public rather than private space) that is permissible only because the prisoner is "bad" and therefore beyond shame or concern. Official punishment disguises the brutal intention to dehumanize, to control.

As Tasker states, the display of muscular prowess takes place within "the territory of identity, the process of the forging and reforging of ways of 'being human,' or of 'being a man,' in which a point of certainty is never ultimately arrived at."[12] This implies that masculinity is a kind of zero sum game in which the compulsively driven male fears being brought back to zero again and must therefore gamble all on a greater and greater share (that macho doubling-down on bad luck which Frank pursued in *Pusher*). Refn reveals Bronson as the pure fist which Nietzsche suggests is the only honorable way of greeting a world that demands to know why we are as we are, and that relentlessly judges us: "Honest things, like honest men, do not carry their reasons in their hands in such fashion. It is indecent to put forth all the five fingers."[13] Or the five fingers, separated like the senses and forced to be in conflict with each other, are fragile as an insect's antennae. But when one closes them together in a fist, when one obtains solidarity of the fingers, of the senses, then one can put them forth *as an idea*, a fully fledged reason in itself binding the disparate senses into harmony.

• • •

In *Discipline and Punish*, Michel Foucault states that it became necessary in the early days of prisons for the punitive arm of justice to achieve an autonomy from the judicial one. He calls this "the Declaration of Carceral Independence" and views it as a stage in which the prison system could claim complete control over its inmates.[14] Bronson represents a kind of extreme test case of this carceral independence: he is originally sentenced to seven years for petty theft, but because of his assaults on guards and other inmates his sentence is doubled. This further demonstrates the idea of the prison as a separate, alternate world within (or even outside of) the true world; this prison world establishes its own truth claims. The separations by which the prison world attempts to certify its power are manifold but always come down to the monitoring and spontaneous judgment of behaviors: this is "the sovereignty of knowledge possessed by the warder." As in Bronson's case, it is finally the prison that determines the convict's sentence and duration, not the original judiciary: "The juridical gravity of a crime does not at all have the value of a univocal sign for the character of the convict, whether or not he is capable of reform."[15]

Prison is where the claims of humanism are comprehensively turned against the human. No human activity is foreign or unnamed within the prison, which has "seen it all." But this is not to celebrate or liberate human energies, instead it serves to bring those energies to complete submission. It incubates the full growth of antisocialness in the prisoner to complete definition in order to keep him perpetually segregated from society. It knows him only as a record of crimes and punishments—this, in itself, becomes a kind of economy outside of the capitalist system which reigns in civilian life. The strange debits and credits (crimes and punishments) substitute for capital within a framework of semi-public ambition, a kind of backwards ladder to "success." Hence, the phenomenon of someone becoming famous for being "the most violent prison inmate."

If anything, crime is muffled and allowed for by being countenanced not strictly as a breaking of laws but as an alternative economy, an alternative society, an alternative law. It is often said that we live in times that have reached a nadir of amorality, in which criminal violence is no longer the exception but the rule; however, this is a phenomenon which Nietzsche traces back to the dawn of human reason, the ancient Greece of Socrates. "Everywhere," Nietzsche writes, "the instincts were in anarchy; everywhere people were within an ace of excess: the monstrum in animo was the universal danger ... the universal trouble—namely, that nobody was any longer master of himself, that the instincts became mutually antagonistic."[16] Like the senses, represented by the five feeling fingers held hostage by a lack of liberating synaesthesia, which turns out to be, among other things, a moral transvaluation. For each sense corresponded to specific sins—to commit one of which was grievous enough; to commit two or three in tandem, and to thereby naturalize their synergistic congruities, was nothing less than meta-sinfulness. With the birth of reason came the notion that we were all sinking fast into a state of hopeless unreason; it was reason's figurative carte blanche, as it were, its own ace in the hole. Because "every yielding to the instincts, to the unconscious, leads *downwards*," Nietzsche writes, the "tyrant of reason" arises to crush wayward impulses by subjecting them to the "*absurdly rational*"; but this is "pathologically conditioned," the result of "a desperate situation."[17]

The enclosed world of prison, cut off from every other world and enforced as the only possible environment, as well as a daily drudgery from which one longs to escape (even in the form of death), becomes a powerful metonymy for the way religion (as Nietzsche charged) miscategorizes the real world and the better world—the world to come, the world of an eternal elsewhere:

> To fable about "another" world than this has no meaning at all, unless an instinct of calumniation, disparagement, and aspersion of life is powerful in us: if that be the case we take revenge on life, with the phantasmagoria of "another," "better" life.[18]

Prison exemplifies what Nietzsche traced as the movement by which "the 'true world' finally became a fable," by the way that a powerful, immanent truth was degraded into a weary, intangible and fantastical "hope." In the real world, hopes have the power to become truths: "The true world attainable by the wise, the pious, and the virtuous man—he lives in it, he embodies it."[19] In the fabulistic world, vain, unfulfilled hopes are made to substitute for truth, "the old sun still, but shining only through mist and skepticism."[20] Or sealed off, as it is for the criminal: in all the prison scenes in *Bronson* where windows are visible, they are always remotely placed and overlit with bright-white artificial lighting, blank and even sinister, like a bullying heaven. (This picks up from the tension between "free" and imprisoned domestic light in *Nemesis*.)

That fable world demands Bronson's sacrifice. As Adorno states, in Nietzsche's conception of the fable world there is always an element of resigned sacrifice, of amor fati (love your fate).[21] Adorno writes that

> the origin of amor fati might be sought in a prison. Love of stone walls and barred widows is the last resort of someone who sees and has nothing else to love.

Both are cases of the same ignominious adaptation which, in order to endure the world's horror, attributes reality to wishes and meaning to senseless compulsion.[22] The prison becomes an objective correlative for the tendency of Christianity, in Nietzsche's view, to denigrate and cast aspersions on this, the only world, in the name of an amorphous, unreal elsewhere which is moreover synonymous with the moral judgment of ruling elites. The real world becomes a dire quagmire whose only purpose is to accustom one to the threat or promise of an eternity to come. (Foucault cites the Pennsylvania Quakers, for whom the prison cell ideally represented "hell in anticipation" and "the very cradle of blessed immortality."[23]) We recognize in Bronson something of a departure from prior Refn heroes who failed to break out of a toxic system, even to the point of finally dying in its name: Frank in *Pusher*, Harry in *Fear X*. Unable to exert their own will over circumstances, they told themselves they were acting with the borrowed will of a greater meaning: business for the former; justice for the latter. With Bronson, this self-deception is rendered impossible. He understands that his will is pointless and meaningless, but he refuses to stop exerting it. Bronson's lonely failure is preferable to him than an ironic capitulation to the very system that would remove his will altogether and thus remove him entirely from the world.

Bronson, in refusing to bow down before his captors, restores Nietzschean truth to the idea of hope. "In the end hope," Adorno writes, "wrested from reality by negating it, is the only form in which truth appears. Without hope, the idea of truth would be scarcely even thinkable, and it is the cardinal untruth, having recognized existence to be bad, to present it as truth simply because it has been recognized."[24] Unlike the tamed circus panther in Rilke's famous sonnet, who comes to see no world between and beyond the bars, Bronson never stops seeing the world, his world, our world (which is also to say: the idea of a better world within this flawed, immanent world). The recreated docudrama footage of a prison riot which Bronson instigated during one of his sentences is a moving tribute to this radical immanence; the prisoners have managed to reach the roof of the prison, where they have a kind of basic freedom in the open air, however limited.

As if to punish specifically Bronson's wish to defend the true immanent world against the fable of another, better one, the prison wardens shrink his physical space more and more. Bronson is brought back to zero or less, again and again, confined more and more intensively (straitjackets, restraints, smaller and smaller cages, etc.) or released back onto the streets to be revealed as the ridiculous misfit that he is: striding down the street in a three-piece suit that is at least one size too tight, clutching his suitcase like a baby blanket, or cowering on the bottom during sex with an aggressive female. The elusive point is the anarchist's realization of true and total freedom, which cannot occur within any known system, and which never materializes for Bronson except fleetingly when he is calling down on himself an impossible fight against a herd of guards. Again, muscularity is finally not the anxiety of the system (nationalist, judicial, military, etc.) expressing itself in the individual male body; it is the anxiety of the lone male body against the oppressive system, which is always better protected, just as Bronson's stripped, muscular body is always outmanned and outgunned.

Refn always problematizes Bronson's musculature and reveals it as *never-enough*: bloody, begrimed, spastic, drooling, isolated, prone, lying in slop and sewage, or literally in the dark. Thus, *Bronson* extends and tries to overturn that obligatory prison moment which Tasker calls attention to—the prisoner's stripping for his captors—into an endlessly reified series of confrontations in which the protagonist, in some form of undress, comes into violent contact with uniformed and armored captors. It is like a restless, unforgiving vengeance against an original state of vulnerability. And during the course of these con-

More than any of Refn's previous films, *Bronson* (2008) has a sophisticated, multi-leveled aesthetic, mingling formal theatrical artifice with nearly choreographed scenes of lurid violence set to Verdi and Scott Walker. Refn also employs complex tracking shots to illustrate the confining vicious-circles experienced by a terminally violent prison inmate, viscerally played by Tom Hardy (pictured, right).

frontations Bronson becomes soiled, the soles of his bare feet noticeably blackened in one scene, emblemizing the way in which the stripped prisoner stands in (in a kind of Victorian social-imaginary) for damaged physical-sexual goods.

Tasker observes, "The performance of a muscular masculinity within the cinema draws attention to both the restraint and the excess involved in 'being a man,' the work put into the male body."[25] In *Bronson* we often see Hardy clenching his fists and letting his face harden into a monolith, a flat-line on a heart machine. The impassivity is stoical, or schizophrenic; but it often interrupts, or gives way to, more maniacal expressions, such as a frozen grin or a slurry of silent, mirthless laughter. With these other, complicating emotions, we see Bronson as more aware of playing to his audience, that shadowy, formal-dress crowd whose responses are as shifting and sudden as the grimaces and spread-eagle poses which Bronson offers up. He plays every possible emotion, all the time, as if uncertain which one is expected or believable. In one dizzying sequence Bronson sits looking down with fists clenched as his young wife visits him in prison; then we see him going alone into his cell and beginning to weep, one hand covering his face; then we see him onstage, in clown make-up and a tuxedo, giggling like a jackal on a jag. On one obvious formal level we recognize all of these actions as being "acted" to one extent or another; Bronson's cackling self-mockery is no more or less sincere than his private tears, and both, of course, are being displayed for an audience. It is as if Bronson's yearning for fame, combined with a certain inner emptiness, his voided humanity, has caused him to live out every moment as if it were an archetypal moment in a spectacle. Here is the scene where the Young Convict weeps bitterly in his solitude: the detail will be remembered as a crucial part of the accumulating legend because it is already part of a generic (and legendary) convict-narrative.

This is not the same as saying that Bronson merely represents the nth degree of a new kind of aberrant norm in a profoundly abnormal age. We are meant to see Bronson as someone who would have been an extreme case in any age, hence an enigma. And enigmas, when we have contained them and rendered them harmless, are inevitably clowns. Just as Bronson's emotional displays often devolve in self-mocking laughter, so his conscious attack mode in its impossible repetition becomes slapstick. We wait for the frenzy to begin, or start up again. Refn plays much of the fighting for comedy: the guards club him to the ground and Bronson seems to wave them off, surrendering, but in the instant that they begin to stand down, he tries to slip through their ranks and escape the cell, still naked, shiny with soot and blood and feces. Of course, the guards surround him and club him down again. But that fake-out is a moment of wit that signals us to see this as a kind of uncontainable sport, or at least a sharpening of playful and creative instincts.

• • •

Bronson is an exemplar of what has been called a "surplus-active character type. This implies a repression of passivity."[26] It is rooted in an extreme fear of being passive: "To be passive again is to stress one's helplessness, to be waiting for the next blow and wondering if the humiliation will be bearable."[27] The phobia of weakness is potentially paralyzing and includes the terror of being somehow complicit in, responsible for, the assaults which the world carries out against oneself. One must control everything, and, furthermore, one is plagued by the sense that this should be within one's capacities. However, there is an internal awareness that even if one beats the world, so to speak, one is still shirking the most difficult task: confronting passivity in all its terrors. This is the Achilles' heel of the surplus-active character. Bronson uses surplus activity, in all its mayhem, to draw negative attention to himself and place himself in a position where greater strength is brought to bear so as to render him, finally, definitively passive, against all his will, a position in which he is forced to bear the pain and humiliations of passivity, to go all the way through it to the other end.

There is something manic-depressive, if not suicidal, about Bronson's bizarre self-expenditure of flashing rage and strength only to be slammed back into his true place, a place of control and punishment, symbolized by solitary confinements, elaborate restraints, and smaller and smaller cages. It takes on the inevitability of purgatorial myths in which people who have stepped too far across the line are condemned to eternally confront their own helplessness, the undoing of their hubristic plans: Sisyphus with the uphill boulder; Prometheus disemboweled nightly by eagles. Bronson exemplifies Maurice Blanchot's intriguing distinction between passive and active submission, the latter having, in its violence, a creative and regenerative function, like that "abnegation understood as the abandonment of the self, a relinquishment of identity, refusal which does not cleave to refusal but opens to failure, to the loss of being, to thought."[28] Active submission meets its overpowering foe more than halfway, and in doing so, becomes an agency. Thus, Bronson, in a sense, condemns himself to the solitary confinements and extra punishments, makes himself something more (or simply other) than his nominal identity of prisoner. In this way he retains something of the nub, as it were, as Blanchot defines true passivity as "being when being is worn down past the nub."[29]

We might think of it in this way: passivity is enforced by the penal system, therefore it is Bronson's default position, his artificially conferred essence. The only way he can retain any personal sovereignty is to engage in Blanchot's active submission. His life still takes place outside of a fulfilled existence, outside of hope, in that forlorn place where "destroyed men come and go,"[30] but Bronson is not defined by this afflicted state to the extent that he revolts against it and forces his oppressors to reveal themselves at every turn.

For Blanchot, passivity is a condition of grotesque loneliness; it denotes "the servitude of the slave bereft of a master,"[31] finally no longer appreciated even to the slight degree that a master's witness and approval might bestow. The passive slave no longer needs even to be watched over by another because he has fully internalized all regulations. The form of his servitude is repeated not only as a meaningless gesture but as one which the self must accept as its own sustaining mission—it is the self turned against itself. This is the truly intolerable element of complete passivity and what Bronson seeks to avoid at all costs. By constantly starting brawls, Bronson keeps himself surrounded by external enemies who can take the blame for his pain; he keeps the otherwise remote, invisible eyes of "justice" steadily trained on him, still their slave but at least acknowledged as such in all unfairness. His continued existence is marked, attended upon, defined in a way that it would not be in that truly passive submission, "which has no purpose, no end, no starting principle."[32]

Bronson has more than a little to do with existentialist man's need to provide a meaning and purpose for his own life, since the ones handed down to him seem absurd, ill-fitting, or tragic. He epitomizes what both Eugenio Barba and Lesley Stern have written about "the decided body." Barba, who coined the phrase, was speaking in terms of the physicality of radical theater; Stern is more interested in how the phrase can be applied to philosophical issues of identity. "This body," she writes, "performs by virtue of training, discipline, almost as an involuntary essence."[33] She is referring, among other things, to the body of the boxer, whose training must become a kind of second nature without ever losing consciousness of itself as a set of skills to be summoned at will: "It is to do with the particular way of deploying energy, and includes context—the presence of an audience, the marking out of a quasi-ceremonial or ritualistic space."[34] The Western body is so highly overdetermined by the process of labor that it has no spontaneity to act without immense premeditation. Part of the fascination with athleticism, with muscular physiques, is that we can temporarily attribute the thrilling feats of which these bodies are capable with an *instinct*, one which illumines and ennobles humanity itself, rather than remembering that we are seeing the production of a long, strict tutelage in the perfecting of shape, reflexes, timing. We want to see athleticism—or cathartic acting, for that matter—as an escape from the regime of work, when in fact it is simply a different kind of labor turned toward a seemingly more individualistic accomplishment.

Thus, Bronson's melees can be seen as conceptual or situationist performance-art pieces. He is one of those men whom Joel Black calls "typically active, demonstrative exhibitionists whose 'work' can be regarded as an extreme form of performance art."[35] Here we are led to consider that *Bronson* might be Refn's self-portrait as an artist. When he made the film Refn had come through a long embattled period in which he had to recoup the losses from *Fear X* and in some ways reinvent himself as a director. Bronson's demeaning incarcerations might reflect the idea of cinematic art held hostage to the need for raising capital, for making a profit, for placating powers that be; this need weaves through all the times in-between actual filmmaking, as well as during the filmmaking process, and becomes inextricably bound up with the director's creative energies. The rage and frustration that build up from this process release themselves in films that are predominated by those tense, conflicted emotions. If one can thrive on such frustration and rage one might have a leg up, so to speak, in the world of current cinema. The revenge for all of the waiting around, ideally, goes into the making of the film itself, its ultimate aesthetic. All great aesthetics within commercial art forms are essentially aesthetics of revenge: willful obscurity, cheeky and even disrespectful casting, unaligned narratives, form as a violent reclaiming of the creative act from the sensible monetary demands placed upon it. The bouncy, "feel-good" film has never seemed so hypocritical and morbid as it does today under the sweating tension of capital raised and gambled; the fervent prayers of box office and opening night. Violent films are not merely a way of insuring return on investment, they are a commentary on the seething nature of investment itself and the artist's haphazard reduction to businessman. The visual style of Refn's film attacks the expectations of mild, humble "good behavior" in much the same way Bronson attacks the same expectations placed on him by the penal system.

Indeed, Refn's cinematic instincts are sharp and sure in *Bronson*, perhaps nowhere more so than in the numerous elegant tracking shots which bear a strange lucidity in the midst of an often frenetic film. Technically, these dense patterns display a real understanding of how the tracking shot is not merely decorative but a way to build tension and even create symmetrical beginnings and endings for small dramatic arcs within the main narrative. For example, the camera tracks with Bronson as he staggers toward an exit, only to be waved back by orderlies; a few scenes later, like the resolution of a melodic line in music, the camera tracks Bronson from the opposite angle as he is dragged toward this same exit by the same orderlies—dragged not to freedom but to a new sentence in an insane asylum. Through the spatial organization of these two book-ended tracking shots, the film establishes Bronson's yearning for freedom and its ironic, false fulfillment. Likewise, the prisoner whom Bronson assaults is introduced to us entering the day room in a tracking shot from left to right; in the later scene where he is nearly killed by Bronson, he reenters the same dayroom from the right this time, and the camera tracks him left. This graceful symmetry gives the assaulted inmate's fate an inevitable air, like keeping an appointed date with destiny. The attack almost seems instigated by the perfect alignment of the prowling camerawork as much as by Bronson himself.

In this veiled portrait of the artist, Refn seems to discover one of his great themes—that art is "an act of violence." This is one of the disorganizing principles that we looked at in the introduction to this book. Far from being destructive of society, violent crime and art refashion the bonds of society by selectively snipping at them. They raise awareness of the public self and its relation to others; they strengthen lines of social force by enabling the public to play judge, or critic. Nonetheless, what Bronson produces, as art and as crime, is a gesture that cannot be explained, much less expiated; for there is none of the blame or guilt which might attach itself to Bronson's destructiveness in the form of linguistic meaning, dogma, conscious will. Bronson is as free of responsibility as an involuntary reflex. Refn's artistry assumes all of the responsibility by choosing Bronson as subject—again, we see the anarchist at work. Of course, this is art that refuses to stem from some sublimation of antisocial impulses; it is the Nietzschean genius of reckless self-expenditure, the river that "involuntarily overflows its banks,"[36] and which betokens what Nietzsche calls hardness: "For all creators are hard.... The noblest only is perfectly hard."[37]

In his refusal of sublimation, Bronson is also refusing to internalize the Foucauldian panopticon, the self-censoring structure at the heart of the punitive social order. This extends beyond mere prison culture into the realm of all interaction within an ostensibly free society. Sublimation is bypassed in favor of a consistent self-truth which absorbs all new data into its foundational antisocial essence whose primary purpose is fighting. Indeed, if we note the women and the seemingly gay-coded men in the film, they represent the only new data that can occasion a movement toward sublimation, or at least restraint; and thus it is possible to view them not as new data per se but as part of Bronson's foundational essence, so to speak. There is a part of Bronson which seems almost female; he attacks men almost in the way of a wounded or violated woman who has the physical prowess to stand up to males. This is reinforced by the theatrical entr'actes, during a number of which we see Bronson interrogating himself, dressed as half man, half woman, turning first one side to the camera, then the other. This is not the signal of a fully fledged orientation but a grotesque piece of business meant to reference those "bearded lady" hermaphroditic sideshow attractions whose bodies are shaved on one side and smooth on the other, whose hair is long on one side and short on the other, and who wear specially tailored outfits in which half of a tux has been stitched up to half of a dress. (This is exactly how Bronson appears in one scene of the film.) Bronson's sometime androgyny is also aligned with criminal insanity, since the hermaphroditic self-dialogue occurs around the revelation that Bronson is being moved from prison to a maximum security insane asylum.

However, we can see in this female side an affirmation of Bronson's removal from patriarchal authority: he displays himself as being, to a strong degree, outside of patriarchy and even victimized by it. In the feminist anthology *Kiss Me Deadly*, Lesley Stern writes about the masculine hero's internalization of the femme fatale's status as "bad-fatal object" in film noir, after which he must find a way to continue to uphold patriarchal hegemony in the face of his own alienated weakness: violence is "a repetitive attempt to negate the horror opened by this internalized bad-object. The desperation, obsession and violence are born of engagement in a game that can never be mastered."[38] Likewise, Bronson's masculinity is rabid and self-destructive even as he upholds a violent rejection of all-male orders. Coming into contact with other males, Bronson becomes female in a spirit of sheer opposition, then lashes out to protect his own internalized femaleness.

The dilemma is this: we do not know for certain whether he fights because he already feels at a disadvantage, the way of justice, or whether he fights in order to place himself at a disadvantage, the way of masochism. Perhaps there is an affinity between these seemingly contradictory purposes? In order to seek justice, one must first be able to see oneself as having been harmed or betrayed; for a tough man, this admission might be difficult to get over. One must ask for compensation and at the same time prove that one is deserving of that compensation because of insult and injury, a double process of humiliation. This factor of humiliation, the admission of having been victimized and then the uncertainty that the claim will be credited, gives us insight into Bronson. Possibly it requires a certain degree of what I would call healthy masochism ("healthy" in the sense of being beyond wallowing in enjoyment of pain). To publicly seek justice for a feeling of loss or victimization, one must be able to relive the agony, to name and acknowledge it as one's own. Scholar Barbara Mennel suggests a link between masochistic fantasy and the ideals of liberalism in precisely this seeking to identify abjection and injustice, in the former as a celebration of passive survival and in the latter as causes against which to actively fight.[39] Where the tendency to fight is strong, so perhaps there is a natural balance in the tendency to be dominated or subdued. In any demand for justice one must retain enough iron in oneself to not be swallowed up by the agony, to separate out the self that suffers from the self that leads its life (or changes the world). In being beaten again and again, Bronson is perhaps learning this healthy masochism in a very hard way, but also compensating for the feeling of weakness which it gives by appearing to impose himself on the world as an aggressor.

• • •

We can see that at the heart of Refn's Bronson is an unnamable thing, but we are not entirely certain what this is. Deceptively open, a figure for whom everything must seemingly be made concrete, Bronson is nonetheless defined by this unnamable thing. It is tempting to reduce this to "queerness" and read Bronson in much the same way that Robin Wood taught us to read *Raging Bull* in his groundbreaking essay[40]—as an examination of how the fear or presence of latent homosexuality accounts for an overabundance of violent aggression against women and other males in the character of heavyweight boxer Jake La Motta. Cannily, Refn has partly foregrounded this idea so that we will not miss it, but also so that we will not seek it out as the only possible explanation. Queerness is not hidden or riddled in *Bronson* the way it is in *Raging Bull*; it is part of the world that Bronson inhabits. In fact, Bronson's fight manager, the epicene Paul Daniels (loftily played by Matt King), is the person who baptizes him "Charlie Bronson," so we have a right to consider queerness or effeminacy as being associated with the heart of Bronson.

But just as the film foregrounds the issue of queerness, so Bronson understands that he is a denotation of the male as commodity: in modern stardom, male actors and athletes make naked appeal to their ability to universally attract. We expect them to have gay fans as well as female and heterosexual male fans. Actually, to the extent that attention is gender-neutral, or rather open to all possibilities of gender, we could say that this is part of why Bronson likes to perform—it opens the floodgates, as it were. It excuses male attention as part of the general floodlight of fame.

And yet, unlike La Motta, who can only respond to the thought of male lust by demonizing a woman or beating up a rival male, Bronson is not so simple in his self-deception. Bronson's passivity toward women and gay men is as extreme and disturbing as his aggressiveness toward all others; it is as though he had no selfhood, at bottom, or rather no sexual selfhood, no sexual will. Bronson seems more secure in his masculinity vis-à-vis women and gay men than Jake is, but also more removed in general from the world of sexual expression. As with legendary screen monsters such as Frankenstein or Leatherface, Bronson is possessed of a lack of sexuality, not a conflicted or an unresolved one but simply a nonexistent one which is poignant and painful in its absence.

When Refn's camera looks into Bronson's eyes, an emptiness stares out. It is not even frightening the way Jake's face sometimes is in *Raging Bull*, screwed-up, bearing down on some idea, shaking with the intensity of tangible repression. Jake is always "acting" (as De Niro is), therefore dissembling among possible truths; Bronson, on the other hand, presents a series of masks whose purpose seems to be to limit our expectations of his depths. The masks are all there is.

That asexualized emptiness is the real heart of *Bronson*. Refn manages to make us see the film through his protagonist's wild eyes and to discover how much more he knows about the (film's) world than we do. In this sense, Refn pushes the character and the situations far beyond an easy nihilism into a kind of Zen that stills us in the midst of chaos. In response to our frustrated hopes that Bronson will become free or at peace, Refn confronts us with the character's obstinate and incongruous truth—that Bronson already is. Bronson has given up on the objective hope for happiness or success in order to pursue a deeply imbedded, subjective hope that his personal truth, whatever it might be, will prevail at any given moment. In *Raging Bull* we are watching Jake as we would watch an animal in a cage, primed to spot his inadequacies and delusions. "Lighten up," we often want to tell Jake. Whereas with Bronson, we find ourselves astonished at his playfulness. "Take life more seriously," we want to tell Bronson. This points back to the lack of sublimation. In the fight where he cheerfully urinates on his beaten opponent we see a lack of repression that allows us to feel that Bronson is at least happy in his animalistic, anarchic world—something we never feel about La Motta. Again, as Adorno states in relation to Nietzsche's conception of amor fati, the world can be recognized as flawed, compromised, bad without our using this as the basis of a truth claim, a belief-system in a wholly other world. The spare or excess worlds of Christianity (heaven, limbo, purgatory, hell, etc.) are reminiscent of multiple land holdings, vacation homes, sublets, rentals, the paid-for change of scenery being an antidote to the misery with which the Christian greets his or her immanent surroundings. Bronson embraces confinement as the proof of immanence.

The fabulizing of other worlds, other realities, never entirely dies away even in that purist immanence which is exemplified by the bare cage. It is a crucial element of hope to imagine something; what Adorno comes very close to stating is that secular myth itself represents a kind of adaptation to the world, a transformative forward movement that spans from truth to hope. It reorients the fabulizing in a more productive direction. The function of myth, let us say again, is to discover and point out the pathway by which a collective hope can become a collective truth. Indeed, it is more important to look at how Bronson's aggression actually is an extreme kind of adaptation to the world, one which calls the larger world into question, throws it into various crises of meaning, without ever being able to resolve its own relation to the world or change the world itself. For it is frustrated protest, frustrated revolution, that we detect in Bronson's constant flailing against authority and punishment.

Again, this denotes a sense in which Bronson is definitively powerless, in spite of the fact that he can beat people up, take a beating, etc. This is a quintessential Refn paradox. A gangster in *Pusher II* describes an occasion when he attacked and killed four men as arising from a feeling of weakness: "Something had to be done. I felt powerless, I guess." This gangster character goes on to characterize violence as a way of conquering fear. But fear is almost never conquered permanently, especially as one moves in increasingly violent circles; fear demands more crimes, more acts of violence, and thus social acceptance grows further out of reach.

Marilyn C. Wesley has commented on this dichotomy of violence and powerlessness in the male heroes of Western narratives:

> The similarity of violent world and violent man does not symbolize a connection, but instead effects a separation [whereby] personal violence is a stopgap that cannot institute permanent private authority, fix the terms of masculine identity, or protect the limited individual from larger powers.[41]

Bronson's absurd tragedy is that he is condemned, by his own truth, to fight against and be crushed by a patriarchal order that initially wants to include him in its power, wants to accept him as a son as it were. However, once Bronson's bad faith toward patriarchy reveals itself, the patriarchal order shows no qualms in tossing him on the scrapheap. Thus, in Bronson's embracing of his fate to be the outnumbered, outcast, underdog fighter, we see a more nuanced critique of patriarchal power: its terrible quality is not that it belongs to any and every man, like an aggressive instinct or an extra chromosome, but that it indoctrinates itself in mankind as a whole through forms of intimidation, abuse and punishment. It does not finally need every man in order to go on holding its unique power over the human species. It nearly goes without saying that some men who symbolize what Wesley calls "the male ideology of violent power"[42] are shut out of the putative rewards of that ideology, their lives rendered futile and meaningless, because the patriarchy has seen how these men's violence is directed as much against the systemic order as specific, weaker, territorialized victims. Deterritorialization, indeed, is what undoes patriarchy (and normativity) most of all; and there was never a single hegemonic "male ideology of violent power," only overlappings of more and less privileged discourses of violent power espoused by more and less privileged men.

In this sense, *Bronson* can be called a "psychotic parable," after Wesley's evocative phrase, a narrative subgenre which she characterizes as having two essential conditions. The first is the subject's inability to develop healthy identification with both mother and father, i.e., with either gender. This is seen as a larger failure of socialization in which the subject, as a young man, is torn from family and other social enclaves, or forced to confront the evil that exists within these structures.[43] (We visited this idea already in relation to *Pusher*.) The psychotic parable presupposes a kind of "psychotic society" given to manufacturing versions of its own psychosis in individuals. The second condition is almost in contradiction to the first, from a normative standpoint; it is the eternal moral of the psychotic parable, so to speak: "Social value cannot develop out of personal or public aggression."[44] Put otherwise: the bleak capitulation to the mass-societal psychosis is not an overcoming of the circumstances of life; one gains no place or promoted position, no refuge and no peace of mind.

This is because the society itself, being psychotic, has only an illusory order which dissolves on closer inspection. Take a few steps back from any social institution, or from any policy debate on the issues, and you see how a kind of relentless and deeply entrenched madness holds everything together, arising from the paranoid need for expediencies. In the thick of it, and perhaps inured to it over a period of time, we no longer regard it as madness. Prisons, as *Bronson* suggests, are a good example. There is nothing more commonplace than looking at the prison systems of earlier ages or of different regions of the world and finding them to be harsh, unduly punitive, cruel and unusual. We look at old drawings of people shackled by the neck to the stone walls of dungeons, without due process or habeas corpus; but when we look at our own current prison system there is no such objectivity. The questions become hysterical and insistent: How do we keep them locked up? How do we build more facilities? How do we appease the victims and the victims' families? Whereas we never think of "the victims' families" when looking at Goya's shackled or hanged men; quite the opposite, we think of *the convicts* as victims.

Blanchot suggests that this is essentially a problem of severely limited options in modern societies, which are left to confront age-old human flaws and dilemmas from a fortress of totalitarian bureaucracy. He writes, "If it weren't for prisons, we would know that we are all already in prison."[45] How does one escape from modernity and its discontents, its hypocritical denials, as the gladiatorial, irreducible Bronson seems to want to do?

As long ago as 1888, Nietzsche was able to take his peers to task for having irreparably lost that nobility and efficiency of purpose which define eras of high civilization. "The entire western world," he writes in *Twilight of the Idols*, "no longer possesses those instincts out of which institutions grow, out of which futurity grows; perhaps nothing is so much against the grain of its 'modern spirits.' We live for the present, we live very fast—we live very irresponsibly: this is precisely what we call 'freedom.'"[46] To find freedom—and the future—Nietzsche was saying we already had to start turning back the clocks.

Without debating too strenuously the competing ideals of freedom which have, to some extent, always existed as a Western dualism (freedom as purpose versus as purposelessness; freedom as perfect order versus as natural chaos), we can see that high modernism itself was born under a cloud of lapse, of degeneration, of having botched the whole enterprise. The current tendencies to see the world as falling apart, as in decline, are hardly unprecedented. But this also has to do with the negative teleology of Christianity, the idea that the flawed world will grow worse and worse until it implodes into the "true world" of God's eternity. (This is not much different, actually, from scientific predictions in the era of global warming.) According to this view, there has always been a distinct albeit benighted temptation to view modernity itself as a fiction, a swindle, a lie that was told and re-told until taken for granted. Much liberal-minded art depicts situations in which the atavistic returns to briefly disrupt our engineered security and peace. The moral is always ambiguous; modernity has paved over primitivism. But primitivism is a lost art; wherever it insists on breaking through, like kudzu through concrete, all that is required is stronger concrete. At the same time, the bad faith of modernist art is that the return of barbarism galvanizes a narrative that would otherwise be as flat as a highway or a parking lot. The thrilling monster of our primordial dreams gooses our secret heart then perishes as a sacrifice to our less secret designs for living.

This is a defining problem of our day, and it keeps us trapped on a loop of doomed irruptions and returns to order. Originality and creativity themselves are bound and gagged by the inability to see anything as a permanent or viable direction, only a blind chicken run to the cliff's edge. Even as the forms of work and leisure grow more streamlined, efficient, gadget-driven and "virtual," there remains a concomitant problem (to borrow from tech language) of "generating new content" in life as well as art, a problem all the more starkly revealed by the unabated advancement of forms. Our viewing matter comes in new configurations (Blu-ray, HD) while consisting largely of permutations on the same stories. Content is primitive, it belongs to another era. It was the primitives who concocted the Ur-myths that we still raid as the basis for our games, entertainments and stories, just as Bronson himself is a man out of time, a dislocated caveman in a social order that has repressed the cave.

The violence with which we castigate and punish the Bronsons of the world is no longer the response of a civilized society who has everything coolly under control but rather one which can offer little more than an impotent, self-loathing shrug in the face of real brutality. In every philosophical sense we no longer even pretend to occupy a moral high ground from which to judge (and how could we?). Meanwhile, the alienated warrior's struggle against modernity, a struggle as doomed as a suicide bomber's, affirms that many of us have never found our way out of a bewildering labyrinth of changes. We who consider ourselves developed and modern can no longer deny that our life (which, admittedly, we have not given up trying to improve) is deeply connected to those ones who never sought, or found, a place for themselves within modernity, just as Earth's atmosphere is breathed by all of us alike. For the anti-moderns, their irrelevance, impotence, and inability to produce are cruel tricks of fate; their only hopes for a world that they can stand to inhabit (and which can stand them) are the fantastical afterworlds that they have been promised by their ancient religions.

In our shockproof world it is the keepers of shock who possess momentum today. They are the ones who still want to ban *Madame Bovary* and *The Idiot*. They never got over the nude painting, or abstraction for that matter. They maintain the boundaries of a struggle that most of us have resolved in our own minds; they maintain the lingering emplacement of taboos which booby-trap a Western discourse that has taken pride in its sophistication and self-knowledge. Amidst us blasé people, they are the only ones who still perceive the boundaries of the struggle and that lingering emplacement of taboos. The taboos to them are signs still visible and burning to their eyes. They are infused with the bitterness of never having gotten what they wanted. They are like the king who lives on long after the king is dead. The tyranny of their moral objections forces us to go back, grudgingly to be sure, and fight the same battles again and again. To do this, we must acknowledge what they see—we must find a way to understand the dire judgment with which they still balefully regard our Emma, our Olympia, our Maldoror, our Prince Myshkin. Instead of the shock of the new (which is probably phenomenologically impossible now anyway), we need to rediscover the shock of the old.

– 7 –

Valhalla Rising

> The mole digs tunnels under the earth, looking for the sun. Sometimes, he gets to the surface. When he sees the sun, he is blinded. —Alejandro Jodorowsky in *El Topo*

After the neo-expressionistic phantasmagoria of *Bronson*, where disparate levels of reality and unreality freely mix within a theatricalized zone outside of diegetic time and place, and where modernity itself is thrown into question, Refn turned to the distant, barbaric, pre-modern past for his next film, the bleak and beautiful *Valhalla Rising*, set in the 12th century A.D. The contest between reality and unreality, however, continues unabated, now inflected with a tone of hallucinatory mysticism, partly inspired (Refn has acknowledged) by Andrei Tarkovsky's *Stalker* (1979), and by Alejandro Jodorowsky's *El Topo* (1970) and *The Holy Mountain* (1973).[1]

In some ways, *Valhalla Rising* attempts to reimagine the warrior-hero represented by Bronson, affording him a greater measure of meaning and dignity, and also a possibility of transcending his own nature (and the world). Bronson never permits himself the ultimate dignity of accepting, and therefore rising above, his constant sense of defeat; in fact, futility is what keeps Bronson going. It is the basis of his shifting, metamorphic identity. As Refn says, "*Bronson* was about a man who creates his own mythology; *Valhalla Rising* is mythology."[2]

Like *Bronson*, One Eye (Mads Mikkelsen), the protagonist of *Valhalla Rising*, is an inveterate fighter; yet he gradually comes to question his own preternatural tendency to violence, whereas Bronson was a Schopenhauerian figure unable to act against his own innate, unalterable will, his characteristic violent response. For Bronson, will is the alpha and omega, which the philosopher of *World as Will and Idea* would certainly have noted as typically human albeit regrettable. For One Eye, though, there will be something higher than the helpless exercising of his will, something like transcendence and even divinity.

Schopenhauer expressed his sense of human fatalism in this statement, "The man who has no conscience in small things will be a scoundrel in big things."[3] The human psyche, ruled and defined by self-interest and will, lacks all middle ground behaviorally, drawn ever back to the same foundational need, the same preternatural and personal vision of the world. Refn's cinema is filled with examples of these compulsive "scoundrels," self-derailing hotheads in whom insensitivity is merely an opening karmic gambit in a game that becomes inexorably more and more destructive. They are, in a word, bullies. We think of Frank's strong-arming drug deals graduating into actual violence; Louis' verbal abuse of Leo escalating into physical assault; the Duke's callous neglect of his son Tonny building to a point where he thinks nothing of trying to use him to kill a woman; or indeed Bronson, who can never progress from "enmity" to "sympathy," those pole opposites which Schopenhauer, in a fascinating passage, identifies as being mutually exclusive and, as we would say, hardwired into each individual's psyche:

> For there are men in whom the sight of another man at once rouses a feeling of enmity, since their inmost nature exclaims at once: That is not me! There are others in whom the sight awakens immediate sympathy; their inmost nature says: That is me over again! Between the two there are countless degrees. That in this most important matter we are so totally different is a great problem, nay, a mystery.[4]

With *Valhalla Rising* Refn finally breaks away from Schopenhauer's polarizing bind by creating a warrior-hero who comes to learn empathy, mercy and self-sacrifice, much as Schopenhauer counseled Buddhist spirituality as a way of breaking down the ego and as an antidote to rampant self-will.

• • •

Refn has said that he wanted to make *Valhalla Rising* since the age of seventeen, when he first envisioned Vikings as space travelers, even though, he adds, "oddly enough, I didn't have an interest in Vikings." But the ancientness would be a way of simulating the strangeness of hyperspace, since for the Vikings, Refn reasoned, "America would be like going to the moon."[5] This is why Refn has called *Valhalla Rising* "a Viking science-fiction film, in a metaphysical way"[6]—an outrageous-sounding but ultimately accurate description.

The space travel theme in *Valhalla Rising* takes different metaphorical shapes. For example, Refn conceived the scene where the Vikings are adrift in a longboat on their way to the New World as "my spaceship concept ... like they're sitting in a space capsule."[7] Literally, to achieve the effect of what Refn calls "traveling into outer space, but on the world," *Valhalla Rising* was filmed in extremely remote locations in Scotland. Refn has said, "I had this obsessiveness of going to the most remote areas of the world to make a film." The shoot involved the entire cast and crew hiking for two hours up mountainous terrain every morning, then another two hours hiking back down before nightfall, a procedure which assistant director Saskia Pomeroy calls "quite challenging." "Nature was controlling us, not vice versa," Refn says.[8]

In addition, there were none of the "on-set" accouterments that make life easier during a shoot—no trailers, no catering; everything was designed to heighten the actors' weariness at being battered by rugged nature. Apparently even the cinematographer, Morton Søborg, who had worked on documentaries in the icy steppes of Greenland, complained about the grueling shooting conditions of *Valhalla Rising*.[9]

Refn became more and more determined to discover "places where there were no people and man had never been." This led to the film's climactic scenes being filmed by special permission in heavily restricted nature preserves around Loch Ness. (Some of these scenes appear to be taking place on the surface of the moon rather than earth.) Refn says, "I was the general each morning, saying 'All right, troops, let's walk! We must go up the mountains!'"[10] Still, Refn admits that he spared himself much of the arduousness and endurance: his situation, he has said, "was different from what the actors were going through, because I had two personal assistants and a lot of survival clothes and gear, and I would take a shower each morning and each night."[11]

Be this as it may, *Valhalla Rising* is perhaps the most potent proof of Refn's sheer lust for film. *Valhalla Rising*, much like *Fear X*, is a film which Refn claims to have rescued from the threat of some kind of blindness, the inability to see what needed to be filmed. Such a claim taps into what has always been at stake in the visual sensibility of the best films: a refusal to take seeing for granted. As with Harry's flashes of sight in the darkness in *Fear X*, *Valhalla Rising*'s depiction of One Eye having prophetic dreams and hallucinations becomes a metaphor for the filmmaker's work of "second sight," of bringing visions into reality, into literal focus.

At the risk of sounding hyperbolic, the images of *Valhalla Rising* seem not so much filmed as literally conquered from raw space and landscape. As in the prehistoric scenes of Stanley Kubrick's *2001: A Space Odyssey* (1968), perhaps, or the runic desert of Werner Herzog's *Fata Morgana* (1971), the camera feels like the invisible witness to a time before its own invention.

Indeed, the remote, uninhabited locations in Scotland where *Valhalla Rising* was made could be said to be terra incognita that Refn and his cast and crew literally did have to conquer for cinema, much as early "invaders" conquered for power, wealth and religious belief. All three of these latter motives for conquest are referenced and critiqued in *Valhalla Rising*, even as Refn's camera serenely appropriates the drama and stillness of the wilderness in one pictorial triumph after another: red pools reminiscent of the river of blood in the beginning of *El Topo*; rocky outcroppings; moody, panoramic cloudscapes that seem to stretch forever. Never has this poet of urban spaces displayed such restless affinity for nature at its rawest.

So one meaning of "space travel" is this impossible geography of earth, perhaps a reference to the statement in Deodato's *Cannibal Holocaust* that the earth is the first alien planet that we need to explore and understand. *Valhalla Rising* is also about the idea of space travel as an individual's journey of faith through a continually shifting and internal frontier.[12] Similar to Tarkovsky's *Stalker*, as well as *Solaris* (1972), the inner journey of faith is represented by remote and hostile places where the human being is tested. This testing of the body yields distilled knowledge of the extra-physical, the metaphysical. Not that these metaphysical pursuits have caused Refn to abandon his trademark taste for bloodletting, mutilation, bare-handed killing, etc. (In many ways *Valhalla Rising* was more violent than any of Refn's previous films.) However, he has focused the action here to hypnotic and surprisingly meditative effect, "like taking your heartbeat down to a trance."[13] What happens to physical bodies in *Valhalla Rising*—albeit graphic and gory—has a way of pointing outside of the body toward the spiritual. The film intuits, long before its hero One Eye does, that there is something within life that shines forth in our good deeds and which finds its glory in a dignified acceptance of inevitable death.

This intuition emerges from subliminal depths, an allegory of the historical emergence of Christian faith from a supposed spiritual chaos. Citing LSD in particular, Refn has stated that he wanted *Valhalla Rising* to act on the viewer's nervous system like an hallucinogenic drug: "It's almost like: how do you create a movie like a drug?"[14] Disorientation is woven through the film's form and content, as the mainly nameless characters span two continents, wandering across desolate primordial wilderness, barely speaking, staring inscrutably into the distance (or directly into the camera), ostensibly the first European people to set foot in the pristine wilds of North America. The experience of being alone on an unsettled continent is a kind of radical test of that comfortable core identity which many devoted acid-trippers believed it was their duty to challenge and even shed in drug-propelled diffusions of self and sudden revelatory breakthroughs of past lives and future destinies. *Valhalla Rising* is the nth degree of such an existential dare, in which some characters find a common chord and merge with the universe around them; while others resist, cling to their delusional self-beliefs, and generally have, in acid-lore terms, a classic "bad trip."

But this is not necessarily their fault. One Eye, the only character who exemplifies complete transcendence, is marked for this destiny not only by his prophetic visions but perhaps more importantly his unique background as someone who was never either pagan or Christian—in other words, without orthodoxy. Both religions are infected by violence and Schopenhauerian enmity—namely, the difficulty of these primitive men to trust anyone, even their closest friends. All experience is essentially violent experience, swift and brutal—stabbings, skull-crushings, many broken necks, even one scene of male rape.

In a by-now-familiar Refn motif, violence becomes a way in which the film's male characters—inarticulate, barely bonded into societal or familial units—attempt to communicate with or change each other. This film reveals a historical conception of violence as the original common ground of humanity, out of which later, modern refinements—such as language, sexuality (in the Foucauldian sense of a coherent discourse as opposed to opportunistic, discrete, "meaningless" acts), philosophy and religion—evolved without ever fully leaving behind their distant violent origins.

Indeed, general lack of trust, and fear of violation, mutilation and death, combine to ensure that the social order as such will be based on total subjugation to provisional, megalomaniacal leaders who hoard the power to crush all predatory instincts or, indeed, wherever possible, subsume those predatory instincts into the basis of tribal law. This law is more materialist than moral in nature. It is related to an economy of bodily integrity and monetary protection, an economy for which One Eye himself is presented as the synecdoche: he begins as a prizefighter, kept by one clan to do battle (for the economic benefit of his keepers) against fighters from other clans. These are fights to the death, winner take all, the ancient roots of zero sum economy.

Appropriately, One Eye's body begins as more of a thing than a person. A slave, he bears numerous battle-scars. Even his face is scarred, his gouged-out eye a constant reminder of the suffering he has survived and, by implication, inflicted on others. In an early scene he must battle two men, both of whom he kills. Although he always fights from a place of disadvantage (usually chained by the neck to a pole while his opponents can move freely), he never loses.

When the different pagan tribes watch One Eye prizefighting, the action and their way of reacting to it do not have the escapist character of a modern sporting event. Rather, in this, as in everything else in *Valhalla Rising*, Refn has his actors studiously underplay. They sit stonily, aware that every moment might mean death for their fighter; the acknowledgment of this, rather than filling them with crazed bloodlust, seems to bring on an almost meditative equanimity. Refn shows us that, for the pagans, these mortal combats are close to being a kind of religious ritual. The pagans derive their meaning from the subjugation of One Eye's killing force, from having his nearly superhuman power at their constant command; he is an energy resource in a world before fuel.

Although he is in some form of bondage in all of these early scenes (ropes, cages, an iron collar fitted with poles by which the pagans push and pull him when they must transport him somewhere), his body is also a kind of venerated object. Before a fight, we see One Eye kneeling, his hands bound, while his body is anointed. He has been given ornate tattoos. The pagan chieftain seems in awe of his own fighter; the height of the pagans' ideal seems to involve identifying something stronger, more invincible, than themselves, and then finding a way to harness it and exploit its energy. This parallels the pagans' relation to their gods, who all have special powers and functions of protection, and who are "owned" by their human worshipers more than the other way around. The chieftain boasts of having "many gods who protect us," while the Christians "have only got one." When the chieftain speaks the words "many gods," Refn cuts to a shot of One Eye asleep in his cage, further reinforcing the idea that One Eye already represents a kind of divinity.

We see this divinity-in-flesh, so to speak, more nakedly in paganism; however, between paganism and the emerging Christianity, it is arguably only a difference in the degree to which the believers attempt to exert their own power through and over the entity that they have chosen to worship. In Christianity the power of God is already accrued to that of wealth. In this ancient culture war, the pagans are sufficiently troubled by the violent zeal of the Christian missionaries to worry about whether they will have enough money to buy them off. Money, one pagan says, "is the only way to reason with the Christians." This is the potential downside of the pagans' energy-scattering plethora of gods: it is suggested that the monotheistic focus on a single deity allows for the concentration of human energies and the accumulation of wealth, since in monotheism the things of the world are not separated into their own conflicting realms but subsumed within one all-encompassing power, which can and does become a metonymy for the concentrated power of the individual. The tragic fact that money became *the* single yardstick of civilization is concomitant with the exclusivity of value and meaning in monotheistic belief, in which only one entity can prevail over the rest, and in which power flows from a central, universal-symbolic source.

One Eye is sometimes referred to as "the Monster." As Timothy K. Beal has pointed out in his interesting work on the relation between horror and religion, the English word "monster" derives from the Latin "*monenere* ('warn' or 'portend'), which sometimes refers to a divine portent that reveals the will or judgment of God or the gods. In this sense a *monstrum* is a message that breaks into this world from the realm of the divine."[15] This is fitting, for One Eye's progress is a series of remonstrances against everyone whom he comes into contact with, and also against himself—judgments expressed non-verbally and usually through a violent act.

There is a pagan boy, Are (Maarten Stevenson), who develops telepathic communication with One Eye. One Eye is mute, so Are becomes a vessel for his thoughts. The warrior has mystical visions when he dreams; later these visions increase in frequency and intensity, becoming waking hallucinations. The plot of the film valorizes these visions (much like Harry Caine's in *Fear X*) as prophetic in nature. But One Eye is, in the beginning, a visceral rather than mystical creature; we are told that he is "driven by hate; that's how he survives, why he never loses." All gods, here, are gods of wrath; the idea of a god of love is one which is tentatively born only at the very end of *Valhalla Rising*, after the definitive failures of pagan and Christian structures.

"Who are you?" the pagan chieftain asks One Eye before selling him off to a different tribe. The problem of subjectivity is posed in this question, which is also a kind of command by the chieftain for One Eye to embark on a new phase of life, a new identity to go along with a new owner. However, led through the countryside bound and hooded, One Eye suddenly breaks free and murders his captors. This seems to be One Eye's answer to the chieftain's challenging question. He is now the one who will kill at will on his own behalf.

Even though One Eye grasps his own potential to become a free individual fairly early, his clearest sense of identity remains stuck at the level of brutish slaughter. He ties the new chieftain to a boulder. This chieftain stares at One Eye and declares, "What do you see—yourself? When I die, you will go back to hell." One Eye promptly disembowels him. In a sense, paganism entailed just this rupture of identification with others due to the fact that death was experienced as solitary, frightening, meaningless, and incapable of being shared. The disemboweled chieftain can only face his own imminent death by implying that One Eye is really killing himself, and also that the dying chieftain will actually send One Eye "back to hell," as if, when the pagan dies, the world dies with him.

Specifically, here, the power of hell is being invoked as a weapon on the side of the pagan chieftain. Beal writes: "In this way the monstrous other who threatens 'us' and 'our world' [One Eye, in this case] is exorcised from the right order of things and sent to some sort of Hell."[16] One Eye returns to the old chieftain who sold him, cuts off his head and places it on a pike. This is, again, One Eye's embodied attempt to answer the chieftain's original question, "Who are you?" We see One Eye stalking across the landscape, carrying an ax and trailed at a cautious distance by Are. Set free from tribal bondage, One Eye and Are adopt each other, so to speak.

They stumble on a pagan encampment overrun by Christian Vikings who have killed all the men, and stripped the women and chained them together. A great heap of bodies is burning amid hastily erected white sheets with crosses painted in blood. Robert Muchembled has advanced the theory that for the early Christians the "constant reiteration of the visible 'proofs' provided by the ritual of execution, was necessary before the [non–Christian] crowds could accept the Christian perception of the body and the non-return of the dead."[17] Massacres and auto-da-fés were deployed to break the lingering pagan superstition that death was merely a continuation of life in a different realm, or even something like an indeterminate period of slumber from which the dead might return to wreak vengeance. Because of this, the "more dead" the early Christians could make someone—by pulverizing, dismembering, burning to ashes—the safer they felt about having placed the dead spirit successfully at bay.

In spite of their violence, the Christian Vikings see themselves as missionaries and herald One Eye's coming as fortuitous proof of God's will. If the pagan chieftain understood One Eye as a demon driven by endless rage, the Christians see in him a potential ally or arm in the implementation of their dream of a boundlessly wealthy and forgiving Holy Land. In both belief systems, One Eye's raw, wordless power is used as a pawn.

The Christian Vikings explain that they are planning to set sail in search of this Holy Land, a new Jerusalem across the sea. They promise One Eye, "Your sins will be absolved.... You will see your loved ones again." The Christians' expectation (not much different from the pagans' as it turns out, in terms of the denial of death) is that people who have died are transported to this other land and wait there to be found again. This other world is a Paradise where peace and joy reign, and all one's needs are satisfied. But Are explains to the Christians, speaking for One Eye, that One Eye was "brought up from hell" and has no one in the world. In this sense, One Eye is immune to the sentimental impulse behind the Christians' belief in an afterworld Paradise with an eternal reunion with their kin. In fact, One Eye is reluctant to go on the pilgrimage at all. However, One Eye is welcomed by a proselytizing Viking, who tells him, "We are more than flesh and blood, more than revenge.... You should consider your soul. That's where the real pain lies." One Eye turns and stares at him in recognition; this acknowledgment of inner pain, spiritual pain, and of something distinct from and theoretically more enduring than the body, stirs a response in the warrior.

The next sequence, which takes place on a Viking longboat sailing across the Atlantic Ocean, is the only one in the film shot inside a studio, and is evocative of silent expressionist cinema. The angled shots of bodies and ship's rigging against a blank background are reminiscent of Murnau: the ghost ship in *Nosferatu* (1922), as well as what Eric Rohmer called the abstract "pictorial space" of the Heaven Prologue in *Faust* (1926).[18] One also thinks of the frontality of close-ups against blank backgrounds in Carl Dreyer's *The Passion of Joan of Arc* (1928).

In fact, much like Dreyer, Refn uses close-ups to emphasize what is literal, immanent and corporeal about spirituality—what critic Bodil Marie Thomsen has called Dreyer's "haptic vision." She writes about Alois Riegl's distinction between the haptic vision of medieval times and the optical vision of the Renaissance, translating these, in cinematic terms, into close-ups (haptic) and wide-angle deep-focus (optical), but suggesting as well that something beyond the aesthetic is at stake in these "visual preferences":

> Haptic is the tactility of vision, so to speak. We use haptic vision when seeing an object in extreme close-up: the structure of the skin seen in a mirror, for example. Haptic vision excludes outlines, profiles and figurative isolation from the background. This discussion about the optical and the haptical was, according to Riegl, very much related to the fall of the Roman Empire, and the struggles on whether or not the body could be a vehicle to divine grace. The outcome of this we have all experienced: the body had to be transcended in order to gain a more spiritual point of view.[19]

I do not find the presentation of context in the form of background/foreground problematic in itself, but instead a welcoming of universality and interrelatedness; yet I am intrigued by the idea that there was once a cultural longing—one which cinema now reawakens and refines—for a sense of spiritual divinity that could be exuded through, and visible in, the surfaces of the body. For both Joan of Arc and One Eye, as medieval entities, faith and action are inextricably linked. This enables certain distinctions to be drawn between false, power-driven religiosity, embodied in Dreyer by the holy inquisitors and in Refn by the Viking chieftain, and the earthy, inchoate religiosity embodied by Joan (also a warrior given to visions) and One Eye. The former are physical presences who do not touch us in the sense of reach or move, and whom we do not wish to touch, unlike, perhaps, One Eye or Joan. For Thomsen, Dreyer's realignment of spirituality with a direct appreciation of human physicality, human beauty, is a leap forward toward a less repressive, body-phobic Christianity.

However, this tactility is somewhat more recessive in *Valhalla Rising*, since, according to Thomsen, it is Dreyer's use of tight and frontal close-ups which makes his film haptic ("not separating the figure from the ground" and the subsequent denial of "normal distance"),[20] while Refn freely uses a mixture of what Thomsen would consider haptic and optical perspectives throughout *Valhalla Rising*.[21] Also, the all-male context of Refn's film does not allow us to see anything like Joan of Arc's femaleness, which becomes the most obvious element that separates her from her male tormentors (a crucial distinction, as Thomsen argues[22]). In this sense, the figure of Are becomes strategic, since, as *Valhalla Rising*'s youngest and most vulnerable character, his witness to violence is that much more appalling; Are's vulnerability is similar to Joan's. But One Eye, too, although stoically refusing to completely surrender until the moment of his ultimate sacrifice, becomes a figure whose vulnerability we glimpse more and more beneath his solid build and primal masculinity. As a body, One Eye does not seem like a body so much as a gruelingly forged response to trauma; and after his emancipation he never appears naked, as he did throughout much of his time as a pagan fighter-slave.

At the risk of oversimplifying Thomsen's argument, there is recognition in Dreyer's contrast between Joan of Arc's luminous face and the "monstrous" physical presences of her inquisitors; the most spiritual body is also the most physically beautiful. Thomsen defines the later denigration of this truism as an example of patriarchal church sexism in which female spiritual truths are especially denied.[23] But if anything, One Eye's masculine ventriloquism of "Joan of Arc" (if he can be said to be doing this) complicates the issue, turning physical beauty into something like brute strength and stony impenetrability.

But does this make One Eye any less beautiful or less spiritual? It is the nature of male, masculine beauty to be (rather than a passive attribute which might go unnoticed) the record, etched on the flesh, of an active prowess. Now this beauty of strength can belong to women as well, or to the androgynous, but male and female genders have never been as wholly constructed as Judith Butler and others assert. The places at which gender roles mix—machos with a feminine side, tough ladies, etc.—are behavioral nuances that we have come to view as increasingly normalized in our time; however, they always have been normative for untold people throughout history. It requires a certain hubris to imagine that gender confines are overthrown only through postmodern conceptualization, or that one has suddenly drawn some sexual Excalibur from the stone, so to speak. Everything that can be, is, and has always been.

In fact, strictly speaking, "essentialism" already accounts for varying degrees of androgyny which occur naturally in some people regardless of their sexual history or orientation. The idea that gender embodiment (or perform-

7. Valhalla Rising

The beauty of strength is the record, etched on the flesh, of an active prowess. In *Valhalla Rising* (2009) the body of One Eye (Mads Mikkelsen) is a symbol, like the cross, in a world that is largely pre-symbolic. His internal journey brings him to a place where he can transcend the physical to discover a spiritual dimension based on sacrifice, love and trust.

ance) is constructed arose largely from a too-literal reading of Foucault's archaeology of knowledge, with its revelatory insight that the expression of human sexuality is conditioned by social codes and therefore malleable in different epochs and societies. Also, gender-construction theory seems to partake of wishful queer thinking about the "G.I. Joe man" and wishful feminist thinking about the "Barbie doll woman"—e.g., that there would be no such man or woman unless society somehow demanded it.

But real people anywhere have never been as blindly hegemonic as academics like Butler imply. For me, the insistence that masculinity and femininity are tendentious constructs that no one would choose for himself or herself apart from social brainwashing is a case of placing the cart before the horse. Our beings, essences, genders all predate any modern social coding, and history tells us that there has always been a recognizable spectrum of human gender affiliations, making it difficult to see how any comportment or performance of gender could fail to be essentialist (i.e., natural) at the deepest level.

When masculinity possesses strength, it is sometimes denigrated as patriarchal out of hand; whereas a butch lesbian or transgender is seen as having somehow earned her prowess through rebellion while nonetheless claiming her masculinity as an organic part of herself (not chosen). Empirically speaking, the beauty of strength is still an issue of power whether it is the man or the woman who possesses the musculature, and the love of strength is the same no matter whose strength is being worshiped. (And for myself, as a gay man who loves men, I do not separate psychical maleness from muscular beauty, nor would I want to. Nor am I dismissive of those masculine traits denoted as representative of "essentialist maleness.") Whether we are talking about musculature made through hard work and exercise, or reflexes honed by athletics and combat, human strength measures a rugged distance that has been crossed, a world that has been experienced and engaged with. "Are you collecting scars or what?" someone asks the careless Tonny in *Pusher II*. In *Valhalla Rising*, wherever the male body is most scarified and damaged, and his senses most deranged, there ends up being the greatest transcendence and spiritual awareness. "As the microcosm of the body crumbles in pain," writes Beal, "so does the cosmos itself.... [Individual pain] undoes the world."[24] It is the moment where the strong must begin to ask for help, for something that will mend not only body and soul but the sundered, undone weft of the Real itself.

This is religion's sometimes manipulative appeal to frailty, damage and suffering. It is reminiscent of *Stalker*, in which the stalker's longing for the peace and healing powers of "the Zone" is motivated in part because he was raped while in prison. The Viking chieftain's son is raped by another Viking after the tribe grows lost in the New World and falls apart. Are witnesses this rape and screams in horror. His traumatized reaction is depicted by Refn as a loss of innocence, a kind of threshold loss, the way Bronson in the insane asylum is exposed to the sight of an inmate defecating into his own hand: in both, there is the sense of males confronted with inappropriate gestures centering around male anality. In *Valhalla Rising* the threat of male rape, particularly for weaker or younger males, is the visceral ne plus ultra of savagery, defined, in a complex way, as the death of honor itself and giving rise to a certain need for faith.

In general this need for religious solace is more acute, perhaps, in survivors of calamity. True suffering is coin of the realm, what the Holy Land "wants" in order to prove and augment its supposed power. We spoke before of LSD bringing its users into harmony or alienation with their environments; to the user, the environment itself might seem to play an active role in this rapport. Like the Zone in *Stalker*, and like the idea of heaven itself, the New World in *Valhalla Rising* is a geography invested with the supernatural authority to accept or reject those seekers who arrive there: "I think it lets those pass who have lost all hope," the stalker says about the Zone, "not good or bad, but wretched ones."

How blissful could it ever possibly be, this heaven of the wretched ones which seems more like a depression ward or recovery center? It is quite easy to imagine a heaven still haunted by the fear of death, for example, whether through memory trauma or residual uncertainty about the future. In the New World the Vikings' first contact with the existence of the native population comes through the grim sight not of living people, but of how the natives represent and treat death. In the middle of the woods the Vikings come across a clearing where tall wooden catafalques have been erected; upon each one there is a dead body, most of them skeletonized, but bedecked in opulent-looking furs. Flies buzz around the decayed cadavers. The Vikings react to these unburied, fetishized corpses with distaste, concluding that they have reached another "ungodly" pagan realm rather than the Holy Land. But it is merely another kind of death fetish—the crucifix—which they use to confront the pagan spectacle of decomposition.

For the most part, the Vikings find only reflections of their own inner demons; Refn indicates this by showing that they do not encounter external enemies at all, at most occasional volleys of arrows which periodically sail from the forests and which they attribute to various things (fog, their own God striking them down in displeasure). In a triumph of sound design, the ambient background music mutes out, only to have the sudden silence torn by the amplified whoosh and thwack of an arrow piercing one of the Vikings, who begins to scream at the top of his lungs. The enemies within grow stronger and take over. The chieftain's determination to claim and conquer this terra incognita for God has an increasingly obsessive and reality-denying cast. This strange push and pull of the early Christians' faith—sometimes acting impulsively in defense of their moral absolutes, and sometimes passively waiting to accept whatever comes as God's will—is evinced by the chieftain's hubris, that he is privileged to know the difference between a situation in which God wishes him to intervene and one in which God wishes him to show acceptance. As with other Refn heroes, the Viking chieftain becomes a compulsive gambler hurling good money after bad.

Since religion grows from calamity, it must remain in crisis in order not to lapse into self-righteous complacency and superiority. Thus, to return again to Beal, true spirituality is not the effect of an a priori or always-already sense of grace, but instead the messy, tenuous ground that will permit grace that is only complete and visible in failure. The meta-power of this faith guarantees solace where human power might break down; yet it places any sense of real power out of reach. At bottom, this is the meaning of all religion: it must die before it lives. And here again we find Frankenstein, the moment when the dead "it" is shocked "alive," in Paul Morrissey's version seeking flesh to authenticate an abstract idea of life.

• • •

Before they arrive at North America, the chieftain's son rapturously tells One Eye what his father has told him about the Holy Land, "all about its beauty, its wealth." Religious lore is a kind of escapist entertainment in a harsh, primitive world where untamed nature is, in effect, the only show in town. It is the grudging imaginative triumph of an essentially non-imaginative people, fighting with might and main to keep their literal physical integrity in a world of constant danger and death. Nothing transpires for the Christians that is not symbolic and also pregnant with divine meanings. There is also no middle ground between seeing One Eye (or anything) as a promise of Paradise and then seeing him likewise as a promise of Hell. In fact, the stronger the reminder of one, the more likely it will be that the opposite will soon come to mind. Belief in heaven enables and compels equal belief in hell, in a different kind of zero sum economy, just as there can be no "all" without the "nothing" that defines it. Thus, the wished-for reunion with angelic loved ones in an otherworldly haven threatens to become a rendezvous with living demons; the limitation of the religious imagination is that all-consuming damnation feels more vivid and plausible than the wild hope of eternal bliss.

Spiritual development is possible only in a state of blatantly superior strength or else in completely protected isolation. The Vikings are not much different from the modern gangsters in other Refn films in the way they bully and foreclose upon each other's attempts to gain individual status within an established group. (Also in the way they reinforce restrictive ideations as a group, which the individual members find themselves questioning. Convulsive movement against the pack is the essence of any taboo, somewhat like the paranoia that can accompany the use of drugs that one knows to be illegal and condemned.) As if to underscore this, we see One Eye off by himself, striving to erect a tower of stones; it collapses, and he doggedly begins again, pursuing a private vision. Is he trying to show dominion over the landscape? Is he trying to express the stony core inside himself? Is he mourning something lost, or attempting to purge and change, or create a balance? The reason does not matter as much as the fact that what he is doing is for himself alone, not for the others. It must be rehearsed outside the confines of the tribe. The tower of stones is presented as a kind of art work, an individualized statement within a world that has not yet invented the true individual.

This tower also suggests the "obelisk" which Bataille calls the "calmest negation" of the death of God:

> The obelisk is without a doubt the purest image of the head and of the heavens.... It was the surest and most durable obstacle to the drifting away of all things. And

even today, wherever its rigid shape stands out against the sky, it seems that sovereign permanence is maintained across the unfortunate vicissitudes of civilizations.[25]

What is important, for Bataille's purpose, is not that the tower attempts to rise into the heavens, but that it remains *rooted*; it is the body of man trying to have it both ways. It bulwarks a fragmentary transcendence while yielding little of the stability provided by solid ground. It is an impotent, would-be enduring fetish representing man's fleeting sense of his own earthly potency, his own power and potential. The erecting of this tower turns out to be a false feint for One Eye, but it is part of his growing intuition that man could possibly transcend the insulting brevity of life by creating things (or people) who will live on, and that this speaks to the ultimate dignity of man.

During the Vikings' collective downward spiral, the chieftain's tall cross presides over their madness, agony and futile striving. The cross, like the tower or obelisk, is also an erected structure which invokes the death of God, but it pointedly lacks Bataille's "calm" finality and instead stirs up opaque, chaotic and primordial responses. It is, of all static, inanimate things, the one most dynamic and in upheaval. The fact that it points in four different directions at once is only the beginning of its sibling-like relation to a windmill or gun-turret. The men circle this cross, looking or turning away; it is like an externalized part of the wounded human psyche, always on display and drawing out raw negative emotions. Is the cross exerting a constant promise of benediction, forgiveness and redemption? Or is it a sinister presence driving the men to increasingly desperate acts and gruesome sacrifices? In *Nemesis*, the high, cross-shaped stained-glass window was the only light, amid droves of windows and lamps, that shone with an undeniable truth on the lovers Verity and Michael, and later on the nun's confession. So, in *Valhalla Rising* the cross sees as much as it is seen.

Belief in God presupposes the necessary element of the death of God, in whose all-encompassing sacrifice we are meant to read all other ordeals as trivial and able to be overcome, even individual death. But if every suffering pales beside the crucifixion, then what could ever compete? To an extent, this endgame has caused religion to place a kind of inevitable cap on compassion (at some point the crucifixion will always be invoked as a trump card) and also why various manifestations of "evil" have become the bearers of a seemingly purer and more open-ended compassion in the modern era. Although slightly counterintuitive, it is clear that what needed to be done was to restore to immanence some of this commanding, awestruck suffering, and with God holding a monopoly on that, the Devil was the only possible way to go. This is why Sartre called Baudelaire's Satanism a mirror reflection of his lapsed Catholicism: to the religious mind, faith imposes the only terms by which we can imagine rebelling against it. It must be *worse than the crucifixion*, worse than the death of God, the most unbearable of losses in religious terms; thus there is some comfort in worshipping a devil whom we are already certain has been more or less defeated, and whose total defeat (and, by extension, man's) can be made to mirror that death of God. Throughout Refn's extended montage of penetrations and erections (the planting of the sword; the male rape; One Eye's tower), nothing equals the preeminent erection of the cross, whose power to shame the men and make them feel small has already worked its way into their consciousness, regardless of the fact that most of them are engaged, in these scenes of the film, in actively defying spiritual influence.

Toward the end of *Valhalla Rising*, Kare (Gary Lewis), a Viking priest, begins to question the logic of trying to conquer this vast new land, which he now realizes may not even be the fabled Jerusalem. "We need to follow [One Eye]," Kare tells the chieftain. This is heresy to the chieftain, and, more viscerally, a personal betrayal. He calmly embraces Kare: "My lifelong friend ... will you turn your back on me?" Then he draws his sword and stabs Kare in the back. Kare staggers away, bleeding, as the chieftain says, "Go on, then. Turn your back on God." This is the same betraying, violating embrace between men that occurs among the gangsters in the *Pusher* films, between Leo and Louis in *Bleeder*, and between Harry and Lt. Peter in *Fear X*; and it will occur again in *Drive*.

After breaking away from the doomed Viking band, One Eye carries the boy up a mountain on his shoulders. This is an homage to *El Topo*, specifically the scene where the itinerant gunfighter (played by director Jodorowsky) carries the Niño (Brontis Jodorowsky, the director's son); it is also an homage to a similar moment in *Stalker*. The mortally wounded Kare and the chieftain's son trail behind, and these four survivors end up on the mountaintop, where they have something like a final regrouping. Refn pares the ensemble down to two sets of mismatched father-son duos in the last fifteen minutes of *Valhalla Rising*. The love between father and son is confessed only obliquely in scenes where the son of one man ends up consoling the father of a different one. One Eye, of course, has become Are's father-like protector. But also the Viking chieftain's disillusioned son has a conversation with the dying Kare, himself disillusioned after failing to meet his own dead sons in this new land: "I came here to beg forgiveness from *my* sons. I was not there when they died in battle." "Could I ever forgive my father for bringing me to this place?" the chieftain's son asks. There is still a sense that separate subjectivities cannot yet merge in complete empathy; again, death is the existential crisis which prevents this. There are no likely words of comfort. Not only does the survivor miss and mourn his beloved dead, he now feels the problem of his own meaning: for what purpose was he spared? For both Kare and the chieftain's son, survival is seen as painful, even shaming. Now the survivor must carry not only his own purpose, his own burden, but the purposes and burdens of the dead. (Harry Caine in *Fear X* feels this in relation to his murdered wife.) To be reunited with the dead is always to ask their forgiveness and to inquire whether they approve of how one has carried on without them. Most ghost stories, for example, are actually tales of atonement, belonging to the religious imagination more than the secular one; the living must discover what the ghost "wants" and help achieve this so as to ease its passing into afterlife. "A life acquires its clearest meaning only in the light of death."[26]

Only the bond between One Eye and Are escapes from self-pitying fatalism. Their united front, throughout the film, has a revolutionary dimension. One Eye, as slave, and the boy occupy a similar, even enmeshed, subject-position. For childhood is generally equated with a state of something like enslavement: a child is helpless to the commands of the adult world and must come to reclaim his own freedom through an act of revolt. In fact, all types of child abuse involve a crossing of the conditions of the slave with what should be the conditions of a free and happy child. Helpful in drawing this distinction is Canetti's approach in *Crowds and Power*, in which the ideal child is presented as the direct opposite of the slave:

> In its play the child practices all the transformations it may be able to use later, and its parents help it with these and continually encourage it to acquire fresh ones. It continues to grow in many different ways, and when it has mastered its transformations it is rewarded by being promoted to adult status.
> This is the opposite of what happens to a slave. Just as its master does not allow a dog to chase whatever it wants, but confines its hunting to his own needs or wishes, so the slave's master puts out of his reach one metamorphosis after another. The slave must not do this and must not do that, but *some* things he must do over and over again.[27]

Canetti emphasizes, likewise, that enslaving men is equivalent to turning them into animals.[28] Refn unequivocally states the same premise in regard to One Eye: when he escapes from slavery, "he escapes from being an animal ... he starts off as a creature and he becomes man in the end."[29] The slave is already allied with mystical energies by virtue of his sacrificial status: "Like a death figure or revenant, the slave can cross the boundaries 'between life and death, community and chaos, the sacred and the secular ... [with] supernatural impunity.'"[30] The slave's life is not his own, it is an open vessel, so to speak, and One Eye's entire life has been a long preparation for his martyrdom. We could say that the same social order which requires slaves in the first place also requires martyrs as a way of reinforcing the foundational principle that true equality in this world is an unattainable, ineffable fiction.

Thus, ironically, in spite of the arc of change that One Eye goes through in *Valhalla Rising*, his character essentially exemplifies what Canetti has identified as the terminal process of enslavement, a curtailment of the slave's ability to go through the series of normative "transformations" natural to human development. Impaired in literal and figurative ways, he is always striving to discover where he "ought to be" at any given moment, and then to arrive there; this is the beckoning nature of One Eye's prophetic visions. Yet, he must go through "rituals of purification and martyrdom"[31] which have no precedent; by definition, then, these are creative, transformative moments, even if they are circumscribed by hopeless constraint, isolation and failure. The victim of assault or murder is, finally, an uncanny audience for a unique, improvisatory artist.

The commitment to faith arises not from finding answers but in spite of not finding them—*because* of not finding them. This is why faith and fallibility, faith and failure, go hand in hand, the ultimate failure being death, which is also the most urgent locus of faith itself. Again, the birth of what man has called the soul begins around the intuition that one should venerate, rather than fear and hate, the dead. The dignity of the dead must be equal to the dignity of the living; they must somehow be allowed to go on living. There has been Hell in this world all along, but it has taken the entire film for the characters to conceive an alternative: a paradise that emerges from and returns to human contact, and whose purpose is to exalt the sanctity of love.

• • •

In the end, the natives finally make their appearance, having come to kill the only ones left, One Eye and Are. In the end, before he gives up his life to save Are, One Eye reaches out and places his hand for a moment on the boy's arm; the importance of this gesture is underscored by Refn, who isolates it in a close-up. From telepathy and implicit trust we have finally moved to the bonding of touch. Never before has anyone touched another in this film without a violent, murderous or rapine intention, or because some ritual labor required it (the ceremonial painting of One Eye's body before a fight). The body of the Other is mainly to be ignored or destroyed. Here we see the discovery of touch as consolation, as an embodiment of empathy.

Bataille defined the sacred as "a privileged moment of communal unity, a moment of the convulsive communication of what is ordinarily stifled"[32]— or, in the case of *Valhalla Rising*, what has never known how to find expression before. This touch between One Eye and Are is the film's sacred moment: again, a discovery of tenderness, a gesture neither violently destructive nor compelled by strict necessity. As gratuitous as a gift, it is One Eye's final spiritual discovery, the completion of his life's journey. He wants the boy to live on after him, and to find peace and safety. In the boy One Eye has a posterity, one who has shared his past and will carry knowledge of him into the future; also, unlike the others in the film, One Eye is the only one who will not die utterly alone or in vain, but witnessed by Are and as a direct sacrifice for his sake. Are is placed in the position of being what Giorgio Agamben has called "the voice's daughter" or "the oral tradition," which succeeded the ancient days of prophecy and the exceptionalized prophetic voice.[33] "Those who act and produce must also save and redeem their creation. It is not enough to do; one must know how to save that which one has done."[34] Rather than describe what he believes is destined to happen in the future, Are will carry the memory of the sacrifice, the rescue, the salvation; he will pass it down to future generations, ensuring that One Eye is never forgotten. Indeed, the last image of the film is of One Eye's face briefly superimposed on the sky.

• • •

In Norse and German mythology, of course, Valhalla is the castle where warriors went to live after being killed in battle. It had 640 gates to accommodate the entrance of 800 men at a time.[35] In *Crowds and Power*, Elias Canetti names Valhalla as one of the great "invisible crowds," or crowds made up of the dead, whose continuously increasing numbers (through new wars) and whose corporeality in afterlife (the dead warriors feast and drink and continue to do battle) foster the comforting notion among the living that death "is not real death."[36] Canetti distinguishes this from later Christian conceptions of afterlife which "exhibit a superior degree of certainty and clarity" by promoting the idea that the invisible crowd of the dead is subject to moral qualifications, dividing more or less into devils on one side and angels or saints on the other: "With the latter [angels and saints] everything is calm. There is no more striving, for the goal has been reached."[37] The afterlife becomes an abstract realm of affect rather than a simulacrum of active life. The Christian function of the spirit in death is no longer to perform its former earthly tasks but to reap the somewhat abstracted benefits or torments of those tasks. Religious belief comes in to determine whether the afterlife will be "monstrous" or "calm."[38] But, whether pagan or Christian, the invisible crowds of the dead "are the life-blood of faith. The hopes and desires of men cling to them."[39]

To depict One Eye passing through monstrousness to a Zen-like place of calm, actor Mads Mikkelsen fully commits to the role, which became (Refn acknowledges) a test of their director-actor relationship:

> It was very much about trust, in terms that when Mads realized that he had no voice, only one eye, and ... was more like a monolith that mirrors everyone else ...

that was kind of challenging.... From an actor's point of view, I took everything away from him that he could ever use, so for him, it was a great search of how do you play this.... Because when you are no longer human, anything that was human behavior didn't work.

Gunnar Hansen, who played Leatherface in *The Texas Chain Saw Massacre*, has expressed similar difficulty with that role, also a man "who couldn't talk"; Hansen claims that his audition consisted of director Tobe Hooper asking whether he was "violent" or "crazy" and seeming discouraged when Hansen said he wasn't either of those things.[40]

A characteristic of *Valhalla Rising* is the starkness of its *mise en scène*. Refn may have been influenced, again, by Dreyer's approach to recreating the medieval world in *The Passion of Joan of Arc* by studiously avoiding the overstuffed trappings and detail of "epic" or costume films. "Handling the theme on the level of a costume film ... would have merely resulted in a comparison with other epochs," Dreyer wrote. "What counted was getting the spectator absorbed in the past ... the spirit of that time. In order to give the truth, I dispensed with 'beautification.'"[41] Although Refn's film is not un-beautiful in its sweeping land- and skyscapes, and its hallucinatory images, what predominates above all is the grime of wilderness living. This was accentuated by the fact that the actors were not permitted to shower, and wherever natural dirt was not sufficient, it was enhanced with make-up technicians' "dirt spray" in a can.[42]

The bleakness of Refn's recreated 12th century is compelling and total. It is an almost entirely pre-symbolic world. Apart from One Eye's tattooed body, and the sculptural tower of rocks which he builds, the only symbolic signifier which this world has given birth to, the only thing permitted to enhance or substitute for literal meanings, is the ubiquitous image of the cross. Refn reanimates this symbol by depicting it at its most primitive and schematic, sometimes merely two sword blades held together at right angles. Through this swordblade-cross, Refn reveals the cross itself as simultaneously bringing separate things together while also keeping the rest of the world at bay. The cross begins as a promise of unified wholeness and also as a weapon meant for the opposite, for dispersal and disarticulation. It creates not only a point of intersection (where the beams connect) but an inside and an outside. One can stand behind, beside, or beneath a cross (all of these positions are evoked in *Valhalla Rising*) as a way of defining its power as well as deriving personal power from it. (And when one stands beneath a cross, one has the comforting certainty of not being nailed up on it, an excluding vantage point that reminds me of Roland Barthes' witticism about liking to eat lunch in the Eiffel Tower because it was the only place in Paris where he did not have to see it.[43]) Like literal weapons, too, the cross can also be wielded to bludgeon or "stab," to clear a path or threaten. Inspired perhaps by the cross-shaped "Christian gun" in Jodorowsky's *The Holy Mountain*, this double image of peace and war, sacredness and desecration, cross and weapon, is obliquely dramatized by Refn in the scene where the Viking chieftain hugs Kare (bringing-together) only to accuse him of betrayal and stab him in the back (dispersal-disarticulation).

Indeed, cross and sword pollinate each other throughout *Valhalla Rising*. Upside-down swords frequently double as crosses, with the ornate hand-grips on the hilt of the sword forming the cross-beam and the blade forming the main shaft. The Viking chieftain sometimes brandishes his sword this way, and sometimes with the blade out, both gestures meant as threatening; he also drives his sword into the ground on numerous occasions as a way of claiming new land for God—land that he is under no illusion about having to take and defend by bloodshed. It is as if he were killing the land itself to make it his own.

Violence and crime are not born with Christianity, but they are cemented in place as an intrinsic part of an ineffable system whose workings are unknowable and who requires sins that it can absolve and punish. Bataille has written: "Perhaps Christianity is even fundamentally the pressing demand for crime, the demand for the horror that in a sense it needs in order to forgive. It is in this vein that I believe we must take Saint Augustine's exclamation, 'Felix culpa!,' Oh happy fault!, which blossoms into meaning in the face of inexpiable crime."[44] Thus, the Viking chieftain's question, "Will you turn your back on me? Will you turn your back on the Lord?" leads him to immediately stab his friend in the back, as if murder were finally far more incidental on the moral scale than apostasy or moral betrayal. "Christianity implies a human nature which harbors this hallucinatory extremity, which it alone has allowed to flourish.... It may be that Christianity would not want a world from which violence was excluded."[45]

One Eye stands at the crux of this intersection—this cross, if you will—where violence and honor, crime and virtue, produce the Big Bang needed for monotheism to take hold. He grows less violent as he grows more spiritual, but he never escapes from violence itself. He does not remove it from the world so much as hallow it as part of the legend of martyrdom. It remains a "kill or be killed" world, never more so than when he passively surrenders to his own murder. He has even foreseen his death in one of his mystical visions, the exact nature of which remains somewhat obscure and open to interpretation. Such visions are often allied with purity and holiness, a non-immanent form of sight. But they could also be a reflex evolved for simple survival. William C. Reeve has characterized the trope of a warrior's prophetic dreams (in a different context, specifically the writings of Kleist) not as the emblem of higher, much less "divine," powers of reasoning, but rather as a connection to the bestial unconscious, "barbaric roots" and "a deep-seated aggressiveness."[46] We might think of One Eye's visions also as representing "the pure destructive force of the unconscious ... in whose interest social laws are transgressed in moments of ecstasy and violence."[47] Like the unconscious, the violent rage that sustains his life churns unabated in One Eye no matter what he is doing, even at rest, even dreaming. And rather than having control over his dreams, as higher reasoning would imply, One Eye is controlled, taken over, by them; they act upon him like the bodies of his enemies in combat.

In any event, it is not accidental that his visions frequently relate to combat, violence and blood. Perhaps, then, such dreams would relate more to animals' instincts for survival, a sixth sense evolved through testing confrontations with the wilderness and with antagonists. One Eye could stand for a diachronic moment in the evolution of human reason, in which reason does not wholly supplant animalistic behaviors but coexists with them. The bestial is always there to take over whenever, as Reeve writes, "a reasonable approach could prove inadequate"[48]—i.e., risky or dangerous in terms of survival. Literally, One Eye's gift of second sight seems to stem directly from attributes that could be considered grotesque behaviors and brutish deformities: he has killed more people than anyone else in the narrative, and he is mutilated.

In terms of survival, then, One Eye's mind wants to act for his body even in lulls and times of waiting, as if to speed up events or to bring the most dreadful forecasts to culmination. We could say this is a pre-historical form of historical awareness. For the warrior, even passive contemplation is linked to action; thought must become action, unable to maintain itself in the impotent suspension of merely disembodied consciousness. This is also, to a great extent, Harry Caine's problem in *Fear X*; Caine, too, has psychic dreams and visions of his dead wife, and although he is only a mall security guard, what seems to drive him is the ageless and unconscious sense that his life as a man should be an impassioned, warrior-like quest.

Nonetheless, it is not enough for One Eye to embody spontaneous mythology, his mythology must also be preserved and disseminated through pre–media age storytelling: the boy must survive him, as the future teller of the tale. It is not One Eye's action but the boy's eventual description of that action which will found a future civilization. Here Refn is at odds with his own medium of film, since the visual proof of film has speedily derailed man from the former, agonizingly slow pace at which knowledge and belief could be passed down through time and certified as precious. It was precisely the fact that the handing-down was manual, so to speak, rather than technological, and depended largely on an older generation beating certain ideas into the children until they could accept an abstract law or an unproveable deity, that made the cementing of the indoctrination so effective over the ages. It was part of how people lived, not merely a story. It was a labor, an overriding labor within the life of social man. It was oral retellings of the same narrative. It was patient copying and recopying of texts by scribes (ancient sacred texts bear in their very aura an overwhelming responsibility; they parallel the passing of generations themselves). We are weary, stultified even, to think of how any book today could have such single-minded, endlessly reified power, and we cannot, and do not even want to, imagine a future in which such a thing could be allowed to happen again. Knowledge now, being instantaneous, is not held as precious or enduring; no one's life depends upon it. This is how knowledge is kept safe from itself.

The significance of this is, however, not only to enshroud faith within a form of ineffability from which it cannot be easily rationalized or reduced in meaning. It is also to suggest that familiar postmodern "pointing" toward something extratextual, which nonetheless gives weight and structure to the text itself, and to further suggest that this postmodern extratextuality actually has roots in the superstition of divine authorship, even as Joyce's *Ulysses* keeps its faith with Homer. Each work is the précis of an event or a philosophy whose origins cannot strictly be accounted for. Thus, the new work proclaims its worthiness through the urgent need to connect its own temporal existence (as text) with something beyond provisional authorship itself, the "proof" of something which predates and postdates the new work itself.

• • •

According to Beal, death can be "refuge from divine besiegement and divine obsession"[49]—paying back the wages of a too personal or too assuming relationship with the divine, perhaps, or indeed that crushing, saga-like weight of bearing endless generations of the past and the future. In more secular terms, the faith for which One Eye ultimately dies is that faith in the "invisible crowd" which Canetti identifies as "posterity" itself. This is the hope that one's immediate tribe or family group "must increase, first gradually and then with growing acceleration." This is a way of ensuring ongoing visibility through a pattern of phased invisibilities, or deaths, but deaths which leave behind future generations to carry life onward. Posterity is allegorized in Tarkovsky's *The Sacrifice* (1986), for example, in the story of the old monk who plants a barren tree on a hillside, making his young acolyte promise to water it every day until it comes to life. Canetti: "Tribes and whole peoples trace their origin back to a common ancestor, and the promises claimed to have been given to him show how glorious, and how numerous, a progeny he desired."[50]

In this sense, Refn builds into the myth of primal origins a unique breaking-out of those endlessly connected bloodlines which carried the thought of posterity in ancient times. Actual fathers end up separated from their actual sons; fathers and sons die far apart, without each other, or unrelated males take on makeshift father or son roles toward each other. Posterity becomes willed, an intellectual decision to choose to be part of this or that lineage; it also takes on an element of fate, of randomness. It is closer to what Canetti sees as the modern derivation of the ancient concept of posterity as innumerable descendants or "unbroken succession—a kind of density throughout time."[51] In modern times, "the image of abundance has detached itself from our own progeny and transferred itself to future humanity as a whole. For most of us, the host of the dead are an empty superstition, but we regard it as a noble and by no means fruitless endeavor to care for the future ... [and] to want their good and to prepare for them a better and juster life."[52] We think of Tonny wanting to rescue the baby at the end of *Pusher II*, accepting a protective fatherly role toward the boy not because he believes he is biologically the father but because he comes to understand that he could be a better father than anyone else. At the same time, actual father-son bonds go awry in that film and crystallize in patricide. "Unlike the Homeric 'imperishable glory' or the Christian belief in resurrection, however," modern conceptions of a noble posterity are typically "presented as having very little palliative effect."[53] Something greater must be at stake, some decisive change for the better, rather than merely the repetitious preservation of the past.

Thus, One Eye's death by violence is a hopeful attempt to abolish violence in the future, in the form of Are, the film's true hero and the witness, the survivor, an unassuming character sometimes barely noticed by the others but who derives his importance from sheer endurance. He is what Canetti calls "the ancestor": "It is part of the strength and glory of this ancestor that he was once left as the only human being alive.... Whilst he lived amongst his fellows he may not have distinguished himself particularly; he was one man like many others. But then suddenly he is entirely alone.... Humanity begins again with him and is built on him alone."[54] We note that Are begins and ends the film, thereby denoting in visual language his incipient and finally realized destiny as keeper of (the film's) time. The first shots are of him alone, struggling to carry a pail of water across an empty heath. In the final shot he is alone again, by the ocean with its promise of fertility. The domesticated water inside the bucket has grown to immense proportions, a metonymy for the spiritual growth traced by the film.

• • •

The warrior has this fatal weakness: he takes every sign of life as an affront against the mystery of life itself, which stands most fully revealed in the fraught emblem of the corpse. Any corpse "simultaneously occupies two places, the here and the nowhere. Neither of this world nor entirely absent from it, the cadaver thus mediates between these two incompatible positions."[55] The "nowhere," or what has been evacuated of animate life, thus serves to measure transcendence or spirituality as a negative quantity: utter lack of life is the most efficient and effective reminder or explanation of what actual life looks like, moves like, feels like. There is nothing fake or potentially betraying about it. It is only when the warrior can see a corpse (particularly one that he himself has made) that he can, internally, smile upon life itself.

One source of his accusation against what is alive is that people are more passive than they should be, too matter-of-factly or casually alive; they derive their meaning from random externals in too received and unquestioning a way. "Being is ... present only as a block of inertia that persists anyway, independent of signifying chains."[56] Put otherwise, the still corpse makes one suddenly value life. This motivation is implicit in warrior culture generally, and I call it a fatal weakness because it is usually defined, in narrative terms, as bringing the warrior to an impasse where only the production of his own corpse will serve the urgent need of reanimating the lost drive or purpose in life. The killer saves himself from the threat of death by killing but also, as Canetti writes about the figure of the executioner, "anticipates the ultimate penalty which hangs over himself."[57] Hannah Arendt identifies this same syndrome as the ultimate certification of depersonalized totalitarian violence: "The climax of terror is reached when the police state begins to devour its own children, when yesterday's executioner becomes today's victim."[58] One thinks back to Lt. Peter in *Fear X*, killing in the name of a spurious justice and finally being killed in a similar act of justice/revenge. All power is, at bottom, a perceived mastery of death, but although death may be deferred for a time it is never vanquished—the killer's (or police state's) dependency on death itself ensures this.

Passivity is already a kind of crime and a source of guilt. Ernst von Alpen suggests a direct link between passivity and guilt, at least in the witnessing eye: "The similarity between tree and criminal could be, for example, that both are imperturbable. Trees grow on as if nothing had happened [beneath them], just as the perpetrator, untouched by the destruction he committed, the death he dealt, went on with the violence."[59] This evokes the extension of the warrior's transference of other life energies to himself through killing. Primitive tribes believed in a "supernatural and impersonal power, which can pass from one man to another.... By killing his opponent the survivor becomes stronger and ... capable of new victories."[60]

The understanding that life is only able to persist and become enhanced through destruction cannot be ameliorated in the idealistic vision of people who simply come to live and love more strongly; a greater sacrifice is always required. "There is probably no more universal signpost of urgency and magnitude than body counts."[61] There is also nothing more stultifying and benumbing; man's greatest adaptations throughout history have always been to mass deaths, wars, disasters, genocides, plagues, and also to those shadows of mass deaths, slavery and prisons. It is individual crimes that fascinate and become difficult to forgive; whereas the suffering of any collective contains the democratic means of managing the grief and finally growing more and more indifferent to it—"indifferent" as in the fact that one no longer feels the need to act in retribution, or one grows simply weary at the prospect of so large an atrocity to redress. One forgets without ever truly forgetting, the worst kind of forgetting. At the same time, indifference is always maddening to the warrior, who can tolerate anything but this, since it mirrors too closely the serenity with which he himself has cultivated his own destructive inclinations. He is a man who can only feel by being forced to acknowledge how little he actually feels. Numbness is his tragic burden; therefore it must be an actively, outwardly displayed numbness, through lashing out in omnipotent violence.

The dichotomous One Eye suggests the fact that there have always been two schools of thought in modern culture regarding religion and in particular paganism. One is that the soul is in danger of being engulfed and swallowed up, killed off, so to speak, by the body and its exigent needs. The other school of thought reverses this fear and stems from the threat posed to the body by the concept of the soul: that the body's needs will be curtailed, will go unsatisfied, will be forgotten utterly in abnegation, a foretaste of complete nonexistence. The first way expresses, in schematic form, the animating emotion behind Christianity; the second way, likewise schematically, attempts to reclaim and defend a space for pagan sensibilities (although, by definition as archaic discourses, neither is truly authentic in a modern context). Refn has astutely stated that, in fact, Christianity, where it could not outright conquer and convert, contented to fuse itself with pagan beliefs so that the widely held superstitions of the one became inextricably mingled with those of the other. The pagans were not proselytizers or missionaries, unlike the Christians; yet they bore an influence simply by virtue of being a kind of obstacle which the new Christianity had to work around or else assimilate.[62] Ultimately, there was a certain consolation in creating a religion that was a patchwork of beliefs that people were already comfortable with, rather than creating one whole out of alien cloth. It is hard to retrain entrenched iconographies, those representations of the real that mankind had addicted itself to in its prehistoric days and against which the prescription "Make unto thee no graven image" never stood much chance of demolishing. Cinema is the living proof of this. Indeed, both violence and religion—as epistemic breaks with reality—are reduced to the status of sibling metaphors for the way the image becomes overloaded with the meaning of our repetitive thrill of surviving the death of the real that occurs whenever we look at the image. This is why Carl Dreyer and *Cannibal Holocaust* can bear equal weight within Refn's aesthetic-philosophic sensibility: in both, the pure passion of what the image reveals bears witness to that radical exhilaration of survival.

– 8 –

Drive

> Such is the new and difficult feature of the plot. The other ... is the relation that I cannot sustain, and whose approach is death itself, the mortal passivity. —Maurice Blanchot[1]

A number of Refn's films center on protagonists who bear a special skill over which they can claim some mastery. For Frank in *Pusher* it is drug dealing, although things spiral out of control for him; similarly with Bronson, whose natural ability to fight (or is it more just willingness to give and take beatings?) lands him in increasingly narrow confinements. Not all antisocial skills are self-destructive, however. The same warrior skill of fighting gives One Eye greater and greater freedom, which he uses for his gradual spiritual development. Treasuring movie lore, for the socially-challenged Lenny in *Bleeder*, becomes a gateway to being able to love. Furthermore, two other Refn protagonists are remarkable sleuths: Harry in *Fear X* is an amatory amateur who learns sleuthing to solve his wife's murder, while Miss Marple is quite simply the world's greatest detective. But perhaps in no Refn film is the idea of the specially endowed skill more central than in *Drive* and in the figure of its main character, called Driver (played by Ryan Gosling).

Drive is a film that has a scent of paradise about it, of serendipity. It is that rarest of things anymore: a happy film, not in the sense that everything in it is happy but rather that it is happy with itself, and also that it seems to have been a happy experience for the artists who made it. "I was quite happy at that period of my life," Refn admits.[2] The director had recently moved to L.A. and rented a house in the Canyon with his partner Liv and their two children. Once assembled, the cast of *Drive* would come to this house to run lines with Refn and work out their parts. Gosling had been given "his own key, so he could come and go whenever he wanted." The director and the star had met not long before and bonded during a strange, now legendary night of antihistamines and '80s hair ballads. Cinema was the sealant. The first film that Refn and Gosling watched together was Kenneth Anger's *Scorpio Rising* (1964), inspiring them with its slow tracking shots of shiny classic cars and its scorpion decal on the back of a biker's leather jacket. *Drive* emerged initially from this meeting of minds between Refn and Gosling, in which Gosling was to play "a man who drives around in a car at night, listening to pop music that gives him emotional relief."[3]

From that evocative seed came a film that ended up being much more universal than any of its key inspirations—as universal as the longing for propulsion itself. There is every kind of car chase in this film. The opening one, which takes place at night, has Driver's souped-up baby darting into tight spaces to elude police cruisers like a kitchen cockroach dusting the broom. It also includes a spectacular flight from helicopters across a freeway bridge. Later, there is an old-fashioned ram-and-slam jalopy-style pursuit with billowing dust (and some amazing backwards driving). Energized by the idea of driving and its heady American connotation of freedom (although it is highly arguable that the world's freest drivers are to be found in the United States), Refn displays his own prowess at directing action scenes, here proudly in the adrenalin-spiked tradition of car-fetish classics like *Bullitt* (1968) and *The French Connection* (1971).

So it is difficult not to imagine Driver's skill as being closely related to Refn's own skill as a filmmaker—now unleashed with bigger, brighter toys to play with. And just as driving and filmmaking are extroverted for the most part, they both have an introverted side—namely, driving is what keeps Driver isolated from others. His living comes from driving—he is auto mechanic, movie stuntman, stockcar racer—but ultimately not his life, which is somewhere beyond the road, as he comes to realize without losing his gift. If anything, Driver achieves his ultimate mastery of driving only after he has discovered something even more fulfilling, an undying love. And with *Drive* we feel it is much the same for the director: he has connected his craft with a renewed excitement and energy, and perhaps a sense of being happy with himself.

• • •

Drive was Ren's first U.S.-based film since *Fear X*. However, it is essentially an independent film with an A-list Hollywood cast, since studio backing (even with Gosling on board) chickened out and Refn had to seek funding in France.

The good side of this, as Refn has stated, was that he and Gosling had total control over the overall making of the film. *Drive* was, he has said with some satisfaction, made in "a cocoon" without "focus groups," second-guessing, or Hollywood interference of any kind.[4] It has a certain sui generis quality. And the Euros were safe: *Drive* ended up being a titan at Cannes, where it premiered, winning Refn the Best Director award. Refn's vision and artistry had triumphed once more over doubts and delays. Again, the smoothness of Driver's driving and the sinuous smoothness of *Drive* itself are succinct, compact reflections of each other, and there is something almost classically Hawksian about this fable of men doing what they do best, doing what they love, and becoming heroes in the process.

Heroism is one of *Drive's* explicit themes. A techno ballad featured prominently on the soundtrack ("A Real Hero") underscores this, but the presence of heroism itself should not be surprising, since it has been an ongoing concern of Refn's since *Fear X* at least. The ideal of the credible and real hero, who nonetheless possesses or attains a certain mythic quality, rises to its perfect pitch in *Drive*. Indeed, it is one of the largest aspects of reclaiming myth for the modern sensibility. The classic hero saga has largely been jettisoned as socially and politically naïve, if not worse (its characteristic individualism seen as an elitist promotion of anti-egalitarian values), though its hold on storytelling and its possibilities for cathartic intensity have yet to be replaced by compelling alternatives. (It should be said, however, that Refn himself has already found ways of moving beyond the central individualism of the classic hero saga in his most recent film, *Only God Forgives*.) The problematic of the hero is that he or she acts alone; the hero does by definition what others cannot, thus no one can assist him or her.

Yvonne Tasker writes, "The hero of the action narrative is often cast as a figure who lacks a place within the community for which he fights."[5] The hero feels compassion for the threatened figures whom he or she must protect; but it is usually an unnatural, learned compassion based on logical deduction rather than actual felt empathy. Weak things get crushed in this world; this given family, or this mother and child, are weak; thus they will be crushed if "I" do not protect them. This is the decisive element which forces the hero out of passivity and into action. The fight against injustice, in action cinema, is always a fight against no less than mortality itself, and the dazed realization that the thing one loves can be harmed and will one day perish anyway, regardless of any efforts to keep it alive. Feelings of love immediately go to feelings of needing to protect the loved object from inevitable violation; in this, the numbed hero often gives the aura of also being traumatized, violated—the painful and sometimes buried memory of what Blanchot calls "the blow always long since received which makes us all the more sensible to all blows."⁶ Like Refn, whose violent men (as we have seen) engender new ideas of themselves and other men through their violent acts, Blanchot understands this life-changing "blow" to be, among males, an alternative birth process.⁷

There is some projected messianic paranoia here, a demonization of weakness per se; but this, too, is essential to traditional myths. The bonds which appear among ordinary humans are precisely what restrains them from being able to rise up against the threat of evil forces: their love for each other brings fear of risk and the tendency toward general tolerance of others. They are civilized and comfortable; their purpose is to enjoy their way of life no matter how threatened and to demonstrate it as peaceful, virtuous and worthy of preservation. The hero, on the other hand, is one who exists outside these bonds, almost inhumanly but with solemn and undying love for the human (as he or she perceives it). The hero enacts an imitation of compassion built up from gentle envy and the fierce longing for a sacred otherness. As Michael S. Kimmel writes, the hero's "compassion is social and generalized, [and] he [or she] forms no lasting emotional bonds with any single person."⁸

• • •

Drive works admirably as a kind of swan song of the individualistic hero, one who is not as lofty and self-righteous as one might fear. To a large extent, Driver is not even particularly individualistic. We will get to some of his oddities a little later, but for the moment I would like to describe the crucial role of *environment* in hero myths, for this is an aspect of the myth structure which Refn has clearly updated and modernized. In classic hero-myth structure there is always a toxic or dangerous environment, a literal area of land or realm of existence which has been invaded or always-already occupied by forces hostile to fragile life. In *Drive* this is the modern urban world controlled by organized crime.

Refn's mostly unglamorous L.A. is vaguely dystopian, presided over by a West-coast Jewish mafia network who take their orders from the East-coast Italian heads of the family, and are therefore driven by a frustrated "second-rank" status. Bitterness curdles the air around these glorified bagmen, Bernie Rose (Albert Brooks) and Nino (Ron Perlman), ersatz and deracinated, eating Chinese takeout in the little pizza joint that they use as a front. "The family that calls me a fucking kike, to my face!" Nino sneers about the *cosa nostra*. "I'm 59 years old.... They still pinch my cheek like I'm a fucking kid." With time seeming to slip away from them, Bernie and Nino can see no other choice but to ratchet up their immediate power over L.A.

This is the environment which requires a unique hero to make it safe for life, progress, and the future, represented in *Drive* by the threatened figures of Irene (Carey Mulligan) and her young son Benicio (Leon Kades). It becomes Driver's mission to protect Irene and Benicio after Irene's husband Standard (Oscar Isaac) is killed while trying to repay a debt to Bernie and Nino. This turns into a vendetta for Driver when it becomes apparent that Irene and Benicio will not be safe unless both mob bosses are killed.

So far this is classically mythic, or classically enough. But the hero's suppression of human bonding is not necessarily something that Refn wholly retains for his modern fairytale, *Drive*. For Driver, it is more a question of bad timing and bad luck that he cannot join the community. However, even though Driver is reconfigured so that he is not so completely outside of human community, he is still defined mainly by the extent to which he is shut out, and thus behaves like a classical hero.

For one thing, the insider love within the community often seems wounding and strange to the chivalrous hero. The nature of romantic love inside the community is that it has been tested; it has the wisdom of experience behind it. Actress Carey Mulligan describes the love between her character and Driver as being mutual but "respectful" and "not physical." Scriptwriter Hossein Amini describes their love as something "they both want ... so badly, but it's so repressed for both of them."[9]

Because the traditional hero is not permitted to take part in emotional bonds with others, two features emerge in him, both of which are present in Driver. First, he lacks the timidity and restraint which the bonds (really tokens of civilization) have inculcated in the community. He can do battle against evil forces with little to lose and with a killer's ability to overcome taboos about the sanctity of life. Second, his inability to experience social bonding for himself has given him a nearly undue respect for that bonding. It amounts in his mind to something close to a religious experience or paradise; when for the people who actually exist within the bonded community everything is more normalized and everyday. Driver's love can triumph over the bad guys but never over the bonded community, since his love is in itself nothing more than a tribute to that community and a hypervigilant misreading of its values. Such great renegade loves are doomed because they only serve to remind the lovers of that purity which only the community can bestow. At the same time, love may be stronger outside of the community; whereas there is an element of duty always present within the community—the duty of keeping a family together, for instance. As Mulligan explains, "[Irene is] trying to keep focus on the fact that this is her family [Standard and Benicio]."[10] The hero's love, however, is strictly passion, a passion which he can only re-channel into the fervent duty of protection: a hysterical overcompensation for his inability to perform the smaller daily duties.

Thus the hero's unique and nearly inordinate respect for women and children as the rightful property of another, as well as a proof of purist intentions. (Driver is not programmed to steal these things, or anything, directly from another man.) *Drive* steers well clear of the patriarchal doldrums; but in traditional myths, the child protects the woman from being fallen, even if she lacks a husband. Tradition always positions a child as being the living memento of the father, the "first man," the man to whom the woman initially gave herself (with a boy-child, he becomes even closer to a memento of the father's literal genitalia). The child becomes for the hero a flesh and blood talisman of the bond that is so sacred to him and which he cannot imagine for himself or herself. The hero cannot create it, he or she only knows it when he or she sees it, a kind of critic, perhaps, parsing the sweep of the humanities for exemplary avatars. The hero is concerned with last things: the widow who shall never take another man; the orphaned lineage; the Manichean confrontation which is meant to symbolize the end of days writ small. And it follows naturally that the hero is thus engaged with death more than with life. We can look at it this way: the community's love is largely passive and invested in the production of living beings, children; the hero's love is active but invested solely in the production of corpses. The future, of which he or she must deprive the villains, returns as a precious thing in the community's children, like the return on an emotional investment.

Somewhat paranoiacally, the hero can imagine himself or herself far more easily as another one of the community's enemies; attacking all other enemies draws as clearly as possible a line of separation. The hero already feels that whatever love is given him or her by the community is essentially stolen, that he or she is being predatory and presumptuous in all moments except the decisive ones in which he or she risks life and limb to confront and scourge the community's enemies. When the hero darkens the door of someone's home, he or she marks it as a place of jeopardy merely because he or she is there.

If the male hero speaks to the wife of another man, especially if he likes this woman, he is careful not to taint her in any way, not even in her own eyes. Driver has very few moments alone with Irene, and then they are almost always accompanied by Benicio, the memento of Standard's prior claim to Irene. (For female heroes this chivalry can also extend itself to women, both in sexualized and platonic ways; it can even extend itself to weaker males. Movies which contain female heroes who conform closely to the male-heroic archetype include *Red Road, Point of No Return, Haywire, Million Dollar Baby*, the *Aliens* franchise, *The Girl with the Dragon Tattoo, I Am Number Four, Kill Bill, The Brave One, Bound*—to cite only a few offhand.) Driver immediately bonds with Irene's son. In fact, the nearness of the situation to an "actual" ready-

The tender and respectful love between Driver (Ryan Gosling) and Irene (Carey Mulligan) in *Drive* strikes a romantic, fairy-tale chord in the midst of what is otherwise a hard-hitting crime drama. Love temporarily humanizes Driver, a classic loner hero, and also gives him incentive to become what Refn calls "a superhero, a scorpion."

made family seems to be part of what fuels Driver's devotion. He first falls in love with Irene after overhearing her and Benicio saying "I love you" to each other in a grocery store. He is, appropriately, one aisle removed from their bonded ritual, listening in. As a salutary gesture, he takes them on a play date in a park away from the city; it is the film's only peaceful interlude, as they sit by a lake skipping stones. This is also the only sequence in *Drive* that suggests that there can be peace in stasis, in standing still. In all other scenes of stillness something ominous is about to catch a stalled, unwary person off-guard.

• • •

In essence, then, the hero is already close to that which he or she fights against; the hero is vaguely dirty in the same ways that "it" is dirty. When Driver first meets Bernie he hesitates to shake the mobster's hand, saying humbly, "My hands are a little dirty." Rose gives him a fixed look, nods and says gruffly, "So are mine." They meet under this mutual understanding that both bear a stigma, both stand outside the community.

Although unalike in most ways, both are tormented by a sliver under the skin, the *resentment* of not belonging, of failing some ultimate judgment. When they are reminded of this, they can kill nearly anyone at hand in order to make the bad feeling go away. The fact that Driver *is* accepted by the bonded community does not change him into a domesticated creature nor alleviate his guilt. Under different circumstances the same man who emerges as the hero for a given community might very well be the one who preys on that community.

And this sense of guilt, this slight dirt on the hands, is not merely imaginary. Driver spends his nights piloting getaway cars for criminals who contact him anonymously and contract his services; he shows no interest in committing crimes himself, but he does live off the criminal enterprise of others (as L.A., perhaps, participates in commerce with businesses that turn out to be fronts for organized crime). It is true that he is not programmed to steal directly from others, but when driving comes into play it is different: his main skill and raison d'être makes all infractions permissible—a wash, so to speak. Here again we can draw similarities with filmmaking: the director must get his hands "a little dirty," so to speak, by raising funds from anywhere he can get them. In fact, Bernie himself was a movie producer in the '80s.

To a great extent, of course, Driver is not truly "with" the criminals, even though he abets them and takes a cut of their loot. Often he makes it clear that when he acts as wheelman on a heist he stands apart from his thieving passengers in objective judgment of their criminal skills. His efficiency is so legendary in the underworld and so deeply ingrained in him that he seems to view the heists as events for his private spectatorship, operations to take pride in for their smoothness and sang froid, or to frown upon for their slip-ups and agonizing delays.

Driver, at least at the start of the film, is invested in the success of crime; whereas the community, in this L.A. night world, knows but does not know. It turns a blind eye and tries to get about its business, since this is much easier than attempting to uproot a criminal organization whose roots are clearly everywhere and whose bosses are perceived (and perceivable) as wealthy local businesspeople. Not pillars of the community, though: "good" businesspeople are represented by Standard's attorney, for instance, or by the diner where Irene waitresses. Not all business is corrupt; but some corruption operates strictly as business, only the means and aims vary from the front room to the back room of the store, so to speak. Even this salutary division is crossed when Bernie and Nino begin to fall apart; Bernie kills a bumbling lieutenant in one of the pizzeria's booths with a fork from the utensils station and a butcher knife from the kitchen.

Within the hero-myth environment, then, a false love is rendered to the villains, either unknowingly or grudgingly; but even though he knows it to be a "blackmailed emotion" (Chryssie Hynde), the hero is nonetheless profoundly jealous of this love. Above all, he or she does not wish to see the sacred bonding of the community tarnished and perverted by the need to pretend to love its overlords and oppressors even as they are forced to pay them obeisance. Again, this is not because the hero can ever imagine having the community's love truly for himself or herself; just the opposite, it is because the hero knows that the love can never be his or hers. This is why it is a point of wounded, defeated pride on the hero's part that this love must not go to anyone unworthy.

Refn permits one epochal kiss to transpire between Driver and Irene to complete their own deep but fleeting bond, since a kiss, he says, is the essential "sensual" ingredient of any couple. It is staged nonetheless like a fantasy, in an elevator where he and Irene are trapped with a mob hitman. Acting fast, Driver sweeps Irene to one corner, shielding her from the hitman. An artificial spotlight falls on them (much like the one that falls on Lenny and Lea at the end of *Bleeder*), and time stops as their lips meet for the first and only time in the film. Hyper-romantically, Driver becomes willing to die if need be for this single intimate moment with Irene. Their kiss is an exceptional moment and an incentive motivating Driver's completion of himself as a sacrificial hero. Refn explains: "He kisses her goodbye because now he knows what he has to do ... to turn himself into a superhero, a scorpion."[11] Hossein Amini states, "She almost makes him human for a very brief moment,"[12] and although this moment is not to last, its impact warms and sweetens the entire film, even if Driver's next action is to immediately turn around and stomp the hitman to death, finally squashing his whole head underfoot like some enormous insect. In slight contradistinction to the traditional individualistic hero whom Tasker tells us never finds a place within the human community, Driver is allowed to taste real love, albeit within a space nearly as confined and dead-ended as one of Bronson's cages or even the grotesque elevator in *Fear X* where Harry finally confronts his wife's killer. (Refn seems to feel about elevators what Hitchcock felt about trains.)

• • •

What is poignant about Driver is that he always acts as a substitute for someone else, a proxy. He goes uncredited for his labor. There is even an extent to which Driver courts a certain deliberate invisibility beyond the required stealth and surreptitiousness of crime films. Tossing Driver the keys to a Chevy Impala for a heist, garage owner Shannon (Bryan Cranston) assures him that it is the "most popular car in the state of California" and "no one will be looking at you." The melancholy tone of this last line suggests a eulogy for the recessive Driver from his friend (Shannon, who is Driver's boss at the garage and who acts as his agent with the movie stuntwork, is also Driver's only friend). Shannon sees his loneliness and feels bothered by it even more than Driver does.

Here we begin to see Driver's lack of traditional individualism, even though he operates alone. Instead of the classic myth structure, heroism is born from a moment of crisis in which the hero actively surrenders to a process of allowing himself to be redefined by and for others. This process occurs in a number of Refn's films: Tonny's attempt to rescue the infant at the end of *Pusher II*; One Eye's sacrifice of himself so that Are can live. Passivity is at the core of the Refn hero, no matter how violent he might be. There is paradox in the way the needs of others take over the hero and become his or her own. It is helpful to note Maurice Blanchot's explications of the contradictory nature of passivity—i.e., an active surrender which becomes regenerative. One first recedes "from the privilege of the first person,"[13] the subject position, the declarative and pronominal "I." In general, a hero becomes exceptional only after he or she has accepted that his or her identity no longer matters. The hero acts as one who no longer quite exists, with nothing to lose; thus his or her actions are able to become exemplary.

Blanchot rightly denotes the hero as a "hostage,"[14] or one who must be detained as a substitute for something else. The hero is a machine, which, once activated, disguises and absorbs the labor of others. On the movie lot, as they get ready to perform a car-crash stunt, Shannon tells Driver, "You're doubling for the star, like a day-player." The hero—as a stand-in, someone meant to run risks (largely without credit) for the real star—can suggest a system in which all labor and its needs are communally shared: *to each according to his needs, from each according to his abilities*. Doesn't this often misunderstood motto make perfect sense when we think about the prowess and mission-work of the classic hero? The materialist aspect has been rendered in its most basic form—it is the apportionment of life itself for which the hero fights on others' behalf. Again, like stuntwork, the risks of life fall upon whomever can handle them the best.

Thus the original logic of the communist motto—*to each according to his needs, from each according to his abilities*—assumes the character of an expression of *justice*. "In other words," Blanchot writes, "I must answer for the persecution that opens me to the longest patience and which is in me the anonymous passion, not only by taking it upon myself regardless of my own consent; I must also answer to it with refusal, resistance, and combat."[15] This "anonymous passion" is what overcomes and fills the self after the self has been willingly voided in the service of justice.

Driver's passion, again, is not forced to remain completely anonymous. Amini describes Driver's love for Irene as coming from "a place of resistance,"[16] which intriguingly extends the idea that the love story in *Drive* is more than the vestigial spark for the "anonymous passion." For Driver, to love in itself is seemingly a forbidden act which goes against his programming, in which it is already an act of rebellion to feel and pursue. Also trying to break out of a kind of programming, One Eye goes through a stage of trying to create monuments that will endure into the future before he realizes that the story of his death (retold at a later date by the boy who survives) will be the only monument he leaves, and the only one he needs. Driver, too, will live on in the memory of those he has saved, and this is finally what a hero *wants* in the same way that others speak of wanting to go to the beach or to get married. It is the only bond a hero can conceive, and it suggests why religious myths stem from hero myths and vice versa. Veneration, the persistent remembrance which preempts and prohibits, the extension of control beyond the span of human life, all of this points to the idea that a single action can contain an ethic, and a single bond can contain all bonds, just as all souls are contained within God, where they find immortalism.

Blanchot explains that, after depersonalization, the hero experiences a return, "if possible—for it may be that there is no return," to "the adverse I" or "the I that knows and that knows it is exposed." We would be correct to see in this a reformulation of the Freudian Superego, which here emerges after the death of the individual ego, as a stern reminder that even this ego-death, this pitiful love of justice, this hanging oneself out as bait for the bad guys (and in Driver's case his love for Irene), is nothing but an obscene exhibitionism, a wallowing in disgraced weakness. This is why the "return" as such is more than a notional one, although it is akin to double checking to make sure one has locked the door on one's way out. Put otherwise, from that voided ego which actively surrenders to the needs of others a remainder of power must be roused to spasm outward against the wrong that must be righted. The adverse "I" is where the emptied ego regains enough individualism in order to be able to feel and direct rage. In active terms, the emergence of the Superego and the return to the adverse "I" gives rise in the hero "to egotistical Omnipotence, to murderous Will"[17]—contrary to Freudian dictates that the Superego manifests checkmate-power over the unruly atavism of the individual. The hero is that sole figure whose basest instincts merge with the Superego, deforming it and being deformed in turn. The hero makes the Superego rousing and bloodlusty (he gives it that common touch, so to speak), while the Superego credits the hero with having denoted the fine line between justice and revenge (although often this denotation is far from clear). At bottom, this is nothing more than the motivation that obtains wherever men choose to kill and die in something's name.

The Blanchotian concept of "murderous Will" (and here we cannot help but hear the echo of Schopenhauer, even as Blanchot deliberately constructs a progression or metamorphosis for the hero which Schopenhauer was content to ascribe to innate and irreversible characteristics) is, in fact, foundational to many action films, in which a man first seeks to remove himself from a battleground, believing that he can remain above the chaotic, painful world, only to find himself pulled back into the thick of battle by an attack which he has undergone, a loss which he has sustained, or an injustice which he has witnessed. This is Michael Corleone's explicit cry in *The Godfather III*—"They keep pulling me back in!"—but we also think of the implicit structure of the *Death Wish* series in which the vigilante architect (played by Charles Bronson) goes through this cycle again and again, to the point where it becomes gimmicky and overcompensatory. Every time he tries to get away from conflict, conflict pointedly follows him, almost as if he himself has wished it, willed it into being through an inner negativity which calls out for a legitimizing mirror, that active and demanding world, as Blanchot writes, "where negativity is the task."[18]

The labor absorbed by the hero without reward is always, so the parlance goes, "dirty work": that which would soil and contaminate a normalized ego. The egoless self is finally not a completely depleted lack but part of a dialectic that pushes and gives. It is, therefore, action "*beyond* being. Only this relation, and not selfhood or identity,"[19] defines the hero.

• • •

But isn't Driver really something more (or less) than a human hero? Isn't he really, in fact, a cyborg?

I can never watch *Drive* without feeling that Driver is a super-sophisticated, top-line species of A.I. He eats real food in two scenes, so this would contradict the existing lore about cyborgs. And yet we never see him sleep, even though he is a workhorse, holding down at least three jobs. In one scene, when he needs to intimidate a loudmouth in a diner, he turns his whole head so stiffly toward the antagonist that it unmistakably recalls robotic body language. And, although stabbed by Bernie in their final showdown, he manages to kill Bernie and drive away; we see him in the film's last images seemingly unscratched and unscathed.

Cyborg or not, Driver represents what Joseph Tabbi has called "technology as an outward embodiment of thought"[20]—his car moves sinuously to the motion Driver imagines. Again, there is no troubled ego here, only holistic reflex. Where the fusion of human and machine becomes complete, there ceases to be that "deep self-division" which plagues "the postmodern ego which goes on romantically asserting its independence from all technological determinations."[21]

The main thing about Driver is that he yearns so much to be helpful. Somewhat sad to say, we do not associate such extreme helpfulness with human characters but with inorganic ones: the androids in *Star Wars*, the unwanted child in *A.I.*, or even Hal in *2001* before he shows his vindictive, destructive side. But perhaps Hal is an exception that proves the rule, going as he does from "good" to "evil." The cyborg redeems our own fallibility by incarnating goodness as a purely mechanical function destined to break down at some point. Of course we betray each other, let each other down—even our machines do this. But most cyborgs, like Driver if he is one, are incapable of violating the trust that is placed in them. They go beyond the passivity of children to the way we might think of life in the Garden before the Fall; and it does not seem coincidental that they are often depicted as the harbingers of a new race of people, presumably as we ourselves once were (according to Christianity). Perhaps the entire fantasy of the cyborg-among-us is really the idea of prelapsarian innocence, the knowledge prior to knowledge.

For example, Driver always does the right thing. By this I mean both the correct thing and the successful thing. But how does he know what it is and how to do it? I have been deliberately referring to him as "programmed." The other characters in the film display knowledge that has come about, shall we say, after the Fall. The mobsters are riddled with shame, self-loathing and envy; the women around them are strippers. Standard is weak, while Irene feels tempted by Driver to cheat on Standard. Only Driver—and here the touching scene of him in the nature park with Irene and Benicio becomes relevant—has knowledge of something primeval, untouched by worldly experience, yet also able to recognize the bad faith in others and do battle with it.

It becomes a riddle. If Driver is a cyborg who has been programmed with prelapsarian, essentially godly knowledge, then who programmed him? Could a mere human simulate the godlike code? And if the code were known, why couldn't it be taught to and practiced by human beings? Why would artificial intelligence be required to flesh it out, as it were? The ineffable, perhaps, is something that can be reflected only in an other. Or Refn might be suggesting that the code of innocence might be something that we all do know but are unable to enact because we have been compromised too much by the world.

This question dates from much further back than the modern age of cybernetic technology. In Mary Shelley's *Frankenstein*, a key text of Romanticism, we see the same attempt to create an exemplary being who would stand outside of humanity and perhaps above it. The Baron Frankenstein (his title puns on infertility) stitches parts of corpses together and reanimates his creature with a divine, or infernal, spark of lightning. But the Creature is a recalcitrant son, ungrateful, unloving, alienated, with an undisguised murderous hatred for his "father." Shelley's novel allows the Creature far more articulation and purposefulness than most of the modern film versions, in which the monster's helplessness is touching and a more precise measure of his creator's confused delusions. There is no natural lineage between Doctor and Monster. In Shelley's novel, the kinship is close enough to act as a repellant.

Perhaps it was Shelley's femaleness that caused her to conceive this guilty male longing to give birth, and also to expose it as a tyranny. The masculine hero, no matter what his putative aim, stands outside of society because he cannot take part in the central function of social organization and continuity: the production of children for the future. Instead, the hero's job, as we have seen, is the production of corpses—enemy corpses, hostile corpses, scientifically revivified corpses, anything to shovel the future into the past as quickly as possible and make both time periods identical as sites of compulsive regression. Enormous swathes of future are cut away like forestation in order to erect the image of individual and collective pasts. Like a serial killer, the modern hero knows who should live and who should die. And like Lenny in *Bleeder*, mouthing along with Udo Kier in *Flesh for Frankenstein*, he wants to use all the corpses to "populate and repopulate the world" in complete and gleeful denial of female biological reproduction.

The highly principled Driver, at any rate, remains true to Irene and Benicio, and, to the extent that his power is embodied in their rescued lives, to himself as well. There is no moment of acclaim or even recognition for Driver; thus, his fate contradicts Blanchot's shrewd assertion of the inevitable pride that lies behind sacrifice, since "the sovereign gift is still only the privilege of sovereignty, an enrichment of glory and prestige, even when it is the heroic gift of one's life."[22] This is why Driver's sacrifice is registered but ultimately downplayed. He may be dead or he may be immortal, tooling around some slick 21st century Valhalla. "Life," as we know it, did not belong to Driver in the first place. What matters in the film's final shots is that Irene is still alive and has the chance to start over with making a life for her and her son; whether Driver is headed toward new missions and adventures, or whether we are only seeing the mythic outline of his lonely night-driving repeated on endless identical streets, to a techno beat, is almost beside the point. Sovereignty, like getting the girl, was never exactly in the cards. Driver's power has always been a matter of duty, the only way he can approximate the dutiful love within the community, and never a question of privilege, since outside of the community there is no real life to speak of, let alone honorific states of being such as "privilege" or "sovereignty."

– 9 –

Only God Forgives

I said, The sky is further away than you think, is it not, mama? It was without malice, I was simply thinking of all the leagues that separated me from it. She replied, to me her son, It is precisely as far away as it appears to be. She was right. But at the time I was aghast. —Samuel Beckett[1]

But what matter whether I was born or not, have lived or not, am dead or merely dying, I shall go on doing as I have always done, not knowing what it is I do, nor who I am, nor where I am, nor if I am. Yes, a little creature, I shall try and make a little creature, to hold in my arms, a little creature in my image, no matter what I say. And seeing what a poor thing I have made, or how like myself, I shall eat it. Then be alone a long time, unhappy, not knowing what my prayer should be or to whom. —Beckett[2]

Perhaps inevitably, given the industry clout that Refn and Gosling had suddenly accrued with *Drive*, there was intense backlash against their second film together, *Only God Forgives*, which they filmed in Thailand and premiered at Cannes in May 2013. Although *Drive* had triumphed at the festival in 2011, a coterie of reviewers greeted *Only God Forgives* with a booing section. The film is challenging; artistically it takes giant risks. It does not show Refn playing safety positions against his own momentum. It is to *Drive* what angel dust is to opium, perhaps. Yet it is more or less "of a piece" with much of Refn's previous work in its basic concerns and its towering, iconoclastic style.

The rotten-egg reviews are telling in their hysteria. The most vehement of the Cannes reviewers wrote: "I felt violated, shat upon, sedated, narcotized, appalled and bored stiff."[3] The extreme moods checked off here belie their own truthfulness; unless one isn't really appalled, or unless one is accustomed to being "violated" or "shat upon," it's impossible to be simultaneously "bored stiff." How closely this description corresponds to a generic list of experiences that we strongly disfavor confronting in our art today: rape, degradation, loss of control, boredom. This review is a rallying cry laying blame on *Only God Forgives* for any and all of these existential problems, which, interestingly enough, are also appraised and judged within Refn's film with great moral wisdom and candor.

Not only the content but the formal elements of *Only God Forgives* came in for excoriation. Specifically, another reviewer harped upon the downplayed, low-affect acting, imagining Refn coaching Ryan Gosling to do more and more takes to get a perfectly impassive quality.[4] In fact, this subdued acting has to do with Refn's affinity for minimalism more than anything, as well as his ongoing attempt to bring out new elements within familiar genre scenarios. As with Mads Mikkelsen in *Valhalla Rising*, Refn gives Gosling one of the ultimate challenges for an actor—to convey emotion not in words but through body language and especially through his eyes, which communicate powerful and nuanced modes of sorrow, resignation, rage, humiliation, and disgust far better than words ever could.

It might have been strange to see an A-list Hollywood star like Gosling giving himself to this very artful and "interior" film, and probably would have been in another director's hands. It is nothing at all like Joe Dallesandro's glorified cameo in Louis Malle's *Black Moon* (1975), where we never stop thinking, "Hey, that's Little Joe trying to kill that eagle with a sword—far out." Refn manages to reveal an unfamiliar quality in Gosling through exotic camera angles, lighting, and the way he poses the actor and has him move. It is almost like encountering a new Gosling, and it says something for how the actor's charisma has matured that he can now, somewhat like a younger version of Brando in *Last Tango in Paris* (1972), step into a more groundbreaking, demanding role that nonetheless depends so much on that reservoir of charisma and the innate sympathies it invokes. In fact, it is quite lovely how well his refinement and gracefulness fit against the Asian background—why didn't anyone think to take Gosling there before?

In so many ways, Refn did not hedge his bets with *Only God Forgives*; he did not undercut his own mysticism (and mystique) with redundant exposition. Indeed, *Only God Forgives* is as far removed from tepid halfway measures as Dostoevsky is from Marvel Comics. There is that element of going for broke which we noted in the introduction as a key personality feature of the anarchist director. Refn's approach is to put his obsessional cards on the table, so to speak, then attempt to pare things down, to do more with less. Peter Bradshaw

The friendship that has developed between Nicolas Winding Refn and Ryan Gosling has proven artistically fruitful for both of them. Although *Only God Forgives* (2013) was met with incomprehension and hostility by many reviewers, my belief is that in time it will come to be seen as a masterpiece, and my hope is that director and star will not be deterred from working together in the future.

of *The Guardian*, one of the lone voices of support for *Only God Forgives* at Cannes, said admiringly, "I'm afraid it's going to be even nastier the next time I watch it."[5] For me, the film has become more serene with each viewing, and not because of "shock" wearing off. In fact, the shock of some scenes still has not abated for me; for example, I always find myself watching with my arm across my eyes during the nightclub scene where a man is mutilated with shishkabob skewers. It is more because, as with all of Refn's films, the characters are compelling, albeit highly stylized.

There is very little middle ground in the film's Bangkok setting between extreme sleaze and extreme spirituality; both are present in abundance. (There are beautifully filmed, rather formal scenes of a karaoke lounge which have a nearly liturgical feeling.) All of the white characters are glorified tourists (they do not speak Thai), existential journeymen with karmic debts to settle. The film's intense negative energy flows from Crystal (Kristin Scott-Thomas), a foul-mouthed, coke-dealing harridan who is generally reminiscent of Diane Ladd's boozy Mafia belle in Lynch's *Wild at Heart*, with perhaps a few dashes of Katey Sagal's iron-backboned Gemma Teller from *Sons of Anarchy* thrown in. Crystal (her name perhaps a reference to methamphetamine) is far more dangerous and vile than nearly any cinema villain in quite some time; yet it is possible at times to be almost touched by her desperate manipulations, her utter lack of self-reflection. Gazing intently at male strippers flexing onstage at a sex club, she seems like an embodiment of what Spinoza called "the sad passions," the state of wallowing in and cultivating everything in life that is shabby, imperfect, enslaved and enslaving.[6] Really, Crystal is a goddess of Chaos; she is shown wearing increasingly plainer gowns and with more bizarre mannerisms as her evil becomes progressively exposed. What exposes her is the source of the film's positive energy, a mysterious cop named Chang (Vithaya Pansringarm). But he is not just any cop. Although physically unprepossessing, he is a kind of Zenmaster with the ability to materialize and dematerialize at will. He hunts down prey like a bloodhound, and he carries a blunt sword down the back of his shirt with which he dispenses gory but exacting justice.

The film's first image is a tracking shot along this blunt sword in extreme close-up, as if the entire film that follows is being enacted upon its steely surface or within its dusky mirror. Chang's blunt sword is one of two central fetishes in the film,[7] as we have come to recognize the fetish in Refn's work, an object soothing in its familiarity and constant presence, to which the voyeuristic sensibility returns to lessen the fear of loss and to accomplish the work of mourning. However, Chang's blunt sword goes beyond the other fetish objects in previous films in that it is an object that has a special relation to death. It is a fetish from which death itself streams, almost sweetly. With this sword the gap completely closes between the fear of death and its heady acceptance. Once targeted by Chang's mystical sword, no one can escape. Pleas for mercy are muted on the soundtrack; we see only the targets' hands waving and mouths moving uselessly. Meanwhile, the sword can see whom it will kill from a physical and temporal distance, and nearly every weapon that is used in the film draws upon the blunt sword's Damoclean authority. Refn inserts a shot of a disembodied arm raising and chopping down with the sword at several points as if to indicate that it is a supernatural entity which kills *through* Chang.

The fact that the sword is blunted and foreshortened (it is a type of sword used primarily for the practice of forms of tai chi, which we see Chang doing in one scene) mitigates against what a Cannes reviewer denounced as *Only God Forgives'* "shit macho fantasy."[8] In fact, this is one of the least macho of action films and one which questions phallic authority most directly. (One of the things that mystifies me most about the outraged reviews from Cannes is that, of the two Refn-Gosling collaborations, *Drive* is far more traditionally macho in every respect.) The other prime fetish in *Only God Forgives* are the hands of Crystal's grown son Julian (played by Gosling). There are numerous shots of Julian's hands opening and closing, once (early in the film) against a background of arabesques and later (near the end) against the vibrant green of clustered growing plants that seem to suggest cannabis. Drugged with secret knowledge, Julian's hands are a gateway to the mystical. Like Chang with his sword, the hands have a prophetic quality. We will elaborate on some of the meanings of the hands later in this chapter, but for now we can think of them as a first line of defense (Julian often poses, rather stiffly and unnaturally, with his fists raised like a boxer) and as the repository of immense sexual guilt. The hand substitutes for the penis again and again in the film, and Julian's nightmare is also his most fervent wish: to have it cut off.

This sexual guilt, like the rest of the film's negative energy, comes from the mother, Crystal. Julian is caught between her energy and Chang's. Chang's positive energy is physically violent but emotionally balanced; whereas Crystal's negative energy is emotionally savage and terroristic, but she farms out her killings to any available man, including Julian, whom she had induced years before to kill his own father. What becomes clear at every point in the film is that Crystal has had incestuous relations with both Julian and his older brother Billy (Tom Burke), and that this primal affront is the source of all the mayhem that plays out.

Billy and Julian promote kickboxing matches in Bangkok, but the fights are a cover for their drug dealing. "It's time to meet the Devil," Billy tells Julian very flatly one night. He goes to a brothel and demands to have sex with a fourteen-year-old girl; he offers the pimp 15,000 baht if he can fuck the pimp's youngest daughter. Then Billy runs amok, beating up the pimp and several of the prostitutes. On the street he meets a sixteen-year-old prostitute who he ends up raping and killing. The squalid murder room is a blood-bath of red neon from outside pulsing on the floor's pooled blood. Out of nowhere Chang appears at the crime scene and convinces the prostitute's father (Narucha Chaimareung) that he should murder Billy in revenge.

Julian receives news of Billy's murder after a session with his regular prostitute Mai (Yayaying Rhatha Phongam). Their erotic ritual is one of distance and abnegation: she ties his hands to the arms of a chair and he watches with pained longing while she sits on the bed and masturbates. But Mai is no dominatrix; the light bondage isn't a turn-on but seemingly a precaution on Julian's part, as if he is afraid of hurting her by venting his sexual energy on her. During this ritual Julian has a hallucination of a sinister corridor, at the end of which he presents his hands to be chopped off. When he gets the news about his brother, he seems to understand Billy's rampage as an unleashing of Billy's own inner devil, and perhaps a kind of satanic meeting of his maker (the Devil instead of God, say). But Julian has his own devil (and maker) to meet now, in the form of Crystal, who arrives in Bangkok for the funeral.

Very apprehensively, Julian walks down another strange corridor, seemingly terrified of what he will find at the end. This time, it is his mother's hotel room, and she sits provocatively on the bed. She motions Julian to come closer and then clasps him around his waist, her face buried against his abdomen and her hands reaching around to press his buttocks. We see Julian looking down, aware of something jarring and wrong but not pulling away from his mother's grasp. He sits on the bed, and she stands and snaps her fingers, as if inducing trance. She announces her intention to kill whoever murdered Billy. "Now get up and kiss your mother," she says. Julian obeys, then lights her cigarette as she strokes his arm erotically.

The prostitute's father is easily tracked down and eventually rubbed out (he is a slum-dwelling vendor of street food), but the instigator Chang proves more elusive. Crystal orders a hit on the cop at a noodle shop; there is an Uzi massacre from which Chang manages to escape unharmed. Never one to miss an opportunity to fuse sex with hatred, or to derive a perverse thrill from betraying a loved one, Crystal sleeps with Chang. Later, Chang tortures Crystal's henchman Byron (Byron Gibson) in a nightclub in order to track down Crystal in turn. Now Chang has the upper hand, like a wall against which the white characters batter themselves to no avail. Julian challenges him to a boxing match, where Chang's superior speed and reflexes dominate. Julian is knocked out, his face bruised and swollen.

At this point the characters become almost like human Tarot cards; it is clear that the psychical energy among them is thickening. Chang seems to understand that Julian is a victim of Crystal, that she has corrupted and perverted him and turned him into a loveless killer. As a last stand, Crystal sends Julian and another assassin (Charlie Ruedpokanon) to Chang's house, where they lie in wait. The second assassin is a scruffy adolescent who might be Crystal's latest plaything; he slips up by telling Julian that Crystal ordered him not only to kill Chang but "to kill them all."

Wandering and waiting inside Chang's empty house, Julian confronts his mother's evil and realizes that she has sent him to his death. His lifetime of servitude to her whims and demands comes to an end all at once. When Chang's daughter returns home with her nanny, the adolescent shoots the nanny; then Julian kills him, thereby saving the little girl and himself. This mainly self-preserving act on Julian's part is registered karmically as a good deed toward Chang and helps cement Chang's willingness to help Julian finally overcome his mother (all of this is telepathic rather than spoken out loud). Chang goes to Crystal's hotel room with his blunt sword and gives her a lobotomy by way of her larynx. Julian arrives later to find his mother dead; with a sword that he took from Chang's house, he slits Crystal from navel to vagina (Refn refrains from showing this directly) and inserts his hand in the opening. This is not a return to the womb so much as a pointedly sexualized violation of it, a reliving, and perhaps an exorcism, of that incestuous intercourse with Crystal that Julian had repressed. The violence and the incest go together, a Gordian knot that only grows tighter with the effort to pick it apart. Still suffering from his endless guilt and afraid of perpetuating the cycle of abuse, Julian encounters Chang in a wooded area and wordlessly submits to Chang cutting off his hands.

At the end, Chang and Julian seem to become almost aspects of each other. Chang has understood from the beginning that Julian wants to confront his demons and become a better man. After the failed hit on Chang, the cop is led into the arcade-like lobby of the boxing gym to look over a silent, waiting Julian. Chang says, "He's not the one," and moves on. In turn, we feel as though Julian has summoned the cop to wage war against his mother, and to help set him free. Uncomfortable with his male role, and disgusted by the sexual abuse to which he has been subjected, Julian prefers a kind of castration, which might be taking place not on earth but on a bardo of his spirit's transit between reincarnations. This is perhaps the first narrative film which is told from the viewpoint of the Vedantic-Emersonian Oversoul, a universal spiritual phenomenon whose energy moves through a number of interconnected persons until the relations among each other crystallize and complete a cycle. At the heart of *Only God Forgives* is the idea of the poisoning of the Oversoul which occurs in incest, specifically in the mother's rapacious sexual devouring of her two sons. Abusiveness, learned and suffered at an early age, gives rise to damaged psyches which then inflict abuse on others.

The Oversoul, as perceived by Refn, takes in ever-revised and changing ideas of pregnancy, since childbirth is one of the Oversoul's primary connecting links to the world. Each life brought to term has a meaning and destiny within the Oversoul, not like the Christian conception of a brand new life uniquely crafted by God, but rather a reincarnated life that already comes from past lives and past sojourns in the Oversoul itself. Nothing is more individualistic than the Christian conception of the fetus: an imago of sovereignty meant to subvert (male) dependency on women.[9] But with the Oversoul, nothing gains life and consciousness until it is actually born, i.e., able to partake directly in (karmic) experience. Whatever individual meaning a life forms is dependent upon the fact that it must first merge with the Oversoul and become essentially nothing, a non-individuated particle of the larger whole. ("It must die before it lives.")

Pregnancy has been a recurring theme in Refn's films. *Bleeder* was an early suggestion that there is a universal atmosphere poisoned by incest, particularly because incestuous sex can result in pregnancy and therefore return fouled

9. Only God Forgives

karma to the Oversoul. The pregnancy porn that is the focus of a key scene in *Bleeder* further clarifies the idea of the human fetus as a product of certain kinds of karma. In *Fear X*, it is the fetus, killed when Harry's pregnant wife is killed, who seems to haunt Harry's nightmares in the form of a hand or even a face (Harry's) pressing against the wall of a veiny, tissue-like sac. Something of the spirit, perhaps, still wants to be born—although, naturally, this can be read as Harry's projection about the paternity that was stolen from him. Or the fetus itself might be a harbinger of death or suicide—the nameless collateral life which leaves the Oversoul to make room when any new person is born. The violence of the birth process (which, as we have seen, is enacted by men as bloody fistfights in which one male returns the other to goo-spattered infancy and the possibility of being reborn, for good or ill) is akin to murder in intensity and bodily vulnerability; it is only very recently, historically speaking, that childbirth has been rendered more or less sterile and safe in the Western world. For most of humanity's life on this planet it was a roll of the dice, with death omnipresent: the woman's or the baby's death on the one hand, the extinction of the family line or species on the other.

In a creepy scene from *Only God Forgives*, Crystal tells Julian, "When I

A terrifying and oppressive symmetry dominates the world of *Only God Forgives*: it is the desperate sign of a broken world trying to hold itself together, and it is most pronounced around the film's white characters. Here, Julian (Gosling) escorts the prostitute Mai (Yayaying Rhatha Phongam) to a dinner date with his mother Crystal. The pretense that Mai is really Julian's "girlfriend" is only one of many lies that ripple outward from Crystal like an immense pool of bad karmic energy.

was pregnant with you, it was strange and different. You wanted to terminate." While we are disinclined to trust most things that Crystal says in the film (indeed, here she is trying to prey on Julian's guilt at letting people down), this odd remark strikes a chord. It is like the vengeance of the incest-produced fetus and porn-star fetuses of *Bleeder*; it is a grim articulation of the fetus which contains seeds of death in *Fear X*. It is also the intriguing disposition of a fetus who resists the violence of childbirth and karmic legacy, a fetus who does not wish to ride the Oversoul's seesaw of life and death, breeding and murder, because it seemingly grasps that its purest way of honoring the Oversoul is to bow out of the endless cycle, to remove the need for a death occasioned by each birth: an ecology of human life, perhaps.

This predominant interest in the Oversoul shifts *Only God Forgives* away from the totalizing, traditional conception of the lone individualistic hero and toward something communal and cosmic. At any rate, it is not Julian (already born, seemingly against his own will, into karmic chaos) who enacts this role. Chang is the film's unlikely hero, but even this is only to the extent that he sets aside his own immediate needs to facilitate the healing of the Oversoul. Other male figures are tormented by self-interest and the refusal to accept, the refusal to forgive themselves and others. Both Billy and Julian are fragmentary men held together by hieratic poses and by a speech that resents having to become verbalized. They have been rendered out of whack with the cosmos, virtual zombies. Refn uses light to make their faces almost look like Francis Bacon portraits: Billy's eyes are lit but his mouth is wiped out, or his mouth flaps inhumanly from the bottom of a head that has been foreshortened by shadow. After being beaten up by Chang, Julian's face has the pulpy, meatlike look of one of Bacon's screaming-blurs; likewise, the bashed-in face of Billy's corpse, whose upper lip appears to be where his nose once was, and whose eyes seem to have been knocked to either side of his cranium. Ultimately, both brothers are consumed by the death drive, but Julian has become implosive, cut off from himself and others, whereas Billy has become explosive.

This is why Crystal immediately takes Billy's side regarding his killing of the teenage prostitute. "I'm sure he had his reasons," she snaps. This is the closest we get to an expression of guilt on her part, an oblique acknowledgment of having damaged Billy in the first place. It also helps explain Billy's rampage: the one whose innocence has been stolen seeks to force this loss of innocence on others. Elsewhere Crystal admits her sexual connection to her sons quite openly, though without any sense of guilt. Her most salty and direct tirade takes place in the restaurant where Julian has brought Mai to meet her. Mai is the closest person Julian has to a girlfriend; in a poignant moment he gives her a special new dress to wear and asks her to pretend that the two of them are a couple. "Can you do that?" he asks in a hushed voice, as if half hoping that she will say no. Gamely, Mai wears the dress and enters the restaurant on Julian's arm. Nonetheless, Crystal sees through this act right away. Having ruined Julian sexually, she knows that the only woman in his life could possibly be a hooker. Then Crystal berates Julian for being unable to fill his older brother's shoes in no uncertain terms. "You were always jealous," she says in front of Mai, "what with Billy being the older brother and having a bigger cock. Julian's was never small, but Billy's, oh!"—she gasps—"it was enormous." She not only wants to shame her son, she wants to force Mai to recognize her territorial scent on Julian.

This is also a kind of twisted "welcome to the family" moment: to become part of Julian's family is not to journey from sexual marginality to a type of normativity, but rather the opposite. "Why do you let her treat you like that?" Mai asks Julian after they have left the restaurant. He shoves her against the wall of an alley and seethes, "'Cause she's my ma." Then he screams at her to take off the dress he has given her. Mai shames him by doing so obediently. Standing in her underwear in the alley, Mai seems more pure, certainly more honest, than Crystal and Julian.

Thus the truce that was made with the maternal in *Nemesis* is violently broken in *Only God Forgives*. Indeed, the blatant and horrified foregrounding of sexual violation in *Only God Forgives* helps us understand some of the more oblique and fraught references in earlier Refn films: the dizzying conflation of motherhood and prostitution in *Pusher II*, the sibling incest which triggers a chain of tragic violence in *Bleeder*, the sense of male violation in *Fear X* and *Valhalla Rising*, the endless rage of *Bronson*.

But loss of innocence, which must be regarded now as Refn's greatest theme and the one that perhaps offers the most potential for his artistic future, comes in other forms besides incestuous sex. The film's most powerful evocation of this comes not from the kinkiness of the white characters but instead during a scene in which Chang has tracked one of the Thai men who tried to kill him back to a seemingly disused industrial space. He finds the assassin there, feeding his small son. The son sits in a high-backed black chair, in which his skeletal, rickety body seems swallowed up. The son is all head and eyes, big slow eyes that watch as his father asks Chang to spare the boy's life. We see the misery and poverty that drives a man to resort to contract killing in order to feed a son who is clearly suffering from malnutrition, retardation, and stunted growth. In such poverty there is no way to preserve family from the corruption of the world; this also links with Bangkok's rampant prostitution of teen children. And Chang does sympathize with the little boy, but he kills another of the assassins—splitting his heart open so that he falls backwards, gushing blood—with the boy watching. Chang's full turn from the force of the sword-chop brings him face to face with the boy, whose eyes flicker slightly in astonishment. This boy is, of course, reminiscent of Are in *Valhalla Rising*, witness to male rape, and also to Benicio in *Drive*, whose sleazy exposure to violence, in the form of a bullet given him by a gangster as a warning, is so outraging to Driver that he returns this bullet by threatening to hammer it through the gangster's forehead and then finally making him swallow it.

In *Only God Forgives*, the high-backed chair where the boy sits suggests a movie theater seat in which a child might be exposed to violent movies. He absorbs it, fascinated, but without fully understanding, perhaps. And there is nothing positive in his world to counteract and mitigate the fearsomeness of the sword and the spurt of blood. Chang's obvious sympathy for the boy is seen as essentially futile, since the boy's future is dim, whether his father remains a criminal or not, or even whether his father remains alive. Yet, there is a running motif of Chang rebuking and threatening parents in order to get them to love and protect their own children. Refn had spoken of this idea around the time of *Pusher II*, with its cathartic scene of patricide: "I knew a lot of people who needed to kill their parents,"[10] presumably because of childhood abuse.

Children hold a special silence in Refn's work, the silence of attentiveness, of the wide-eyed taking in of adult, worldly things that are beyond their immediate understanding but which penetrate their consciousness and sort of "zip up" a piece of them that might otherwise develop more openly. The wordless telepathy between Are and One Eye in *Valhalla Rising* depends on faith and innocence, and is evidence of those human qualities. Likewise, these qualities are referenced in the intense eye contact between Chang and the small boy, and, by extension, in the telepathy between Chang and Julian, who is himself partly a child figure invested in the same enclosed, traumatized silence.

Julian takes to extremes the Refn motif of the speechless hero. One Eye was physiologically mute, but Julian can speak and chooses not to because of secrets he is afraid of uttering. But such reticence has many fascinating roots. We think of Lenny's difficulty speaking to Liv in *Bleeder*, arising from his shyness and basic distrust of words; he seeks an understanding that is already beyond the need for speech, or rather, perhaps, a familiar speech whose content and meaning are irreducible (i.e., the campy dialogue of his favorite cult films, which he mouths along to on his TV in lieu of real and spontaneous relationships). Driver speaks very little, through a meditative passivity and patience that is nearly non-human and as efficient as one of his high-torqued cars: just as he wastes no actions in clumsy or unnecessary gestures, so he wastes no words. Similar to how Blanchot describes the unnatural wakefulness of insomnia as having no beginning or end,[11] we can say that long periods of silence, seemingly never begun or broken off at any point, cast a kind of shadow over the possibility of speech. Silence—or disarticulate sounds—predate human speech both in collective history (the time prior to the development of language) and in individual lives (babies cry before they can use words). Silence in *Only God Forgives* relates to the idealized, near-telepathic bonding between babies and their mothers: the needs that are (ideally) met before the baby even needs to voice them, right at the dawning of the need; the Pavlovian breasts that have timed themselves to lactate at those times of the day when the baby gets hungry.

Julian's dysfunction is that he is trapped within a law of silence because of primal needs that were not met. His psyche has no expectations of connecting with anyone else. The law of silence imposes itself, and while it is interrupted occasionally by speech, these interruptions never completely diminish or cancel the law itself. There is the temptation to view the difficulty of spoken communication (such as it is) as stemming primarily from the fact that it always occurs under this strict and primal law of silence, imposed prior to any kind of language—a refuge much like the womb or pre–Oedipal consciousness. This law of silence is also revealed when the communicative meaning of speech breaks down, giving way to desperate cry. Blanchot on silence: "Surely we feel that it is linked to the cry, the voiceless cry, which breaks with all utterance, which is addressed to no one and which no one receives, the cry that lapses and decries."[12] The cry only strengthens the silence which it interrupts, since it is as primal as the silence, and as restricted in communicative capabilities. Yet it is triggered by a need to try to escape, however briefly, from the shameful taboos upheld by silence, or to articulate, however incoherently, the psychical indictments which rage and fear have frozen over. The only time Julian raises his voice in *Only God Forgives* is when he screams the sexual command, "Take it off!" to Mai. Appropriately, it is Mai, the only person who represents even the possibility of love for Julian, who elicits the uncharacteristic cry, precisely because, in her concern, she has demonstrated that she is the only one who can already hear the things that Julian does not and cannot say.

• • •

I stated earlier in this book that Refn's revenge sagas are searches for a lost symmetry which stands for wholeness and balance. This is especially true in *Fear X*, where Harry's loss of his wife gives rise to his nightmarish entrapment within asymmetrical lines. These lines only seem to straighten and right themselves late in the film, in a single hallucinated image that could represent a revenge killing, an "eye for an eye": the elevator where Harry finally confronts his wife's killer, with its double doors and red lanterns on either side, and a glossy pool of blood on the floor around it. The ending, however, returns us to uncertain asymmetry, as Harry drives away down one side of a forked road.

Much of *Only God Forgives* might suggest, stylistically, that shot of the elevator, but it completely revises the meaning of symmetry vis-à-vis the earlier film. In *Only God Forgives* the visual symmetry is relentless, so omnipresent and oppressive that one sometimes wants to scream. Light sources double on either side of characters' faces; lengths of bright neon tubing extend on either side of characters' heads; bodies are placed in the direct center of converging lines like bull's-eyes on an archery board. People are constantly framed by doorways that are positioned middle-screen, or at the end of hallways narrow enough that we see both walls in equal measure. There is nearly no architectural space in the film that has not been made to conform to this constant alert, this composition that always points at something that occupies its heart like a glittering, provocative ornament, or a cracked jewel elaborately set so as to disguise its flaw. This symmetry is the outward symptom of a world in decay, covered with stretched bandages and illusions. It is entropic symmetry. It becomes synonymous not with the redressing of wrong and the restoration of order, but of a kind of cosmic lie, a desperate and artificial balance whose ordering principle distorts and unhinges the world even as it seems to collect it into perfectly aligned structures.

It is only in Chang's home, in the scene where Julian has his tense vigil waiting for Chang and his family to return, that we begin to see extreme breaks with this symmetrical composition. Julian's dawning cognizance of Crystal's evil and his concomitant liberation from dependency on her is drawn out through a series of shots in which the center of the frame is for the most part skewed. Julian is seen in doorways that stand to one side of the frame or the other, or between a wide, light-colored wall and a narrow green one. The dispelling of the symmetrical is a sign of Julian awakening from his trance, the hypnoid state that his mother has placed him in. It is also a sign of him letting go of his own need to be the magnetic center, a shifting in his sense of his own power from someone who does the expedient thing to someone who does the more difficult and compassionate thing. It is in this asymmetrical house that he saves his own life and the life of Chang's little girl by killing the second assassin, himself a symbolic double of Julian, as the mother's new cat's-paw.

Julian is gaining consciousness of the Oversoul and his own beleaguered position in it as the inheritor and victim of his mother's blood guilts, and also the passive perpetuator of her wrongs. He is becoming aware of something which Refn has spoken of in relation to nearly all his films—the idea that "man is meant to sacrifice himself; that is being human, having a soul."[13] As with

9. Only God Forgives

One Eye, Driver, even the misguided Bronson, Julian is a man who discovers his own soul in relation to the pain that he feels for and because of other people; he is made to learn that his ego is not sovereign but exists in reciprocal relations with other egos. This is the unlocking which leads (corridors and passageways are ubiquitous in *Only God Forgives*) to the acceptance of one's own non-ego, a nearly Buddhist state of enlightenment which can be the same as self-sacrifice and the finding of one's true place within the Oversoul.

Apart from the symmetrical giving way to the asymmetrical, Refn has also worked out a kind of visual editing pattern to depict the workings of the Oversoul. If the Oversoul is like the delta of all sentient beings in the cosmos, then its workings manifest themselves cinematically through fascinatingly interrupted and disjointed actions, sometimes involving people who are physically and temporally removed from each other yet intercut together so that we see a rapport. These edits are like unfinished gestures which segue into other characters' gestures, meld and then reemerge in the next shot as the end results of the "matings" of the disparate characters' convergent intentions. For example, a lingering shot of Julian in blue light, staring into his bathroom mirror and then turning to look off camera, cuts to a shot of Chang entering the frame in an interior with a different lighting and background; the telepathy between Julian and Chang is established, and also their fledgling, nascent ability to work toward each other, to work together for the repair of the damaged Oversoul.

These segues also work to demonstrate ruptures or contaminations of the Oversoul. In particular, acts of killing are never represented as one person acting alone to kill another. The killer is always an instrument of someone else, a more powerful and hidden consciousness who orders and pays for the act. Crystal is seen on her hotel balcony overlooking all of Bangkok in the middle of the failed hit on Chang at the noodle shop, with a distinct element of direct or near-direct gazing between her and the faraway action unfolding. There is a satanic or witch-like element to this—as when the over-the-top mother in *Wild at Heart* "sees" her retribution against her daughter's boyfriend in a crystal ball. The name "Crystal" links additionally to the cinematic Ur-image behind *Wild at Heart*: *The Wizard of Oz*'s Wicked Witch of the West, who harmed people from a distance with her own crystal ball.

We also sometimes see these edits in mafia movies, where the all-powerful kingpin sits and waits in an office somewhere while a hit is carried out remotely. The climactic montage of *The Godfather* (1972), which cuts back and forth between the church christening of an infant son and a series of assassinations ordered by the infant's father, Michael Corleone (Al Pacino), is a set of symphonic variations on this basic editing motif. *The Godfather* limited itself to profaning Catholic ritual or exposing its hypocrisies. *Only God Forgives* places the entire cosmos in balance to the ruthlessly murderous desires of its characters. The terror of remote power is the greatest threat to the Oversoul, since it means that someone can kill another without ever having to confront the essence of that person; the bad karma becomes diluted, spread thin, impossible to assign to the guilty parties with any precise degree of justice. In a poor economy like Thailand's, the rich can pollute an entire nation, an entire people, by extorting them to carry out nefarious plans. Meanwhile, the true motive of the murder becomes illegible; this in itself is a form of terrorism. The disguising of a mercenary motive as a random irruption of hatred between strangers is poison to the world's sense of its own harmony.

Like the mob itself, Crystal has a chokehold on the Oversoul, as it were, since she is continuously seeking male figures to attack and kill other male figures for her own personal reasons. These males are then punished for the crimes that she has ordered. For the Thai characters, there is no sovereignty that could express itself as the desire to kill for personal reasons. Face to face with the man who beat Billy to death, Julian says in English, "Ask him why he killed my brother." The question is relayed in Thai as "Who hired you to kill his brother?" Caucasian and Thai, rich and poor, are held apart here by something more than a language barrier—a profound difference in subjectivity in which the reasons for evil are spiritual or psychological for the former, but commonplace and material for the latter. But it is the Thai, suffering more greatly in the immanent material world, who are ultimately revealed to be the more spiritual and more moral of the two cultures.

Perverse and unforgiving personal justice is itself a crime against the balance of the Oversoul and the workings of karma. In this sense, *Only God Forgives* is as much an anti-mob film as *Drive* was. It views the weft of human life as being ripped apart by sinister, mercenary consciousnesses; gangsters, who induce others to commit bloodshed in their name, infect the entire Oversoul with displaced and indefinable guilt. To be killed without understanding why, no less than to kill hiddenly, is a catastrophe that leaves souls stranded and disconnected, bleeding wounds in the Oversoul's holistic oneness.

Only God Forgives deconstructs one of the essential plot points of revenge cinema—that the avenger must kill "up a chain" so to speak, beginning with underlings and trigger-men until finally reaching the godlike enclave of power from which the violence has originally emanated. But that enclave is never reached in *Only God Forgives*; instead, the center of godlike power, and of forgiveness, is finally revealed, in very Zen terms, to be within Julian (and he himself is not above the violence he commits nor exempted from its consequences).

Thus, the title's meaning is easy to mistake. It is not a way of saying, for instance, "Kill 'em all and let God sort 'em out," or even "God forgives, I don't." It is saying that forgiveness *is* godlike, and only someone who becomes godlike can begin to feel and practice that forgiveness which is necessary to end interpersonal cycles of abuse as well as immemorially entrenched international conflicts. All the predatory, dysfunctional whites are eliminated by the end of *Only God Forgives*: Crystal the tourist from hell, giving a hard time to the concierge (Dujdao Vadhanapakom) at her hotel; Billy and Julian, the pseudo-colonialist exploiters. The final scene shows Chang singing karaoke to a song called "You Are My Dream," to a preternaturally still and peaceful lounge filled only with his fellow Thai policemen. Again, as in Refn, violent revenge has restored an internal balance which is nearly self-justifying. It is up to the young or even the future-born to resolve our ongoing crises in favor of peace, as when Chang's young daughter is arbitrating a dispute among her dolls. Chang asks her, "Then how do we make sure he doesn't cause trouble again?" "By talking nicely to each other," the little girl answers.

Those closest to birth are the wisest and most perceptive, while those who are nearing any kind of death (and here we might recall again the film's somber judgment on its white characters) wander somnambulistically, losing their senses, incapable of saying even what little they know. The death of a spirit-manifestation is harder and more agonizing and more protracted than the death of the body. It might take centuries, dynasties, whole eras of power. Meanwhile, existence clamors and beckons, both to those who know whom they are and those who do not. Here we see the recurrence of hallways as a visualization of the birth process: Julian ventures down numerous hallways—often red and with slimy, oozing walls—toward ends that are blocked or empty or simply uncertain. Once he drags the body of a man down such a corridor, as if purging the blood guilt of killing his father. Twice he finds his mother at the end of a corridor, once alive and the second time dead. Her death returns him to the opportunity to seek a new beginning in the climactic cutting off of his hands, which could also indicate his rebirth into a new soul. To arrive at the mother (the womb) and at death are functionally the same because in the mythos of the Oversoul death leads back into birth, and any "new" life bears karmic traces of old deaths, old wounds: this is the fatal mother as creator and destroyer, as the bestower of enormous cocks and bad luck and every other thing that is randomly generated as part of a human life. It is the mother as clock, the literal keeper of her child's time—the one who knows, but will not say, just how far away the sky is.

Conclusion

> We are devolving.... We have no regard at all for our fellow man; we are statistics. So if someone happens to squash a statistic, so what?—Herschell Gordon Lewis[1]
>
> When you walk down the streets of Mortville, make sure you're dressed like what you really are: TRASH!—Edith Massey (as Queen Carlotta) in John Waters' *Desperate Living* (1977)
>
> In the earliest times, the time of magic and religion, knowledge was both an emotional element and an element of collective wisdom. Then, with dualism, things got separated, and we have on the one hand speculative philosophy, pure abstraction, and on the other hand pure emotion.
>
> We must now go back, not to the primitive stage (the religious state), but toward an analogous synthesis of the emotional and intellectual.
>
> I think film alone is capable of making this great synthesis, of returning the intellect to its vital, concrete, emotional sources. That is our task and the path we have chosen.—Sergei Eisenstein (Sorbonne Lecture, 1930)[2]

If myth is, ideally, a speechifying or storytelling power to render changing social realities legible and acceptable to a given society, then we are myth-impoverished today. Our social realities are changing, yet there is no certification that could help us to see the changes as part of our own collective narrative, something we could tell and retell in our own ways, something in which we all have a stake. Cut off from each other, stalemated by ideological gridlocks, we have only a dry-docked cynicism with which to try to understand events that unfold. If we are ever to have the hope of guiding the immense changes to our world, of becoming active rather than passive participants in the systems that we ourselves build and pay into, then we must first conceptualize in humanist truths that are not shackled to any agenda; for when reality is effectively brainwashed against itself, then stronger doses of the same reality, or realities, have no impact whatsoever.

Relativism, whether moral or any other kind, is not a shibboleth foisted upon us by a left that seeks to abjure prejudice and bias; it is practiced far more by the right. Indeed, the right would hardly exist without that relativism, which they beef up even as they superficially condemn it. It is the political right that benefits most from relativist thinking. So they promulgate the ideas that the Bible should be considered alongside scientific texts because "some people regard it as true"; that Judeo-Christian violence is always justified in a way that other religions' violence is not; that the wealthy are oppressed because they are asked to pay taxes that help the destitute; that black people who defend themselves against discrimination by whites are themselves "racists" (anti-white); that "freedom" as a concept is only embodied within a corporate state in which the vast majority of individuals find themselves enslaved; etc.

Without an objectivity that can transcend subjective biases, what can we do with people (on either side) who divisively claim all of empirical reality for themselves, defending themselves with plain blind facts that hold us in sway even as they contradict each other? Spiny twisted facts stick in the throat like fish-bones, and there is always something new to be swallowed. Intriguingly, in the above quote, Herschell Gordon Lewis (who is credited with the invention of gore-cinema) suggests that we are "devolving" not because we are becoming more irrational and atavistic, but quite the opposite—because we are becoming more blandly factitious. The logic of statistical averages settles over every human enterprise like a net, allowing us to see through to the trapped human contents; but it effectively controls their animate possibilities, their ability to go anywhere. The human is at an odd juncture, neither fish nor fowl—a creature of probability theories, diagnostic labeling, genetic likelihoods, fatalistic stereotypes, and above all that feeling of "so what, what can I do?" which Lewis says is occasioned by everything now, even the most heinous crimes of individuals and of nations.

The opposite of the statistical, I believe, is the mythic: in all their dreadfulness and insinuation, mythic narratives have always helped us to locate ourselves within a larger pattern of meaning. Christianity is only one offshoot of the human mythic tendency, and hardly the most fruitful one—in fact, it is already long into a slow process of withering. But the need for more intelligent, articulate, inclusive and modern myths is still purring away inside our slumber, like an eating dream from which we awake with the realization that we are famished.

Indeed, we live in singularly anti-mythic times. The debunking of hero and villain alike as small, pitiful creatures is a hallmark of this resistance to mythos; as is our seeming preference for ideological non-fiction books that preach to the choir as opposed to fiction, which opens us up to the entirety of the human spectrum in ambiguous, messy, uncategorizable ways. Certainly many myths have been unhelpful. All myths have come from some ideological pattern; the challenge is to find new human myths that challenge preconceptions and limitations. Myths of collective consciousness, myths of intergenerational, interglobal, interpersonal oneness.

In this sense myths are merely resonant stories that allow us to see ourselves as capable and achieving. Stories are needed for this, more than ever perhaps, but we seem only able to remake old ones, naturally subjecting them to ideological and factitious clearance, and thus robbing them of their power to wrench and surprise us, or to bring us together in a common unity. Wherever myth is not dismissed out of hand as being beside the point, it is definitively beyond us, trapped in a sanctum of human imagination whose key, it seems, has been broken off in the lock. Adorno notes the "displacement of philosophy by science [and] by the bustle of universal statistics," a primary casualty of this displacement being the faculty of "speculation."[3] Speculation "is either degraded to a docile echo of traditional philosophical schemes, or, in its aloofness from blinded facts, perverted to the non-committal chatter of a private *Weltanschauung.*"[4]

"Speculation" can be read, here, as another word for myth and myth-making (as it is in the world of literary genres: *speculative fiction* is that which is concerned with fantasy, sci-fi, the supernatural). Narratives of speculation are foreclosed upon, from the start, by the fact that we cannot break out of those patterns of thinking (Adorno likens them to the self-fulfilling prophecies of "free association," a psychoanalytic technique which ultimately aims at an average or normative response to all random phenomenological data[5]) that mitigate against the generation of new myths. Put otherwise: we now ask only those questions to which we already (think that we) know the answers. "Instead of mastering itself by performing the task of conceptualization," thought, as Adorno states, "entrusts itself impotently to processing by the [analyst], who in any case knows everything beforehand. Thus speculation is definitively crushed, becoming itself a fact to be included in one of the departments of classification as proof that nothing changes."[6]

As proof that nothing changes. Here is the hidden social, if not political, dimension to this suppression of speculation or myth: the wish to uphold a certain rigid status quo which benefits some in Western society and impedes many others. Adorno mourned the death of a free rationalism that took responsibility for itself, and which should have been left to perform its rigorous operations in pure sanctity, though what he mourned was basically an ideal that had never been completely realized in Western cultural history. But the loss for abstract philosophy is also a loss for practical art, which was always supposed to arrive at the same exalted Adornoesque conceptual subjectivity not through excessive rationalism but through the opposite: a sense of mystique, of the more random and playful operations of mind, which have also been subjected to a kind of professional know-it-all-ism.

• • •

This loss of conceptual subjectivity has finally had a crippling impact on all forms of creativity, perhaps nowhere more blatantly than in the movies, which have sometimes appeared as the modern personification of myth. Forlorn narrative power flags and seeks real evidence—evidence of the real—to uphold its claims. Today those "historical reenactments" in one form or another, which have largely replaced the production of raw new myths in our culture, have led Hollywood into a kind of remake heaven, a nirvana of recycled plots and characters and ever diminishing Ur-myths.

It is interesting how often these Ur-myths are borrowed from the 1970s, a decade in which the spontaneous creation of myths can be seen as an attempt to process widespread societal upheavals and change—the last decade that seems to have still had the power to perform this kind of processing. This is the converse operation to the protection of a societal status quo through the suppression of myth and mythic thinking. Both processes have a largely unconscious dimension; this is why they become so pervasive and so defining of specific eras. The processes emerge as pure responses to fears that are nearly inchoate. Both myth and anti-myth, though opposite in purpose, are rooted in the same fear of lawlessness. Where traditional albeit unhelpful laws are undermined and questioned, society spawns myths that act as effigies of its own most wayward impulses; there is a cozying up to outlaw figures and a purging of the fears of the worst that might happen. The dynamic change is crystallized in progress through an image or a story which makes it readily legible. Things loosen up, there is a period of liberation, then things settle into their own routine. Once this routine has been recemented in place and rendered coercive rather than liberating, those impulses are held in check merely through fact and reenactment (i.e., reference to a successful history of punishments, remakes of old stories, etc.). I would suggest that this factual, punitive, statistical era is the type of era we have been in since the 1980s.

Mythic eras, by contrast, generally refer, again, to a history of outlaws. Similar to the 19th century U.S. frontier days, the '70s spawned legends at the drop of a hat because a sense of the unknown pervaded all of life—also a sense of destiny. Seldom had so many figures leapt out at the public so colorfully, so fully formed to godlike statures. There was a weirdness mixed with undeniable and refreshing honesty, a series of encounters between the old-fashioned understanding of how things were supposed to be and a kind of brave new real, glitzy, buzzy, tacky, iconic world.

There is something uncanny about the power of '70s iconography that I almost want to liken to a confluence of sacred and secular impulses, again a mythical language meant to intercede in the sharp growing pains of a rapidly changing culture. John Travolta dancing in a white leisure suit. Bryan Ferry posing in white tux. Diane Keaton with her thrift-store vest and neck-tie. Mason Reese and Life-loving Mikey, Benji and Chewbacca. Big-tongued, face-painted Kiss. Gilda Radner doing Patti Smith. Even Nixon, jowly, two fingers in the air—before the '70s were through with him he, too, figurehead of the Establishment, attained the same instantly recognizable, mythic-iconographic status. The bold indelible image flourished in stark contrast to events that were far more amorphous and difficult to assimilate: who authorized the Watergate break-in; what really happened at Jonestown; was it Patty Hearst or Tania; who was Idi Amin and what did he want; could a dog really command a person to kill; and what on earth was a "snuff" film? Hello, private *Weltanschauung*. Meanwhile, women received unprecedented reproductive rights; it was the first decade that officially knew no segregation and disenfranchisement for African Americans; and it was actually, if anything, trendy to be gay (or at least know someone who was). But the results for art and culture were not stunted, not devoid of speculative mythos—quite the contrary. Life was confusing, so myth was allowed to flourish, to become more legible and more perfect. Many '70s TV shows, as banal as the example seems, still seem like fresh intersections of disparate cultural identities guided to come together in the formation of stories and mythic figures: *The Jeffersons, Good Times, All in the Family, Maud, Soap, Welcome Back Kotter, Mork & Mindy, Chico and the Man, Sanford and Son.*

This mythic ascendancy has not happened since. Reality-TV, for example, comes at us fully formed. We are not presented with models of people learning to accept each other and get along; instead, we are presented with people who either do or do not get along with others, and never the twain shall meet. Because the ones who do not want to get along now assert their own "right" to do so. This has had a chilling effect on the growth and coherence of progressivist impulse.

• • •

The salient feature of recent remakes of '70s cult films is that they lack any kind of legendary quality, any inventiveness, any feeling for the archetypal;

they replace the bold strokes of myth with banal pop-psychologizing and de facto sociological comeuppance. Although we may have entered yet another era in which life is difficult to assimilate on a daily basis, this has not translated into a widespread renewal of our mythmaking powers. As Mark Fisher asks, "How long can a culture persist without the new?"[7]

One of the most powerful elements of true myth is that, in narrative form, it never seems to begin or end anywhere. When the film opens, we are plunged into an always-already; when it ends, we are left free-floating, no matter what the body count has been, inside a deathlessness that is exhilarating and transformative. Although not necessarily directly or exclusively political, this kind of catharsis involves an active relation to cultural meanings and changes. An awareness of something new (sexual liberation, say, or female empowerment) was meant to be extracted from the experience of watching the films themselves, even if this awareness was largely unconscious or "tricked out" in mythic trappings of nudity and gore. Furthermore, those very trappings *were* the ways in which the changing social imaginaries were defined and codified *as myth*. Catharsis, in this sense, involved a mental and perhaps even molecular reorganization of the way in which social imaginaries were felt and perceived, a deterritorialization which is, in fact, the essence of what we know as exploitation cinema, both in its sloppy formal style and its sleazy content.

Deterritorialization, in fact, must come to light and receive a form in order to speak to human changes struggling to live and move and have their being. Taking her cue from Philip Rahv, scholar Anne Fleche writes that there can be "a revolutionary notion of 'catharsis,' one that, unlike Aristotle's 'static, passive conception quite in line with the needs of a slave-owning class,' would invite the spectator to action."[8] Not a catharsis, then, that reaffirms the existing order through a paroxysm of stultifying terror and the application of guilt or blame, but one which provokes ecstatically new ways of thinking, feeling and assimilating raw experience; also one which decentralizes the individual protagonist to find a more selfless position within larger chains and cycles of being.[9]

Enter Refn. Refn as an artist savors the violation of certain taboos as a way of reenergizing the power of other taboos which have eroded. His cinema is rooted in the representation of violent acts, but what it attempts to restore, on mythic levels, is the idea, for example, that we should tell the truth, or that we should try to help each other—that there are "consequences," as he once said, to our actions. The violence is always a gestural agony—like the arrows piercing Saint Sebastian—whereas what is left in its wake is the conceptual meaning to be derived: the mortal, the fragile, the perishable; the good, the heroic, the brave. These meaningful qualities perish in cynical, apathetic societies; truth or succor become taboo when they are denied en masse through bigotry, corruption and war.

We might think of sex and violence, then, merely as *secondary taboos*, which conceal far more significant and surprising *primary taboos*, such as basic human rights and equality (discouraged or shamed within an imperialist, corporate state), or ways of living which enhance individual people's freedom through cultivated anarchy. The rights of yesterday often become the primary, underlying taboos of today. When the social-imaginary has changed enough to help society's positive changes to thrive and endure, and when the changes that would be of greatest benefit to the majority of people are no longer primary taboos but accepted and encouraged, then perhaps the secondary taboos will fall away or diminish or transform into something different.

In an interview, director Wes Craven has affirmed that *Last House on the Left* (1972) was created in a spirit of willful irrationalism, the attempt to make a film where nothing was repressed or taboo, not even the film's numerous rapes and murders. Among him and his collaborators there was even "laughter at how outrageous it was." The actors improvised much of their roles, with Craven's encouragement: "It's all right to do this, it's a movie, it's not us." The lack of superego in the film is astounding to this day. Craven describes the making of the film as a personal break from his own Baptist upbringing: "It allowed me to be bad for the first time in my life."[10] This rawness seems to have passed from sight today; yet it is detectable, for me, in the liberating power of Refn's work, which has already been widely recognized as a source of new Western mythologies, new Ur-texts. Consider this: in an age where cinema usually dips into "the '70s Well" for its remake inspirations, Refn's first film, *Pusher*, has already been remade twice since its original 1996 release—one of these in Bollywood, no less (talk about global oneness!).

It is my hope that Refn will go on making only the films that he wants and needs to make. There are so few filmmakers these days who are in a position to be free—to be anarchists—about their work. What we once took for granted, that a director is an author, is true now mainly in name only. To the extent that auteurism was always limiting and oppressive, it is good that we now must transcend it; but we should transcend it only in the direction of making films that are more free and imaginative, more open, more cathartic and healing. Refn, then, should not be seen as one of the last auteurs but as one of the first of a new breed who will rediscover the importance of film as a means of personal expression, and as an unparalleled generator of new guiding myths.

Chapter Notes

Preface

1. Sharon Willis, "Disputed Territories: Masculinity and Social Space," in *Male Trouble*, ed. Constance Penley and Sharon Willis (Minneapolis: University of Minnesota Press, 1993), 267.
2. Brett Martin, "How to Look Like a Movie Star," *GQ*, January 2011, 50.
3. Willis, *Male Trouble*, 266.
4. Roberto Bolaño, *2666*, trans. Natasha Wimmer (New York: Farrar, Straus & Giroux, 2008), 227.
5. Stephen Greenblatt, *Learning to Curse: Essays in Early Modern Culture* (New York: Routledge, 2007), 12.
6. Ibid., 15.
7. Nicolas Winding Refn and Jonathan Romney, DVD commentary, *Pusher Trilogy*, Magnolia Home Entertainment, 2006.
8. "Zach Borst, New York Filmmaker, Gets Picked for Chevy Superbowl Ad with 'Happy Grad,'" www.huffingtonpost.com, January 1, 2012.
9. Julia Greenberg, "'My First Hardcore Song': 8-Year-Old Girl's 'Brutal' Music Video Goes Viral," www.ibtimes.com, January 19, 2012.
10. Richard Wightman Fox and T. J. Jackson Lears, eds., *The Culture of Consumption* (New York: Pantheon, 1983), 5.
11. Ibid., 5.
12. Theodor W. Adorno, *Minima Moralia: Reflections from Damaged Life*, trans. E. F. N. Jephcott (London: Verso, 2002), 207.
13. Greenblatt, *Learning to Curse*, 17.
14. Willis, *Male Trouble*, 279.
15. Bolaño, *2666*, 26–27.
16. I am referring to Margarethe von Trotta's *Hannah Arendt* (2013). This film was widely panned in such U.S. magazines as *The New Yorker* and *Entertainment Weekly*, in which the reviewers seemed to object almost as much to Arendt the thinker as to Von Trotta's presentation. It occasioned the odd wondering that perhaps we have so many more films about fascists than we do about anti-fascists because we can all more or less agree on why fascists are bad, whereas we seem to have reached no similar consensus on what makes the anti-fascist intellectuals, many of whom were historically Marxists and/or communists, "good" or even particularly necessary in a historical sense.

Chapter 1

1. Jack Giroux, "Interview: Nicolas Winding Refn on Violent Men, Valhalla and Pretty Woman," www.filmschoolrejects.com, August 9, 2010.
2. C. Claire Thomson, ed., *Northern Constellations: New Readings in Nordic Cinema* (Norvik Press, 2006), 111.
3. Edward Douglas, "Exclusive: Nicolas Winding Refn on *Valhalla Rising*," www.comingsoon.net, July 20, 2010.

4. Ibid.
5. Jack Giroux, "Interview: Fetish Filmmaker Nicolas Winding Refn," www.filmschoolrejects, September 12, 2011.
6. Ibid.
7. Sean Axmaker, "Nicolas Winding Refn: 'I Don't Make Crime Films,'" www.greencine.com, November 7, 2006.
8. Danny Leigh, "Europe's Very Own Movie Brat," *The Guardian*, www.guardian.co.uk, March 23, 2000.
9. Peter Sobczynski, "Interview: Nicolas Winding Refn on 'Drive,'" www.hollywoodbitchslap.com, September 16, 2011.
10. Leigh.
11. Georges Bataille, *Visions of Excess: Selected Writings, 1927–1939*, trans. and ed. Allan Stoekl, with Carl R. Lovitt and Donald M. Leslie, Jr. (Minneapolis: University of Minnesota Press, 1985), 241.
12. Zachary Wigon, "Drive: Knife Fights, Car Chases, and ... Art Cinema?" www.tribecafilm.com, September 14, 2011.
13. Theodor W. Adorno, *Minima Moralia: Reflections from Damaged Life*, trans. E. F. N. Jephcott (London: Verso, 2002), 21.
14. Ibid.
15. Ibid., 207.
16. This is not to say that the higher education of academia is valueless as knowledge and experience; but this value is difficult to discern outside the confines of academia itself. One is comprehensively prepared for a very narrow role—the narrower the better, for arcane expertise can often ensure tenure in a world where universities wish to boast about having a corner on specific areas of knowledge. Specialization is always in itself a commodity, but one which serves the economic needs of the bosses while limiting and controlling the individual workers. It is like assembly-line workers who only know their specific part in the manufacturing process and thus cannot conceptualize about the bigger picture, the factory system as a whole. And increasingly the economic marginalization of higher education is becoming literal. Mark Fisher writes: "There is a way in which the current education system both indebts *and* encloses students. Pay for your own exploitation, the logic insists—get into debt so you can get the same McJob you could have walked into if you'd left school at sixteen" (*Capitalist Realism: Is There No Alternative?* [Winchester, UK: Zero Books, 2009], 26).
17. Adorno, *Minima Moralia*, 206.
18. I should clarify: I am not referring here to people who possess concrete agendas that might or might not be crypto-fascist, I am referring to essentially apolitical seekers of truth and of new ideas and expressions.
19. Bataille, *Visions of Excess*, 179.
20. Wigon.
21. Leigh.
22. Ibid.
23. R. H. W. Dillard, *Horror Films* (New York: Simon & Schuster, 1976), 113.
24. Ibid., 114.
25. Antonin Artaud, *The Theater and Its Double*, trans. Mary Caroline Richards (New York: Grove Press, 1958), 82.
26. Ibid., 79.
27. Steven Hager, *Art After Midnight: The East Village Scene* (New York: St. Martin's Press, 1986), 13.
28. Giroux, "Interview: Nicolas Winding Refn on Violent Men, Valhalla and Pretty Woman."
29. Kowalewski, 5.
30. Ibid., 6.
31. Ibid., 8.
32. Ibid., 5.
33. Joel Black, *The Aesthetics of Murder* (Baltimore: Johns Hopkins University Press, 1991), 40.
34. Ibid., 52.
35. Ibid., 38.
36. Axmaker.
37. Pierre Mabille, *Mirror of the Marvelous*, trans. Jody Gladding (Rochester, VT: Inner Traditions, 1998), 19.
38. Laurent Bouzereau, *Ultraviolent Movies* (New York: Citadel, 2000), viii.
39. Karin Badt, "A Conversation with Nicolas Winding Refn and Ryan Gosling About *Drive*: A Modern Fairytale at Cannes," www.huffingtonpost.com, May 21, 2011 (accessed April 25, 2013).
40. Ibid.
41. Black, *The Aesthetics of Murder*, 17.
42. Adorno, *Minima Moralia*, 111.
43. John Waters, *Crackpot: The Obsessions of John Waters* (New York: Macmillan, 1986), 46.

44. DVD commentary track, *Cannibal Holocaust*, Grindhouse Releasing, 2005.
45. Quoted in Bouzereau, *Ultraviolent Movies*, 176.
46. Ibid., 148–149.
47. Fisher, *Capitalist Realism*, 10–11.
48. Ibid., 10.
49. Refn and Romney, DVD commentary, *Pusher Trilogy*.
50. Ibid.
51. Fisher, *Capitalist Realism*, 11.
52. Ibid.
53. Intriguingly, a similar pattern of passing from dogma to new narratives/myths has been identified in cutting-edge scientific research: "Successful scientific ideas often begin life as playful and potentially fruitful possibilities (circumventing the received teachings) because they appear to solve a pressing problem [again, the assimilation of collective changes]; they mature into acceptance and then freeze over, if you like, into dogma. ... The creative process ... is caused by 'the essential tension between tradition and change'" (Edward J. Steele, Robyn A. Lindley, and Robert V. Blanden, *Lamarck's Signature: How Retrogenes Are Changing Darwin's Natural Selection Paradigm* [Reading, MA: Perseus Books, 1998], xvii-xviii).
54. Erich Auerbach, *Mimesis, Fiftieth-Anniversary Edition*, trans. Willard R. Trask (Princeton: Princeton University Press, 2003), 3–23.
55. Robert Muchembled, *A History of Violence from the End of the Middle Ages to the Present*, trans. Jean Birrell (Cambridge, UK: Polity Press, 2012), 244.
56. Ibid.
57. Richard Bausch, *Violence* (New York: Vintage, 1994), 206.
58. Ibid., 232.
59. Ibid., 157.
60. Ibid., 170.
61. Ibid., 185.
62. Black, *The Aesthetics of Murder*, 5.
63. Ibid., 10.
64. Bret Lang, "Ryan Gosling's 'Only God Forgives': Critics Really, Really Hate the Crime Drama," *The Wrap* online, posted May 22, 2013.
65. Axmaker.
66. Wigon.
67. Axmaker.
68. Wigon.
69. DVD commentary track, *The Texas Chain Saw Massacre* (Dark Sky Films, 2006).
70. Jean-Luc Godard, *Godard on Godard*, trans. and ed. Tom Milne (New York: Da Capo Press, 1986), 43.
71. Matthew Arnoldi, "Portrait of a Provocative Mind," www.iofilm.co.uk.
72. J. Hoberman, *Vulgar Modernism* (Philadelphia: Temple University Press, 1991), 13.
73. Ibid., 14.
74. Ibid., 15.
75. V. Vale and Andrea Juno, eds., *Re/search #10: Incredibly Strange Films* (San Francisco: Re/search Productions), 4.
76. Black, *The Aesthetics of Murder*, 53.
77. Vale and Juno, *Re/search #10*, 26.
78. Ibid., 22.
79. Sobczynski.
80. Hoberman, *Vulgar Modernism*, 15.
81. Vale and Juno, *Re/search #10*, 30–31.
82. Gary Indiana, *Salò or The 120 Days of Sodom* (London: BFI, 2000), 12.
83. Dillard, *Horror Films*, 59.
84. Ibid., 8.
85. Ibid., 59–60.
86. Mabille, *Mirror of the Marvelous*, 28–29.
87. Ibid., 3.
88. Ibid., 19.
89. Timothy K. Beal, *Religion and Its Monsters* (New York: Routledge, 2002), 190.
90. Ibid.
91. Much of this comes from Roland Barthes, who defined myth as the movement from history to nature, or we might say the naturalizing of things that are historically new and uncertain. Analyzing a 1950s newspaper photo of a black soldier in a French army uniform saluting the French tricolor, he writes, "We reach here the very principle of myth: it transforms history into nature. We now understand why, *in the eyes of the myth-consumer*, the intention, the adhomination of the concept can remain manifest without however appearing to have an interest in the matter: what causes mythical speech to be uttered is perfectly explicit, but it is immediately frozen into something natural; it is not read as a motive, but as

a reason. If I read the Negro-saluting as symbol pure and simple of imperiality, I must renounce the reality of the picture, it discredits itself in my eyes when it becomes an instrument. Conversely, if I decipher the Negro's salute as an alibi of coloniality, I shatter the myth even more surely by the obviousness of its motivation. But for the myth-reader, the outcome is quite different: everything happens as if the picture *naturally* conjured up the concept, as if the signifier *gave a foundation* to the signified: the myth exists from the precise moment when French imperiality attains the natural state: myth is speech justified in excess" (*Mythologies*, trans. Annette Lavers; New York: Hill and Wang, 1972, 129–130). In this remarkable passage, Barthes illustrates why myth is often problematic to the political imagination: the obedient black soldier is freighted with racist connotations that cannot be stomached; he is essentially propaganda. The resort to myth here (and we should remember that this photo is from the '50s) is essentially one preserving of the status quo. I am attempting to differentiate, in this work, between myths that are radical and liberatory, but which follow the same movement of converting social changes into natural states, and dusty images that perpetuate a slumbering or hypnoid condition in the viewer: *pace* Barthes, the black soldier's salute is less a myth than the successful ongoing suppression of a new myth that is struggling to be born, one in which the colonized man of color's resistance to imperialism can be made legible as an heroic and ultimately natural state.

92. This is why true myths are very different from morality plays. Although both would seem to traffic ideas of good and evil, heroism and villainy, etc., myths are not rote reenactments of concrete dogmas, such as morality plays are. Myths predate dogma; they arise from the need to dramatize an *exception*. This exception, once named, becomes a precedent for social-cultural collective assumptions and biases, perhaps, but at the level of the myth itself, there is only an incipient judgment. Often myths disguise even this incipient judgment by courting a sort of blood-soaked immorality. By direct contrast, the morality play, to the extent that it represents a doddering, defanged avatar of a preceding myth, is a symptom of a fallow period in a given culture, a period of ritual, factitiousness, smug certainty, and the withering of spontaneous imagination.

93. Barthes, *Mythologies*, 109.

94. Scott Tobias, "Nicolas Winding Refn," www.avclub.com, September 15, 2011.

95. Belinda Goldsmith, "Danish Director Refn Splatters Cannes Festival with Violence," Reuters online, posted May 22, 2013.

96. Tobias.

97. Goldsmith.

98. Michael Kaufman, ed., *Beyond Patriarchy: Essays by Men on Pleasure, Power, and Change* (Toronto: Oxford University Press, 1987), 93.

99. Giorgio Agamben, *Nudities*, trans. David Kishik and Stefan Pedatella (Stanford: Stanford University Press, 2011), 8.

100. Ibid., 4.

101. Ibid., 8.

102. Ibid., 39.

103. Emily Apter forges a new understanding of "female fetishism" as an essentially post-phallic formation in her essay "Splitting Hairs: Female Fetishism and Postpartum Sentimentality in the Fin de Siècle" (in *Eroticism and the Body Politic*, ed. Lynn Hunt [Baltimore: Johns Hopkins University Press, 1991], 164–190). Her work has inspired my attempt in this section to relocate all fetishism as essentially an aspect of mourning.

104. About the mortal passing of all things, Agamben writes beautifully: "After all, there is nothing in creation that is not ultimately destined to be lost: not only the part of each and every moment that must be lost and forgotten—the daily squandering of tiny gestures, of minute sensations, of that which passes through the mind in a flash, of trite and wasted words, all of which exceed by great measure the mercy of memory and the archive of redemption—but also the works of art and ingenuity, the fruits of a long and patient labor that, sooner or later, are condemned to disappear" (*Nudities*, 7).

105. Apter, *Eroticism and the Body Politic*, 182.

106. Walter Benjamin, *The Origin of German Tragic Drama*, trans. John Osborne (London: Verso, 2003), 157.

107. Ibid., 139.

108. Ibid., 140.
109. Apter, *Eroticism and the Body Politic*, 175–177.
110. Yvonne Tasker, *Spectacular Bodies: Gender, Genre and the Action Cinema* (London: Routledge, 2000), 121.
111. There is a direct basis for this reconceptualization of the fetish in the thought of Benjamin's *Origin of German Tragic Drama*. Benjamin intuitively links the emotional state of mourning with the status of the immanent object-world and with the body: "For whereas in the realm of the emotions it is not unusual for the relation between an intention and its object to alternate between attraction and repulsion, mourning is capable of a special intensification, a progressive deepening of its intention" (139). Mourning can become out of control, and thus necessitates both healthy and unhealthy changes to the reality surrounding it. Benjamin likens this to "pensiveness" and to "stoicism," external manifestations of inward, private states: "The deadening of the emotions, and the ebbing away of the waves of life which are the source of these emotions in the body, can increase the distance between the self and the surrounding world to the point of alienation from the body" (139–140). Feeling and thought are already fetishes, abstractions invested (for safekeeping) with living energies. It is the "tenacious self-absorption" which "embraces dead objects in its contemplation, in order to redeem them" (157), a process driven by the wish to restore evaporated life. Here we think of Dr. Frankenstein as a cultural touchstone, the creator who wished to conquer death by devising and animating an undead giant as the ultimate fetish against mourning.
112. Johann Sebastian Bach, *Matthäus-Passion* [*St. Matthew Passion*], EMI Records, 1962.
113. Scott Indrisek, "'Valhalla Rising': A Q & A with Filmmaker Nicolas Refn," www.artinfo.com, July 15, 2010.
114. Godard, *Godard on Godard*, 184.
115. Murray Pomerance, ed., *Bad: Infamy, Darkness, Evil, and Slime on Screen* (Albany: State University of New York Press, 2004), 8.
116. Douglas.
117. Beal, *Religion and Its Monsters*, 15.
118. Artaud, *The Theater and Its Double*, 74.
119. Arnoldi.
120. Godard, *Godard on Godard*, 27.
121. Leigh.
122. Todd Gilchrist, "Interview: 'Valhalla Rising' Writer-Director Nicolas Winding Refn," blog.moviefone.com, July 30, 2010.
123. Ibid.
124. Douglas.
125. Gilchrist.
126. Ibid.
127. Skye Sherwin, "Boy Wonder Nicolas Winding Refn Grows Up," www.bbc.co.uk, March 26, 2004.

Chapter 2

1. Marilyn C. Wesley, *Violent Adventure: Contemporary Fiction by American Men* (Charlottesville: University of Virginia Press, 2003), 60.
2. Friedrich Nietzsche, *The Twilight of the Idols, or How to Philosophize with a Hammer*, trans. Thomas Common (New York: Dover, 2004), 5.
3. Refn and Romney, DVD commentary, *Pusher Trilogy*.
4. Nietzsche, *The Twilight of the Idols*, 5.
5. Refn and Romney, DVD commentary, *Pusher Trilogy*.
6. Ibid.
7. Tasker, *Spectacular Bodies*, 113.
8. Refn and Romney, DVD commentary, *Pusher Trilogy*.
9. Greenblatt, *Learning to Curse*, 115.
10. Even in different generations and different white–European cultures, the same point is made in both *Mean Streets* and *Pusher* about the gangsters' narrow-mindedness. Just as Charlie could not go through with being seen dating an African American woman in Little Italy, Tonny takes Frank to task for wanting to have sex with the black TV anchorwoman. Indeed, there is no real liberation to the gangsters' sexuality, their sexual urges satisfied mainly by strippers and hookers. For all of their violence and crime, they cannot bring themselves to trade middle-class values for progressive ones.
11. Refn and Romney, DVD commentary, *Pusher Trilogy*.
12. Wesley, *Violent Adventure*, 61.

13. Refn and Romney, DVD commentary, *Pusher Trilogy*, ibid.
14. Ibid.
15. Admittedly, we have not seen this trend much in U.S. gangster films, but three recent films from the UK—*Dead Man's Shoes* (2004), *I'll Sleep When I'm Dead* (2003) and *Endgame* (2001)—depict rape among males as a punishment meted out for the establishment and protection of criminal territories, or as a kind of assault occurring within groups of drugged-up, sociopathic men.
16. This violent aspect of the social is a motif which particularly inspires Refn. During the climactic knife fight in *Drive*, Refn brilliantly cuts back to close-ups of the two antagonists sitting in a restaurant just beforehand; the looks which they exchange—smirking or dead-eyed—correspond to the turns they take stabbing each other.
17. Refn and Romney, DVD commentary, *Pusher Trilogy*, ibid.

Chapter 3

1. Bolaño, *2666*, 698.
2. Arthur Schopenhauer, *The Will to Live*, ed. Richard Taylor (New York: Frederick Ungar, 1983), 261.
3. Sigmund Freud, *Moses and Monotheism*, trans. Katherine Jones (New York: Vintage, 1967), 103.
4. Ibid., 103–104.
5. Georges Bataille, *The Trial of Gilles de Rais*, trans. Richard Robinson (Los Angeles: Amok Books, 2004), 26.
6. Beal, *Religion and Its Monsters*, 29.
7. Jean-Luc Godard, *Modern Film Scripts: Pierrot le Fou*, trans. Peter Whitehead (London: Lorrimer, 1969), 6.
8. Intriguingly, the ending of *Pusher* seemed to be an oblique reference to this parable as well, with its close-up of Frank, eyes wary, staring off-screen on a nighttime street—as if to ask, is the blind man finally seeing, and is there anything to see beyond the darkness of the end, the approach of death?
9. Beal, *Religion and Its Monsters*, 3.
10. Auerbach, *Mimesis*, 81.
11. Ibid., 86.
12. Ibid., 87.
13. Ibid., 90.
14. Ibid., 87.
15. Ibid., 91.
16. Ibid., 86.
17. This diminution of Aryan energies is an overarching theme of the *Pusher* trilogy, whose last installment has no Danes in it at all—the drug dealers are transplanted Macedonians, Albanians, Arabs and Poles fighting for control of Copenhagen. Everything "European" is mere turf, as when an Arab gangster boasts that his Danish is better than a Macedonian gangster's. The cachet of Western European culture survives only in hardier eastern nationalities who show no qualms about exploiting white capitalism and white addiction (to drugs).
18. Radeyhan Simonpillai, "Nicolas Winding Refn Interview," www.askmen.com.

Chapter 4

1. Corey Robin, *Fear: The History of a Political Idea* (Oxford: Oxford University Press, 2004), 165.
2. Euripides, *Grief Lessons: Four Plays*, trans. Anne Carson (New York: New York Review Books, 2006), 248–249.
3. Sherwin, "Boy Wonder Nicolas Winding Refn Grows Up."
4. Skye Sherwin, "Fear and Loathing in LA," *The Guardian*, www.guardian.co.uk, March 24, 2004.
5. Refn and Romney, DVD commentary, *Pusher Trilogy*.
6. Sherwin, "Fear and Loathing in L.A."
7. Arnoldi, "Portrait of a Provocative Mind."
8. Ibid.
9. Sherwin, "Boy Wonder Nicolas Winding Refn Grows Up."
10. Michal Leszczyłowski, *Regi Andrej Tarkovsky [Directed by Andrei Tarkovsky]* (SFI, 1988).
11. Sherwin, "Fear and Loathing in L.A."
12. Ibid.
13. Ibid.
14. Refn and Romney, DVD commentary, *Pusher Trilogy*.
15. Sherwin, "Fear and Loathing in L.A."

16. Ibid.
17. Sherwin, "Boy Wonder Nicolas Winding Refn Grows Up."
18. *The Shining* itself can be read as an expression of dread over lost or effaced symmetrical relations: the husband/wife dyad unbalanced by the child; the father's failure to produce a book versus the wife's successful act of giving birth; the sheer number of the father's bad supernatural contacts outnumbering and overpowering the more limited, good supernatural contacts of the son; the elevator doors which part in the exact middle to emit torrents of blood; the twin little girls versus the only son; even "Red Rum" as an eerie attempt to conceal the atomizing knowledge of "murder" within alliterative and syllabic symmetry. The image of the topiary maze, whose center is penetrated only by the mother and child *as a duo*, and which finally isolates and destroys the renegade father, suggests the inability to appreciate the symmetrical state when one is literally in the middle of it, when the state appears so natural as to disappear and become taken for granted. Thus, one jeopardizes harmony by extending it indiscriminately, in a false way, and the attempted multiplication results only in division of the originary whole (as a hotel is divided up into rooms).
19. Robin, *Fear*, 163.
20. "History of African-American Cemeteries," www.sciway.net.
21. Muchembled, *A History of Violence*, 27.
22. Ibid.
23. Later Davis played one of the state troopers sacrificed to Rutger Hauer's bizarre bloodlust for C. Thomas Howell in *The Hitcher* (1987), a non-speaking, fleeting, ready-victim role.
24. Bausch, *Violence*, 244.
25. Hannah Arendt, *On Violence* (New York: Harcourt, 1970), 65.
26. It is also reminiscent of the turbid and greasy water beneath the bridge, where Hank Quinlan at the end of *Touch of Evil* is brought to justice and an unceremonious death, while the incriminating tape against him echoes.
27. Christian Parenti, *The Soft Cage: Surveillance in America from Slavery to the War on Terror* (New York: Basic Books, 2003), 195.

28. Ibid., 195.
29. Ibid., 6.
30. Ibid., 117.
31. Ibid.
32. Benjamin Mercer, "*Fear* × = Mall Cops and Post/9–11 Angst," www.thelmagazine.com, October 1, 2009.
33. Michael Atkinson, "X, Lies, and Videotape," www.villagevoice.com, January 18, 2005.
34. Lesley Stern, "Meditation on Violence," in *Kiss Me Deadly: Feminism & Cinema for the Moment*, ed. Laleen Jayamanne (Sydney: Power Publications, 1995), 257.
35. Scott Indrisek, "Surveillance as Lover and Art," www.somamagazine.com, April 2006, vol. 20.3.
36. Ibid.
37. Arnoldi, "Portrait of a Provocative Mind."
38. Ibid.
39. Blanchot, *The Writing of the Disaster*, 34.
40. Ibid., 127–128.
41. Ibid., 126.
42. Sarah Webster Goodwin and Elisabeth Bronfen, eds., *Death and Representation* (Baltimore: Johns Hopkins University Press, 1993), 4.
43. Adam Curtis, *The Power of Nightmares: The Rise of the Politics of Fear* (London: BBC, 2004).
44. Goodwin and Bronfen, *Death and Representation*, 105.
45. Sherwin, "Fear and Loathing in L.A."

Chapter 5

1. Refn and Romney, DVD commentary, *Pusher Trilogy*.
2. Uncredited, Refn also directed a second episode of the BBC Miss Marple series *Towards Zero* (2007). Because his name is not on the film, I have refrained from devoting a full treatment to it; however, I have watched it and would like to discuss it briefly in this note. The "zero hour" is described as the moment when a predestined group of people, drawn together over time, consummate long-simmering impulses to murder each other. This is a bit like *Bleeder* or *Pusher III* taken from

the hardscrabble urban gutters and placed amid over-bred British country life. Indeed, *Towards Zero* features a very Hitchcockian scene in which proper people sit around and calmly discuss gory murders over cocktails. Refn includes witty tributes to *Strangers on a Train* (1951) and *Psycho* (1960). *Towards Zero* lacks the relentless tension and imaginative look of *Nemesis*; indeed, it is the most conventional movie to come from Refn and not particularly pregnant with his usual concerns. However, loss of innocence occurs in the numerous incidents of childhood scarring and violence: a woman (Saffron Burrows) had her earlobe nearly clawed off by a cat when she was a little girl; a man (Julian Sands) lost the use of his right arm in childhood when it got "jammed in a door during an earthquake." There is also significant reference to a murder committed (in the characters' past) by one child against another. And Refn pulls off some subtly disturbing images: the look of nearly erotic, hypnotized bliss on a man's face as he contemplates the rocks below from a high cliff; the anguished, sweating, teeth-gritted face of an old man having a heart attack alone on a flight of stairs; a golf club whose metal end is smeared with brain matter and blood.

3. However, in a subtle and deeply ironic touch, Refn has the same cross-shaped light shine in on the later scene where Sister Clotilde is filling the scarred, amnesiac war veteran with false memories of a past that is not his.

Chapter 6

1. Giroux, "Interview: Nicolas Winding Refn on Violent Men, Valhalla and *Pretty Woman*."
2. Ibid.
3. Roberto Bolaño, *The Skating Rink*, trans. Chris Andrews (New York: New Directions, 2009), 7.
4. The will of the stone is of a much lower and more inert capacity than the will of a man, but this only serves to show how will, for Schopenhauer, is a universal force of determinism that is linked to the characteristic essence of each thing. He writes, "Therefore, if I say that the force that attracts a stone to the earth is of its nature, in itself ... then no one will attach to this proposition the absurd meaning that the stone moves itself according to a known motive, because it is thus that the will appears in man" (*The World as Will and Representation, Volume One*; trans. E. F. J. Payne; New York: Dover, 1969; p. 105). The material world of the stone, and also of plant life, for example, can only be comprehended once we release ourselves from our ingrained anthrocentrism; this is also a step toward tempering the more heightened and antagonistic powers of the human will. "I consider the inner being that first imparts meaning and validity to all necessity (i.e., effect from cause) to be its presupposition. In the case of man, this is called character; in the case of the stone, it is called quality; but it is the same in both. Where it is immediately known it is called *will*, and in the stone it has the weakest, and in man the strongest, degree of visibility, of objectivity" (ibid., 126). Again, we should not read this as a superficial justification for the strong preying on the weak, for this recognition of everything being driven by its own innate will is merely a starting point in Schopenhauer's work for a proposal that we attempt to view the world as holistically as possible and beyond self-interest.

5. Schopenhauer, *The Will to Live*, 260.
6. Ibid., 271.
7. Ibid., 260.
8. Deepak Mehta, "Circumcision, Body, Masculinity: The Ritual Wound and Collective Violence," in *Violence and Subjectivity*, ed. Veena Das, Arthur Kleinman, Mamphela Ramphele, and Pamela Reynolds (Berkeley: University of California Press, 2000), 95.
9. Tasker, *Spectacular Bodies*, 63.
10. Nietzsche, *The Twilight of the Idols*, 11.
11. Tasker, *Spectacular Bodies*, 80.
12. Ibid., 76.
13. Nietzsche, *The Twilight of the Idols*, 11.
14. Michel Foucault, *Discipline and Punish: The Birth of the Prison*, trans. Alan Sheridan (New York: Vintage, 1995), 247.
15. Ibid., 245.
16. Nietzsche, *The Twilight of the Idols*, 12.
17. Ibid.
18. Ibid., 17.
19. Ibid., 18.
20. Ibid.
21. Adorno, *Minima Moralia*, 98.

22. Ibid.
23. Foucault, *Discipline and Punish*, 239.
24. Adorno, *Minima Moralia*, 98.
25. Tasker, *Spectacular Bodies*, 119.
26. Kaufman, *Beyond Patriarchy*, 91.
27. Ibid., 133.
28. Blanchot, *The Writing of the Disaster*, 17.
29. Ibid.
30. Ibid.
31. Ibid.
32. Ibid.
33. Stern, *Kiss Me Deadly*, 259.
34. Ibid., 259–260.
35. Black, *The Aesthetics of Murder*, 26. Black also cites prison-writer Jack Abbott as saying that punishment is "a spectator sport" (4).
36. Nietzsche, *The Twilight of the Idols*, 64.
37. Ibid., 76.
38. Stern, *Kiss Me Deadly*, 273–276.
39. One of Krafft-Ebbing's case histories is a gentleman who acknowledges that his masochistic fantasies do not seem to square with his liberal beliefs and social conscience, speaking of "violence or rules that only seduce one into breaking them." Mennel, although ultimately disapproving of masochism even as an outlet, writes that masochism "holds out the promise to resolve the paradox that is inherent in liberalism"—mainly that as human beings we are sometimes drawn to things that we rationally abhor and avoid. In the relentless need to see his or her own goodness punished, the masochist stages a kind of reality check on the delusion of earthly perfection. See Mennel, *The Representation of Masochism and Queer Desire in Film and Literature* (New York: Palgrave Macmillan, 2007), 22–23.
40. Robin Wood, "Raging Bull: The Homosexual Subtext in Film," in *Beyond Patriarchy: Essays by Men on Pleasure, Power, and Change*, ed. Michael Kaufman (New York: Oxford University Press, 1987), 266–276.
41. Wesley, *Violent Adventure*, 31.
42. Ibid., 66.
43. Ibid., 73.
44. Ibid., 79.
45. Blanchot, *The Writing of the Disaster*, 66.
46. Nietzsche, *The Twilight of the Idols*, 60–61.

Chapter 7

1. "Valhalla Rising: The Making-Of," Special Feature, *Valhalla Rising* DVD, eOne Films, 2009.
2. Ibid.
3. Schopenhauer, *The Will to Live*, 263.
4. Ibid., 261.
5. "Valhalla Rising: The Making-Of."
6. Ibid.
7. Lauren Wissot, "Nicolas Winding Refn, 'Valhalla Rising,'" www.filmmakermagazine.com, July 14, 2010.
8. Indrisek, "'Valhalla Rising': A Q & A with Filmmaker Nicolas Winding Refn."
9. Ibid.
10. Douglas, "Exclusive: *Valhalla Rising*."
11. "Valhalla Rising: The Making-Of."
12. Douglas.
13. Ibid.
14. Indrisek.
15. Beal, *Religion and Its Monsters*, 7.
16. Ibid., 6.
17. Muchembled, *A History of Violence*, 141.
18. Eric Rohmer, *L'organisation de l'espace dans le Faust de Murnau* (Paris: Cahiers du Cinéma, 2000), 33.
19. C. Claire Thomsen, ed., *Northern Constellations: New Readings in Nordic Cinema*, 48–49.
20. Ibid., 50.
21. Refn had used haptic vision in *Bronson* and other films. There is a memorable scene in *Pusher II* where Tonny is stoned and riding on a subway. As the subway emerges from an underground tunnel, daylight fills the window behind Tonny's head, making it an abstract, glowing white space in which Tonny is set off in relief. His face gains clarity as if the light is "seeing" Tonny rather than the other way around. Also, in *Pusher III* there is a shot of Milo leaning wearily against a doorframe, with the open door itself a block of vacant white light which ignites the tips of Milo's hair.
22. Thomsen, *Northern Constellations*, 44, 53.
23. Ibid., 50–53.
24. Beal, *Religion and Its Monsters*, 35.
25. Bataille, *Visions of Excess*, 215.

26. Goodwin and Bronfen, *Death and Representation*, 234.
27. Elias Canetti, *Crowds and Power*, trans. Carol Stewart (New York: Continuum, 1981), 383–384.
28. Ibid.
29. Gilchrist, "Interview: 'Valhalla Rising' Writer-Director Nicolas Winding Refn."
30. Goodwin and Bronfen, *Death and Representation*, 8.
31. Black, *The Aesthetics of Murder*, 26.
32. Bataille, *Visions of Excess*, 242.
33. Agamben, *Nudities*, 1.
34. Ibid., 4.
35. Canetti, *Crowds and Power*, 44.
36. Ibid.
37. Ibid., 44–45.
38. Ibid., 45.
39. Ibid., 46.
40. DVD commentary track, *The Texas Chain Saw Massacre* (Dark Sky Films, 2006).
41. Carl Th. Dreyer, *Dreyer in Double Reflection: Carl Dreyer's Writings on Film*, edited by Donald Skoller (New York: Da Capo Press, 1973), 50.
42. "Valhalla Rising: The Making-Of."
43. Roland Barthes, *A Barthes Reader*, ed. Susan Sontag (New York: Hill and Wang, 1983), 236.
44. Bataille, *The Trial of Gilles de Rais*, 16.
45. Ibid., 16–17.
46. William C. Reeve, *In Pursuit of Power: Heinrich von Kleist's Machiavellian Protagonists* (Toronto: University of Toronto Press, 1987), 44.
47. Goodwin and Bronfen, *Death and Representation*, 11.
48. Reeve, *In Pursuit of Power*, 97.
49. Beal, *Religion and Its Monsters*, 39.
50. Canetti, *Crowds and Power*, 46.
51. Ibid.
52. Ibid.
53. Goodwin and Bronfen, *Death and Representation*, 227.
54. Canetti, *Crowds and Power*, 259.
55. Goodwin and Bronfen, *Death and Representation*, 12.
56. Ibid., 99.
57. Canetti, *Crowds and Power*, 330.
58. Arendt, *On Violence*, 55.
59. Goodwin and Bronfen, *Death and Representation*, 33.
60. Canetti, *Crowds and Power*, 251.
61. Goodwin and Bronfen, *Death and Representation*, 5.
62. Gilchrist.

Chapter 8

1. Blanchot, *The Writing of the Disaster*, 23.
2. Special Features, *Drive* DVD, Sony, 2012.
3. Ibid.
4. Ibid.
5. Tasker, *Spectacular Bodies*, 77.
6. Blanchot, *The Writing of the Disaster*, 22.
7. Ibid.
8. Kaufman, *Beyond Patriarchy*, 239.
9. Special Features, *Drive* DVD.
10. Ibid.
11. Ibid.
12. Ibid.
13. Blanchot, *The Writing of the Disaster*, 18.
14. Ibid.
15. Ibid.
16. Special Features, *Drive* DVD.
17. Blanchot, *The Writing of Disaster*, 20.
18. Ibid.
19. Ibid., 23.
20. Joseph Tabbi, *Postmodern Sublime* (Ithaca: Cornell University Press, 1996), 21.
21. Ibid., 19.
22. Blanchot, *The Writing of the Disaster*, 89.

Chapter 9

1. Samuel Beckett, *Malone Dies* (New York: Grove Press, 1956), 98.
2. Ibid., 52.
3. Bret Lang, "Ryan Gosling's 'Only God Forgives': Critics Really, Really Hate the Crime Drama."
4. Ibid.
5. Ibid.
6. Gilles Deleuze, *Spinoza: Practical Philosophy*, trans. Robert Hurley (San Francisco: City Lights, 1988), 50–51.
7. Blunt weapons occur in *Drive* as well: there is a scene where Driver impales a man with a broken-off shower curtain rod. The

force needed to stab someone with such a blunt object is intense, and the impact more visceral; to be punctured by something blunt reminds the victim of his own solid mass (as well as its final breachability) even as he is being killed. It shares something uniquely psychological with the overt and covert images of male (sexual) violations in Refn's films.

8. Lang, ibid.

9. These ideas are broached intriguingly in Gaspar Noé's masterpiece, *Enter the Void* (2009), in which a murdered young man's disembodied spirit hovers over the lives of his survivors and is finally given the choice of being reborn through whatever coupling "suits" him best. In Love Hotel his spirit gazes down on many couples, an otherworldly glow shining from their genital connection. Beautifully queer, the film has him lingering near at least two lesbian couples and also a man performing fellatio on another man. The same glow, of love and truth, shines from the homosexual, non-procreative acts as well as from the heterosexual ones. But what would it mean to reincarnate as sperm passed between two men? Would this break a karmic cycle? Would it feel orgasmic? Also, in a graphic scene of a woman having an abortion, the embryo in the metal tray has the distinct shape of male genitalia, like a small, soft penis atop squishy testicles, as if Noé were saying that what bothers men so much about abortion is not that the woman is tearing out a potential fetus/baby, but rather that she is "tearing out" the cock that was inside her. (Noé is thanked in the end credits of *Only God Forgives*.)

10. Refn and Romney, DVD commentary, *Pusher Trilogy*.

11. Blanchot, *The Writing of the Disaster*, 48.

12. Ibid., 51.

13. Special Features, *Drive* DVD.

Conclusion

1. Vale and Juno, eds., *Re/Search #10: Incredibly Strange Films*, 30.

2. Léon Moussinac, *Sergei Eisenstein: An Investigation into His Films and Philosophy*, trans. D. Sandy Petrey (New York: Crown, 1970), 86.

3. Adorno, *Minima Moralia*, 68.

4. Ibid.

5. Ibid., 68–69.

6. Ibid., 69.

7. Fisher, *Capitalist Realism*, 3.

8. Anne Fleche, *Mimetic Disillusion: Eugene O'Neill, Tennessee Williams, and U.S. Dramatic Realism* (Tuscaloosa: University of Alabama Press, 1997), 11.

9. There have been some moderately effective attempts to create myths like this, such as *Pay It Forward* (2000), which crystallized a concept that we are all interconnected by karma and good deeds. However, so far it is more likely that films about universal and transcendent being are presented as scary and apocalyptic. Darker films that have explored an interrelatedness of human beings along with depictions of alternate realities and possible afterlife scenarios are actually on the rise in recent years, two of the best being Gaspar Noé's *Enter the Void* and Harmony Korine's *Spring Breakers* (2012). In the West, Refn seems unique in his exploration of the Buddhist Oversoul.

10. *Still Standing: The Legacy of "The Last House on the Left*," *The Last House on the Left* DVD featurette, Red Shirt Pictures, 2009.

Bibliography

Adorno, Theodor W. *Minima Moralia: Reflections from Damaged Life.* Trans. E. F. N. Jephcott. London: Verso, 2002.

Agamben, Giorgio. *Nudities.* Trans. David Kishik and Stefan Pedatella. Stanford: Stanford University Press, 2011.

Ambo, Phie. *Gambler.* Tju Bang Films, 2006.

Anderson, Lindsay. *If...* Memorial Enterprises, 1968.

Anger, Kenneth. *Scorpio Rising.* 1964.

Apter, Emily. "Splitting Hairs: Female Fetishism and Postpartum Sentimentality in the Fin de Siècle." In *Eroticism and the Body Politic*, edited by Lynn Hunt. Baltimore: Johns Hopkins University Press, 1991.

Arendt, Hannah. *On Violence.* New York: Harcourt, 1970.

Arnoldi, Matthew. "Portrait of a Provocative Mind." www.iofilm.co.uk.

Artaud, Antonin. *The Theater and Its Double.* Trans. Mary Caroline Richards. New York: Grove Press, 1958.

Atkinson, Michael. "X, Lies, and Videotape." www.villagevoice.com. January 18, 2005.

Auerbach, Erich. *Mimesis* (Fiftieth-Anniversary Edition). Trans. Willard R. Trask. Princeton: Princeton University Press, 2003.

Axelsson, Oskar Thór. *Svartur á leik [Black's Game].* Filmus Productions, 2012.

Axmaker, Sean. "Nicolas Winding Refn: 'I Don't Make Crime Films,'" www.greencine.com, November 7, 2006.

Bach, Johann Sebastian. *Matthäus-Passion [St. Matthew Passion].* EMI Records Ltd., 1962.

Badt, Karin. "A Conversation with Nicolas Winding Refn and Ryan Gosling About *Drive*: A Modern Fairytale at Cannes." www.huffingtonpost.com, May 21, 2011. Accessed April 25, 2013.

Barthes, Roland. *Mythologies.* Trans. Annette Lavers; New York: Hill and Wang, 1972.

Bataille, Georges. *The Trial of Gilles de Rais.* Trans. Richard Robinson. Los Angeles: Amok Books, 2004.

———. *Visions of Excess: Selected Writings, 1927–1939.* Trans. and Ed. Allan Stoekl, with Carl R. Lovitt and Donald M. Leslie, Jr. Minneapolis: University of Minnesota Press, 1985.

Bausch, Richard. *Violence.* New York: Vintage, 1994.

Beal, Timothy K. *Religion and Its Monsters.* New York: Routledge, 2002.

Beckett, Samuel. *Malone Dies.* New York: Grove Press, 1956.

Benardello, Karen. "Interview with Nicolas Winding Refn on *Drive*." wegotthiscovered.com/movies, accessed April 25, 2013.

Benjamin, Walter. *The Origin of German Tragic Drama.* Trans. John Osborne. London: Verso, 2003.

Black, Joel. *The Aesthetics of Murder.* Baltimore: Johns Hopkins University Press, 1991.

Blanchot, Maurice. *The Writing of the Disaster.* Trans. Ann Smock. Lincoln: University of Nebraska Press, 1995.

Bolaño, Roberto. *The Skating Rink.* Trans. Chris Andrews. New York: New Directions, 2009.

———. *2666.* Trans. Natasha Wimmer; New York: Farrar, Straus & Giroux, 2008.

Bouzereau, Laurent. *Ultraviolent Movies.* New York: Citadel, 2000.

Canetti, Elias. *Crowds and Power.* Trans. Carol Stewart. New York: Continuum, 1981.

Coppola, Francis Ford. *The Conversation.* The Directors Company, 1974.

Craven, Wes. *The Last House on the Left.* Lobster Enterprises, 1972.

Cronenberg, David. *eXistenZ.* Alliance Atlantis Communications, 1999.

———. *Videodrome.* CFDC, 1983.

Curtis, Adam. *The Power of Nightmares: The Rise of the Politics of Fear.* BBC, 2004.

Damiano, Gerard. *We All Go Down.* 1969.

Deleuze, Gilles. *Spinoza: Practical Philosophy.* Trans. Robert Hurley. San Francisco: City Lights, 1988.

Deodato, Ruggero. *Cannibal Holocaust.* F.D. Cinematografica, 1980.

———. DVD commentary, *Cannibal Holocaust.* Grindhouse Releasing, 2005.

Dillard, R. H. W. *Horror Films.* New York: Simon & Schuster, 1976.

Dominik, Andrew. *Chopper.* Australian Film Finance Corporation, 2000.

Douglas, Edward. "Exclusive: Nicolas Winding Refn on *Valhalla Rising.*" www.comingsoon.net. July 20, 2010.

Dreyer, Carl. *Dreyer in Double Reflection: Carl Dreyer's Writings on Film.* Donald Skoller, ed. New York: Da Capo Press, 1973.

Drive DVD, Special Features. Sony, 2012.

Euripides. *Grief Lessons: Four Plays.* Trans. Anne Carson. New York: New York Review Books, 2006.

Fassbinder, Rainer Werner. *The Anarchy of the Imagination: Interviews, Essays, Notes.* Trans. Krishna Winston. Baltimore: Johns Hopkins University Press, 1992.

Ferrara, Abel. *Bad Lieutenant.* Bad Lt. Productions, 1992.

Fincher, David. *Se7en.* New Line, 1995.

Fisher, Mark. *Capitalist Realism: Is There No Alternative?* Winchester, UK: Zero Books, 2009.

Fleche, Anne. *Mimetic Disillusion: Eugene O'Neill, Tennessee Williams, and U.S. Dra-matic Realism.* Tuscaloosa: University of Alabama Press, 1997.

Foucault, Michel. *Discipline and Punish: The Birth of the Prison.* Trans. Alan Sheridan. New York: Vintage, 1995.

Fox, Robin Wightman, and T. J. Jackson Lears (eds.). *The Culture of Consumption.* New York: Pantheon, 1983.

Freud, Sigmund. *Moses and Monotheism.* Trans. Katherine Jones. New York: Vintage, 1967.

Gilchrist, Todd. "Interview: 'Valhalla Rising' Writer-Director Nicolas Winding Refn." blog.moviefone.com. July 30, 2010.

Giroux, Jack. "Interview: Fetish Filmmaker Nicolas Winding Refn." www.filmschoolrejects.com. September 12, 2011.

———. "Interview: Nicolas Winding Refn on Violent Men, Valhalla and *Pretty Woman.*" www.filmschoolrejects.com. August 9, 2010.

Godard, Jean-Luc. *Godard on Godard.* Trans. and ed. Tom Milne. New York: Da Capo Press, 1986.

———. *Histoire(s) du Cinéma.* Gaumont, 1988–1998.

———. *Modern Film Scripts: Pierrot le Fou.* Trans. Peter Whitehead. London: Lorrimer, 1969.

———. *Weekend.* Comacico, 1967.

Godard, Jean-Luc, and Jean-Pierre Gorin. *Letter to Jane: An Investigation About a Still.* Sonimage, 1972.

Goldsmith, Belinda. "Danish Director Refn Splatters Cannes Festival with Violence." Reuters online, posted May 22, 2013.

Goodwin, Sarah Webster, and Elisabeth Bronfen (eds.). *Death and Representation.* Baltimore: Johns Hopkins University Press, 1993.

Greenberg, Julia. "'My First Hardcore Song': 8-Year-Old Girl's 'Brutal' Music Video Goes Viral." www.ibtimes.com. January 19, 2012.

Greenblatt, Stephen. *Learning to Curse: Essays in Early Modern Culture.* New: Routledge, 2007.

Hager, Steven. *Art After Midnight: The East Village Scene.* New York: St. Martin's Press, 1986.

Hennie, Aksel. *Uno.* Tordenfilm AS, 2004.

"History of African-American Cemeteries," www.sciway.net.

Hoberman, J. *Vulgar Modernism.* Philadelphia: Temple University Press, 1991.

Hooper, Tobe. *The Texas Chain Saw Massacre.* Vortex, 1974.

———. DVD commentary track, *The Texas Chain Saw Massacre.* Dark Sky Films, 2006.

Indiana, Gary. *Salò or the 120 Days of Sodom.* London: BFI, 2000.

Indrisek, Scott. "Surveillance as Lover and Art." www.somamagazine.com. April 2006, vol. 20.3.

———. "'Valhalla Rising': A Q&A with Director Nicolas Refn." www.artinfo.com. July 15, 2010.

Jodorowsky, Alejandro. *The Holy Mountain.* ABKCO Music and Records, 1973.

———. *El Topo.* Producciones Panic, 1970.

Jones, Grace. *Living My Life.* Island, 1982.

Kaufman, Michael (ed.). *Beyond Patriarchy: Essays by Men on Pleasure, Power, and Change.* Toronto: Oxford University Press, 1987.

Kubrick, Stanley. *The Shining.* Warner Bros., 1980.

———. *2001: A Space Odyssey.* MGM, 1968.

Lang, Bret. "Ryan Gosling's 'Only God Forgives': Critics Really, Really Hate the Crime Drama." *The Wrap* online, posted May 22, 2013.

Leigh, Danny. "Europe's Very Own Movie Brat." *The Guardian,* www.guardian.co.uk. March 23, 2000.

Leitch, Will. "Backstory: Meet Nicolas Winding Refn, the Most Violent Filmmaker in the World." *The Projector* online, posted September 15, 2011.

Leszczylowski, Michal. *Regi Andrej Tarkovsky [Directed by Andrei Tarkovsky].* SFI, 1988.

Lim, Dennis. "Cannes Q. and A.: Driving in a Noir L.A." *The New York Times* online, May 22, 2011. Accessed April 25, 2013.

Lowe, Donald M. *The Body in Late-Capitalist USA.* Durham: Duke University Press, 1995.

Lynch, David. *Wild at Heart.* PolyGram Filmed Entertainment, 1990.

Mabille, Pierre. *Mirror of the Marvelous.* Trans. Jody Gladding. Rochester, VT: Inner Traditions, 1998.

MacCabe, Colin. *Godard: Images, Sounds, Politics.* Bloomington: Indiana University Press, 1980.

Martin, Brett. "How to Look Like a Movie Star." *GQ Magazine.* January 2011.

Mehta, Deepak. "Circumcision, Body, Masculinity: The Ritual Wound and Collective Violence" in *Violence and Subjectivity,* edited by Veena Das, Arthur Kleinman, Mamphela Ramphele, and Pamela Reynolds. Berkeley: University of California Press, 2000.

Mennel, Barbara. *The Representation of Masochism and Queer Desire in Film and Literature.* New York: Palgrave Macmillan, 2007.

Mercer, Benjamin. "*Fear X* = Mall Cops and Post/9–11 Angst." www.thelmagazine.com. October 1, 2009.

Miller, George. *Mad Max.* Kennedy Miller Productions, 1979.

———. *Mad Max 2: The Road Warrior.* Kennedy Miller Productions, 1981.

Miner, Steve. *Friday the 13th Part III.* Paramount, 1982.

Morrissey, Paul. *Flesh for Frankenstein.* Compagnia Cinematografica Champion, 1973.

Moussinac, Léon. *Sergei Eisenstein: An Investigation into His Films and Philosophy.* Trans. D. Sandy Petrey. New York: Crown, 1970.

Muchembled, Robert. *A History of Violence from the End of the Middle Ages to the Present.* Trans. Jean Birrell. Cambridge, UK: Polity Press, 2012.

Nietzsche, Friedrich. *The Twilight of the Idols, or How to Philosophize with a Hammer.* Trans. Thomas Common. Mineola, NY: Dover, 2004.

Noé, Gaspar. *Enter the Void.* Fidélité Films, 2009.

Parenti, Christian. *The Soft Cage: Surveillance in America from Slavery to the War on Terror.* New York: Basic Books, 2003.

Pomerance, Murray (ed.). *Bad: Infamy, Darkness, Evil, and Slime on Screen.* Albany: State University of New York Press, 2004.

Reeve, William C. *In Pursuit of Power: Heinrich von Kleist's Machiavellian Protagonists.* Toronto: University of Toronto Press, 1987.

Refn, Nicolas Winding. *Bleeder.* Kamikaze, 1999.

———. *Bronson.* Vertigo Films, 2008.

———. *Drive.* Bold Films, 2011.

———. *Fear X.* Det Danske Filminstitut, 2003.

———. *I'm the Angel of Death: Pusher III.* Det Danske Filminstitut, 2005.

———. *Miss Marple: Nemesis.* BBC, 2007.

———. *Only God Forgives.* A Grand Elephant, 2013.

_____. *Pusher*. Balboa Entertainment, 1996.
_____. *Valhalla Rising*. BBC Films, 2009.
_____. *With Blood on My Hands: Pusher II*. Billy's People, 2004.
Refn, Nicolas Winding, and Jonathan Romney. DVD commentary, *Pusher Trilogy*. Magnolia Home Entertainment, 2006.
Robin, Corey. *Fear: The History of a Political Idea*. Oxford: Oxford University Press, 2004.
Rohmer, Eric. *L'organisation de l'espace dans le Faust de Murnau*. Paris: Cahiers du Cinéma, 2000.
Schopenhauer, Arthur. *The Will to Live*. Edited by Richard Taylor. New York: Frederick Ungar, 1983.
_____. *The World as Will and Representation, Volume One*. Trans. E. F. J. Payne. New York: Dover, 1969.
Schrader, Paul. *Affliction*. JVC Entertainment Networks, 1997.
Scorsese, Martin. *Casino*. Universal Pictures, 1995.
_____. *Mean Streets*. Warner Bros., 1973.
_____. *Raging Bull*. United Artists, 1980.
_____. *Taxi Driver*. Columbia, 1976.
Sherwin, Skye. "Boy Wonder Nicolas Winding Refn Grows Up." www.bbc.co.uk. March 26, 2004.
_____. "Fear and Loathing in LA." *The Guardian*, www.guardian.co.uk. March 24, 2004.
Siegel, Don. *Dirty Harry*. Malpaso, 1971.
Simonpillai, Radeyhan. "Nicolas Winding Refn Interview." www.askmen.com. 2011.
Sobczynski, Peter. "Interview: Nicolas Winding Refn on 'Drive.'" www.hollywoodbitchslap.com. September 16, 2011.
Soderbergh, Steven. *Bubble*. Magnolia Pictures, 2005.
Steele, Edward J., Robyn A. Lindley, and Robert V. Blanden. *Lamarck's Signature: How Retrogenes Are Changing Darwin's Natural Selection Paradigm*. Reading, MA: Perseus Books, 1998.
Stern, Lesley. "Meditation on Violence." In *Kiss Me Deadly: Feminism & Cinema for the Moment*, edited by Laleen Jayamanne. Sydney: Power Publications, 1995.
Still Standing: The Legacy of "The Last House on the Left." The Last House on the Left DVD featurette, Red Shirt Pictures, 2009.
Tabbi, Joseph. *Postmodern Sublime*. Ithaca: Cornell University Press, 1996.
Tarkovsky, Andrei. *Offret [The Sacrifice]*. SFI, 1986.
_____. *Stalker*. Mosfilm, 1979.
Tasker, Yvonne. *Spectacular Bodies: Gender, Genre and the Action Cinema*. London: Routledge, 2000.
Thompson, J. Lee. *10 to Midnight*. Cannon Group, 1983.
Thomson, C. Claire (ed.). *Northern Constellations: New Readings in Nordic Cinema*. Nordik Press, 2006.
Tobias, Scott. "Nicolas Winding Refn." www.avclub.com. September 15, 2011.
Vale, V., and Andrea Juno. *Re/search #10: Incredibly Strange Films*. San Francisco: Re/search Productions, 1986.
"Valhalla Rising: The Making-Of." Special Features, *Valhalla Rising* DVD. eone films, 2009.
Warhol, Andy. *Blow Job*. 1964.
Waters, John. *Crackpot: The Obsessions of John Waters*. New York: Macmillan, 1986.
_____. *Desperate Living*. Charm City Productions, 1977.
_____. *Female Trouble*. Dreamland, 1974.
Welles, Orson. *Touch of Evil*. Universal-International Pictures, 1958.
Wesley, Marilyn C. *Violent Adventure: Contemporary Fiction by American Men*. Charlottesville: University of Virginia Press, 2003.
Wigon, Zachary. "*Drive*: Knife Fights, Car Chases, and ... Art Cinema?" www.tribecafilm.com. September 14, 2011.
Willis, Sharon. "Disputed Territories: Masculinity and Social Space." In *Male Trouble*, edited by Constance Penley and Sharon Willis. Minneapolis: University of Minnesota Press, 1993.
Wishman, Doris. *Double Agent 73*. Juri Productions, 1974.
Wissot, Lauren. "Nicholas Winding Refn, 'Valhalla Rising.'" www.filmmakermagazine.com. July 14, 2010.
"Zach Borst, New York Filmmaker, Gets Picked for Chevy Superbowl Ad with 'Happy Grad.'" www.huffingtonpost.com. January 1, 2012.

Index

Numbers in **_bold italics_** indicate pages with photographs.

Abbott, Diahann 81
Adorno, Theodor W. 2, 4, 5, 6, 16–17, 18, 24, 136–137, 146, 210–211
Affliction (Schrader) 99
Agamben, Giorgio 39–40, 169
Ambo, Phie 89, 91
Amini, Hossein 182, 187
Ancona, Ronni 126
Andersson, Rikke Louise 69
Anger, Kenneth 179
Apter, Emily 21
Arendt, Hannah 8, 175, 21
Aristotle 213
Artaud, Antonin 20, 48
Ashley, Dustin James 115
Atkinson, Michael 110
Auerbach, Erich 26, 83, 84

Bacon, Francis 29, 200
Bad Lieutenant (Ferrara) 58
Bana, Eric 128
Barba, Eugenio 141
Barthes, Roland 38, 170, 21-21
Bataille, Georges 15, 18, 69, 164–165, 168
Baudelaire, Charles 165
Bausch, Richard 26–27, 106
Beal, Timothy K. 48, 72, 80, 157, 162, 163, 173
"beating videos" 46
Beckett, Samuel 192
Bell, Jeannie 60
Benjamin, Walter 40–41, 21
Berlin Alexanderplatz (Fassbinder) 129
Black, Joel 22, 24, 28, 142
Black Moon (Malle) 193

Black's Game (Axelsson) 65–66
Blanchot, Maurice 113–114, 140–141, 148, 180–181, 187–189, 202–203
Bleeder 11, 32, 44–45, 67, 68–88, **_76_**, 90, 95, 101, 102, 103, 105, 108, 111, 112, 113, 118, 120, 121, 122, 125, 166, 178, 191, 200, 201, 202
Blow Job (Warhol) 129
Blow-Up (Antonioni) 94, 110
Blue Velvet (Lynch) 1, 110
Bodnia, Kim 51–52, **_52_**, 69, **_76_**
Bogart, Humphrey 9
Bolaño, Roberto 2, 6, 68, 129
Boorman, John 24
Bouzereau, Laurent 23
Bradshaw, Peter 193–194
Brando, Marlon 193
Breaking Bad (TV series) 42
Brecht, Bertolt 12, 33
Briggs, Johnny 127
Broch, Nicolai Cleve 83
Bronson 11, 13, 15, 43–44, 58, 66, 93, 95, 128–150, **_138_**, 151, 201, 223n21
Bronson, Charles (actor) 104
Bronson, Charlie (inmate) 128
Brooks, Albert 43, 181
Brothers Grimm 23
Bubble (Soderbergh) 115–117
Buric, Zlatko 25, 54, **_76_**, 77
Burke, Tom 196
Burnette, James 86
Burrows, Saffron 222n2
Burton, Amanda 126
Butler, Judith 160–161
Byrne, David 20

Cage, Nicolas 87
Canetti, Elias 24, 167, 169, 173–174, 175
Cannibal Holocaust (Deodato) 7, 24, 28, 154, 177
Carol, Martine 129
Carson, Anne 89
Carter, Lynda 38
Casablanca (Curtiz) 7
Casino (Scorsese) 44
Cézanne 19
Chaimareung, Narucha 196
Chopper (Dominik) 128
Christie, Agatha 125
Ciment, Michael 24
Close Encounters of the Third Kind (Spielberg) 101
The Conversation (Coppola) 94, 110, 118
Corfixen, Liv 70, 77, 90, 91, 92, 113
Cowan, Omar 115
Cowie, Victor 99
Cranston, Bryan 42, 186
Craven, Wes 214
culture industry, death of 4–6, 45–48
Curtis, Adam 116

Dallesandro, Joe 193
Damiano, Gerard 85, 86
Danova, Cesare 60
Davis, Gene 104, 221*n*23
Dekic, Marinela 64
Deliverance (Boorman) 24
De Niro, Robert 81, 129, 146
Deodato, Ruggero 24, 154
Dern, Laura 87
Dillard, R.H.W. 19, 35
Dirty Harry (Siegel) 117
Disney, Walt 1, 6
Doebereiner, Debbie 115
Dominik, Andrew 128
Doukas, Bill 86
Drasbaek, Laura 54
Dreyer, Carl 159–160, 170, 177
The Driller Killer (Ferrara) 73–74, 75, 76
Drive 11, 13, 15, *42*, 43–44, 49, 56, 58, 67, 69, 105, 113, 166, 178–191, *184*, 192, 195, 202, 206, 220*n*16, 225*n*7
Dugan, John 29
Dürer, Albrecht 41

Eastwood, Clint 110, 117
Eisenstein, Sergei 208
The Elephant Man (Lynch) 129
Eliade, Mircea 37
Eno, Brian 94, 112
Enter the Void (Noé) 225*n*9
Eraserhead (Lynch) 80
Erwolter, Maria 123

Euripides 89
Evidence Locker (Magid) 111
eXistenZ (Cronenberg) 97
The Exorcist (Friedkin) 29

Fassbinder, Rainer Werner 55
Fata Morgana (Herzog) 153
Faust (Murnau) 159
Fear X 11, 13, 15, 90, 91, 93–119, 97, 120–122, 137, 142, 153, 157, 166, 167, 172, 175, 178, 180, 186, 199, 200, 201, 203–204
Ferrara, Abel 58, 73–74
Fisher, Mark 25–26, 213, 21
Fiske, John 51
Fleche, Anne 213
Flesh for Frankenstein (Morrissey) 79, *79*, 118, 191
Foster, Jodie 81
Foucault, Michel 135, 137, 161
Freaks (Browning) 29
Freeman, Morgan 16
Freud, Sigmund 69
Friday the 13th III (Miner) 81
Frost, Lee 35

Gambler (Ambo) 89–93
Gardner, John 37
Gibson, Byron 197
Ginsberg, Allen 94
Godard, Jean-Luc 19, 33, 46, 59, 75, 76, 118
The Godfather (Coppola) 205
Gorin, Jean-Pierre 118
Gosling, Ryan 1, 6, 32, *42*, 49, 178–180, *184*, 192, 193, *194*, 195, *199*
Goya, Francisco 148
Grant, Richard E. 125
Greenblatt, Stephen 4, 6, 58
Gregory of Tours 83–84, 88
Grosz, George 6

Hansen, Gunnar 31, 170
haptic vision 159–160, 23
Hardy, Tom 129, 133, *138*, 139
Harrelson, Woody 129
Harry, Deborah 96
Hartley, Hal 2
Hennie, Aksel 83
Herzog, Werner 153
Histoire(s) du Cinéma (Godard) 19, 59
Hitchcock, Alfred 186
Hjort, Mette 12, 13, 46
Hoberman, J. 33–35
The Holy Mountain (Jodorowsky) 151, 171
Homer 26, 172
Hooper, Tobe 29, 31, 33, 106, 170
Houghton, Mark 104
Hurt, John 129

Hynde, Chrissie 186

If... (Anderson) 84
I'm the Angel of Death: Pusher III 11, 25, 32, 54, 57, 58, 59, 64, 66, 91, 125, 221*n*2, 223*n*21
Indiana, Gary 35
Isaac, Oscar 182

Jensen, Levino 69, *76*
Jodorowsky, Alejandro 151, 166, 171
Jodorowsky, Brontis 166
Jóhannesson, Jóhannes Haukur 65
Jones, Grace 14
Joyce, James 172

Kades, Leon 182
Keitel, Harvey 60
Kelly, Laura-Michelle 126
Kelly, Mary 40
Kelso, Susan 99
Kier, Udo *79*, 191
Kierkegaard, Søren 40
Kimmel, Michael S. 181
King, Matt 145
The King of Comedy (Scorsese) 129
Korine, Harmony 225*n*9
Kowalewski, Michael 21–22, 27, 28
Kristjansson, Thor 65
Kubrick, Stanley 94, 153
Kurtis, Kelly 86

Labovic, Slavko 55
Ladd, Diane 194
Lamprecht, Günter 129
Larsen, Thomas Bo 55
Last House on the Left (Craven) 214
Last Tango in Paris (Bertolucci) 193
Lears, T.J. Jackson 5
Leigh, Danny 49
Leigh, Jennifer Jason 94
Lennon, John 72
Letter to Jane (Godard and Gorin) 118
Lewis, Gary 166
Lewis, Herschell Gordon 208, 209
Litz, Nadia 103
Lynch, David 6, 47

Mabille, Pierre 37
Mad Max (Miller) 31, 33
Mad Max 2: The Road Warrior (Miller) 88
Magid, Jill 111
Mann, Thomas 24
Massey, Edith 208
Matthäus-Passion (Bach) 44
McEwan, Geraldine 125
McIntyre, Stephen Eric 99

McMinn, Terri 29
Mean Streets (Scorsese) 60, 81–82, 21
Mehta, Deepak 131
Méliès, Georges 44
Mellor, Will 126
Mennel, Barbara 144, 223*n*39
Micheaux, Oscar 33
Mikkelsen, Mads 51, *52*, *63*, 69, *76*, 78, *123*, 151, *161*, 169, 192
Mill, John Stuart 12
Miller, George 24, 31–32, 33
Miss Marple: Nemesis 11, 125–127, 136, 165, 222*n*2
Mogé, Daniel 86
Morrissey 94
Morrissey, Paul 79, 163
Muchembled, Robert 26, 102, 158,
Mulligan, Carey 182, *184*
Murnau, Friedrich Wilhelm 159

Natural Born Killers (Stone) 129
Neal, Edwin 31
Network (Lumet) 96
Nietzsche, Friedrich 51, 54, 55, 133, 134, 135–136, 137, 143, 146, 148–149
Night of the Hunter (Laughton) 30
Noé, Gaspar 225*n*9
Nosferatu (Murnau) 159

Only God Forgives 11, 13, 58, 105, 126, 180, 192–207, *194*, *199*, 217*n*64, 224*n*3, 225*n*9
Ooms, Amanda 105

Pacino, Al 205
Palmer, Betsy 81
Pansringarm, Vithaya 195
Parenti, Christian 109
The Passion of Joan of Arc (Dreyer) 159–160, 170
Pearl, Daniel 29, 31
Peckinpah, Sam 66
Penn, Arthur 66
Perlman, Ron 181
Persona (Bergman) 96
Pet Shop Boys 132
Phongam, Yayaying Rhatha 196, *199*
Pierrot le Fou (Godard) 76
Pitt, Brad 16
Pomerance, Murray 46
Pomeroy, Saskia 153
Porter, Edwin S. 35
Proval, David 60
Psycho (Hitchcock) 29
Pusher (1996) 11, 32, 36, 51–56, *52*, 57–58, 59–61, 62–63, 64, 77, 83, 90, 95, 99, 102, 105, 120, 122, 123, 134, 137, 148, 166, 178, 214, 215*n*7, 219*n*10, 220*n*8, 220*n*17

Index

Raging Bull (Scorsese) 72, 77, 129, 145, 146
Rahv, Philip 213
Ramel, Jacqueline 95, 96
Rasmussen, Lisbeth 55
Reed, Lou 73, 94
Reeve, William C. 171–172
Refn, Anders 18
Refn, Nicolas Winding 14, *194*; *Bleeder* 11, 32, 44–45, 67, 68–88, *76*, 90, 95, 101, 102, 103, 105, 108, 111, 112, 113, 118, 120, 121, 122, 125, 166, 178, 191, 200, 201, 202; *Bronson* 11, 13, 15, 43–44, 58, 66, 93, 95, 128–150, *138*, 151, 201, 223n21; and conflicts between art and money 64, 91–93, 142; *Drive* 11, 13, 15, *42*, 43–44, 49, 56, 58, 67, 69, 105, 113, 166, 178–191, *184*, 192, 195, 202, 206, 22n16, 225n7; *Fear X* 11, 13, 15, 90, 91, 93–119, 97, 120–122, 137, 142, 153, 157, 166, 167, 172, 175, 178, 180, 186, 199, 200, 201, 203–204; *I'm the Angel of Death: Pusher III* 11, 25, 32, 54, 57, 58, 59, 64, 66, 91, 125, 221n2, 223n21; *Miss Marple: Nemesis* 11, 125–127, 136, 165, 222n2; *Only God Forgives* 11, 13, 58, 105, 126, 180, 192–207, *194*, *199*, 217n64, 224n3, 225n9; *Pusher* (1996) 11, 32, 36, 51–56, *52*, 57–58, 59–61, 62–63, 64, 77, 83, 90, 95, 99, 102, 105, 120, 122, 123, 134, 137, 148, 166, 178, 214, 215n7, 219n10, 220n8, 220n17; *Towards Zero* 221–222n2; *Valhalla Rising* 11, 13, 15, 69, 93, 95, 108, 151–177, *161*, 192, 201, 202; *With Blood on My Hands: Pusher II* 11, 55, 56–58, 61, *63*, 63–65, 91, 94, 122–125, 127, 147, 162, 174, 187, 201, 202, 223n21
Reich, Wilhelm 88
Reid, Anne 126
Remar, James 94, 104
Riegl, Alois 159
Rilke, Rainer Maria 137
Robin, Corey 89, 98
Rohmer, Eric 159
Romanus, Richard 60
Rosemary's Baby (Polanski) 80
Ruedpokanon, Charlie 197

Le Sacre du Printemps 19
The Sacrifice (Tarkovsky) 173
"sad passions" 195
Sagal, Katey 194
Sands, Julian 222n2
Sartre, Jean-Paul 165
Schopenhauer, Arthur 68, 129–130, 131, 151–152, 189, 222n4
Schrader, Paul 77, 99
Schwalm, Peter J. 94, 112
Scorpio Rising (Anger) *42*, 179

Scorsese, Martin 25, 55, 60, 72, 77, 81
Scott-Thomas, Kristin 194
Selby, Hubert, Jr. 94
Seneca 129
The Serpent's Egg (Bergman) 122
Se7en (Fincher) 16
Shelley, Mary 190–191
Shepherd, Cybill 81
The Shining (Kubrick) 97, 107, 221n18
Shoffuer, Bob 86
Siegel, Don 117
Smith, Larry 94
Søborg, Morton 153
Soderbergh, Steven 115
Solaris (Tarkovsky) 154
Something Weird Video 86
Sons of Anarchy (TV series) 194
Sørensen, Anne 123, *123*
Spinoza, Baruch 195
Spring Breakers (Korine) 225n9
Stalker (Tarkovsky) 151, 154, 162, 166
Stern, Lesley 111, 141, 144
Stevens, Dan 127
Stevenson, Maarten 157
La Strada (Fellini) 62
surveillance 94, 109–112
Sylvester, Leif 63, *63*

Tabbi, Joseph 189
Talking Heads 117
Tarantino, Quentin 25
Tarkovsky, Andrei 93–94, 110, 151, 154, 173
Tasker, Yvonne 56, 133, 134, 139, 180
Taxi Driver (Scorsese) 81, 82
10 to Midnight (Thompson) 104
The Terminal (Spielberg) 102
The Texas Chain Saw Massacre (Hooper) 29–31, *30*, 32, 33, 36–37, 43, 106, 170; innovative sound design of 29–30
theory of primary and secondary taboos 214
Thomsen, Bodil Marie 159–160
The Tingler (Castle) 29
El Topo (Jodorowsky) 151, 154, 166
Touch of Evil (Welles) 101
Towards Zero 221–222n2
Troy, Jayson 86
Turturro, John 94, 95, *97*
2001: A Space Odyssey (Kubrick) 153

Unger, Deborah Kara 94, 104
Uno (Hennie) 83

Vadhanapakom, Dujdao 207
Valhalla Rising 11, 13, 15, 69, 93, 95, 108, 151–177, *161*, 192, 201, 202
Veidt, Conrad 7
Videodrome (Cronenberg) 96–97, 110

violence: and aesthetic representation 22, 28, 29, 31, 74–77; and the development of narrative 26–27, 83–85; and male rape 65–67, 72–73, 86, 87–88, 130, 162, 202, 220*n*15; as a way for males to give birth 130–131
von Alpen, Ernst 175
von Trier, Lars 78
von Trotta, Margarethe 21

Walker, Scott 132
Warshow, Robert 21
Waters, John 24, 208
Wayne, John 64
We All Go Down (Damiano) 85–87
Weekend (Godard) 76
The Weird World of L.S.D. 20
Welles, Orson 32, 101
Wesley, Marilyn C. 51, 61, 147–148

Wiesel, Elie 7
Wild at Heart (Lynch) 83, 87, 194, 205
Wilkins, Misty 115
Williamson, Fred 74
Willis, Sharon 1, 6
Wilson, Ruth 126
Wishman, Doris 19
With Blood on My Hands: Pusher II 11, 55, 56–57, 58, 61, *63*, 63–65, 91, 94, 122–125, 127, 147, 162, 174, 187, 201, 202, 223*n*21
Wonder Woman 37–38
Wood, Ed, Jr. 33
Wood, Robin 145
Woods, James 96
Woof, Emily 126

Yorke, Gabriel 28
Young, William Allen 100
Younger, Damon 65

www.ingramcontent.com/pod-product-compliance
Ingram Content Group UK Ltd.
Pitfield, Milton Keynes, MK11 3LW, UK
UKHW041943140426
5217IPUK00014B/628